SAGES AND SEERS

D1601225

Sages and Seers

by

Manly P. Hall

NOSTRADAMUS, SEER OF FRANCE
FRANCIS BACON, THE CONCEALED POET
THE MYSTICAL FIGURES OF JAKOB BOEHME
THE SHEPHERD OF CHILDREN'S MINDS—
JOHANN AMOS COMENIUS
THE COMTE DE ST.-GERMAIN
MYSTICISM OF WILLIAM BLAKE
THOMAS TAYLOR, THE ENGLISH PLATONIST
GANDHI—A TRIBUTE

THE PHILOSOPHICAL RESEARCH SOCIETY, INC.
Los Angeles, California

ISBN NO. 0-89314-393-6

L.C. 79-2419

Copyright © 1959

By The Philosophical Research Society, Inc.

Second Printing

(Formerly published as *Collected Writings, Vol. 2)*

Library of Congress Cataloging in Publication Data

Hall, Manly Palmer, 1901-
Sages and seers.

1. Biography.   I. Title.

CT104.H32   1979   920'.02   79-2419
ISBN 0-89314-393-6

Published by

THE PHILOSOPHICAL RESEARCH SOCIETY, INC.

3910 Los Feliz Boulevard, Los Angeles, CA 90027

Printed in the U.S.A.

TABLE OF CONTENTS

FOREWORD

In this book is presented a group of eight sages and seers of the modern world (sixteenth to twentieth century), all of whom made important and lasting contributions to man's spiritual growth. Their lives, though surrounded by mystery, stand out as inspiring examples of mystical idealism, devout aspiration, and sincere dedication.

The achievements of mankind in the last five hundred years have been prodigious and highly diversified. Our special interest, however, lies in the descent of idealistic philosophical principles and those mystical aspects of learning generally neglected by conventional historians and biographers. Several of the persons whose lives we discuss have been regarded as "births out of time." They belong not to their own generation, but to past ages or to a future world, the boundaries of which are still undefined. Some were regarded as prodigies and accorded extraordinary honor, even while they were alive; others carried a heavy burden of persecution and ridicule; while a few remained comparatively unknown until the general advancement of learning rescued them from oblivion. In each of these lives, there was something of mystery. They were not all transcendentalists, but they shared a common apperceiving power. Their strength was from within themselves, sustained by

5

faith, vision, or illumination. In his own way, each labored strenuously for the greater glory of the human soul. They served a tradition, as old as man's consciousness, which affirms the reality of a divine power available to those who seek it with contrition of spirit, and use it with high resolution.

As these articles were written over a period of years, the choice of subject matter was not intended as a critical survey or an exclusive selection. In various research projects, certain names presented themselves to my attention. Most interesting persons have interesting lives, and it is impossible to divide entirely between a man and his work. As occasion and opportunity arose, I prepared these biographical essays, inspired by a keen sympathy for the patient humanity of these faithful servants of man's greater good.

Two of these writings, *Francis Bacon the Concealed Poet* and *The Comte de St.-Germain,* were first published in brochure form, but have been out of print for some time. The study of Nostradamus was originally intended as part of a comprehensive work on his prophecies, which was discontinued when World War II made adequate research in Europe impossible. The tribute to Gandhi was published in our journal at the time of his assassination.

The research facilities of our Library have made it possible to depart from usual procedure and penetrate further into the philosophical and religious interests of the persons discussed. We have also been able to add many unusual and rare illustrations. In this way, we come face to face with these departed friends of humanity, and they speak directly to us across the interval of years or centuries.

We gain inner strength and renewed determination to keep faith with the privileges and responsibilities which we have inherited, when we realize that in our striving to live well in a troubled world, we are following in the footsteps of the noblest and the best of men. Reputations entrusted to time either grow bright, or dim to oblivion. It is good to know that the world ultimately honors those most honorable, and takes a kindly interest in the fates and fortunes of its real heroes.

Manly P. Hall

May, 1959

NOSTRADAMUS IN THE CLOSING YEARS OF HIS LIFE.

1503 1566

NOSTRADAMUS, SEER OF FRANCE

Part I

The Saint of the Plague

Shun-Ti, the last of the Yuen Emperors, came to the throne of great Cathay in 1333. The omens were unpropitious. Strange forms were seen in the sky. There were unseasonable storms, and the earth was moved from its foundations. An account of these times, artistically embellished with literary extravagances, has been preserved by Chinese historians. Mountains fell into the sea; wide crevasses opened in the earth; great lakes appeared; fountains dried at their source; streams of water burst forth out of barren hills; cities were destroyed; chasms swallowed up whole towns, and the countryside was laid waste.

In his account of "The Black Death," J. F. C. Hecker, M. D. (April, 1885, Humbolt Library No. 67) describes the natural commotions of that time: "From China to the Atlantic, the foundations of the earth were shaken—through Asia and Europe the atmosphere was in commotion, and endangering by its baneful influence both vegetable and animal life."

After the earthquakes came the famine; tens of thousands died. A parching drought prevailed for five months at Honan. In vain the priests chanted the sutras; the gods were not ap-

peased. Swarms of locusts appeared and destroyed every
vestige of vegetation. At Nan-ch'ang Fu (Kiang-Si) four
hundred thousand perished in floods. Canton was inundated,
and torrential rains washed away entire communities. The
dynasty founded by Genghis Khan was brought to naught
by the anger of the heavens.

Then came the plague. Out of the ruin and desolation
wrought by earthquake and famine appeared the grim shadow
of the Black Death. Like the pale horseman of the Apocalypse,
this fearsome specter rode across the world and left death
and devastation in its wake. The Chinese believed that the
comets and eclipses, earthquakes and droughts were omens
announcing the Great Death. Today we realize that the plague
was the result of these natural disasters. Pestilences, having
their origin in areas of congestion and squalor, migrate from
nation to nation along channels of poverty and malnutrition.

In China, thirteen million died of the Black Death. Re-
lentlessly, the spirit of the plague moved westward across
the face of Asia. India was almost depopulated. Pope Clement
estimated the number of dead at twenty-three million in India
and the rest of Asia, apart from China. In Mesopotamia,
Syria, and other parts of the Near East the dead lay un-
buried. Whole cities perished utterly, not one surviving to
mourn the rest. Many, who did not die of the plague, died
of fear. Madness howled in the streets. The repentant prayed
for forgiveness, and begged God to preserve them from "the
plague, the Turk and the comet."

Hecker further points out that various awesome phenomena likewise occurred in Europe. In 1333, Mount Etna
erupted; in the winter of 1336, extraordinary thunderstorms
were observed in northern France; the following year
swarms of locusts appeared in Franconia, and in 1342 there
were great floods in France and Germany.

During this same period there is a strange account of a poisonous "mist," which was reported in many places. In the East a meteor fell, which so infected the air that all living things within a radius of a hundred miles perished. Noxious fumes and vapors poured out from subterranean caverns and the rotting dead infected the air. Millions of putrefying locusts were responsible for some of the terrifying odors. At one time, a thick, death-laden fog spread itself over the greater part of Italy. (See Mansfeld's *Chronicles*.) This writer describes how a hurricane had blown great clouds of locusts out to sea. Afterward, the tides cast the dead bodies of the insects onto the shore, and they produced a noxious exhalation.

In 1348, the plague reached the Island of Cyprus. First, a pestilential air flowed across the island, so that many died of suffocation. This was followed by an earthquake. Those who sought to escape on ships found the sea strangely agitated, and the vessels were dashed to pieces on the rocks. In a few short months this beautiful and fertile island was changed to a desert.

About 1348, the bubonic plague reached the Continent of Europe. From that time on it made occasional reappearances over a period of three hundred years. The population of 14th-century Europe has been estimated at approximately 100,000,000. Of this number, 25,000,000 perished of the scourge. One authority wrote that during its course of three centuries the bubonic plague destroyed one fourth of the population of the entire world.

The mortality figures for the plague years are almost beyond belief. In England nine out of ten died; 100,000 perished in Venice; 60,000 in Florence; 70,000 in Siena; 124,000 Franciscan Friars died in Germany; 30,000 Minorites in Italy. In many parts of France eighteen out of twenty of the inhabitants succumbed, and 60,000 died in Avignon alone. On December 20, 1348, a pillar of fire hung at sunrise over the Pope's palace in Avignon. The same year a grisly comet appeared in the midheaven over Paris. The astrologers declared this comet to be of the order of Saturn and to indicate a horrible mortality.

The Medical Faculty of Paris met in solemn session to determine the cause of the Black Death and to suggest the most approved scientific methods of combating the pestilence. Their findings are preserved in an old document, which opens with the impressive lines: "We, the Members of the College of Physicians, of Paris, have, after mature consideration and consultation on the present mortality, collected the advice of our old masters in the art, and intend to make known the causes of this pestilence, etc., etc." Their pithy findings include a description of a valiant struggle between the rays of the sun and certain emanations from the constellations.

This celestial warfare, which centered in the Indian Ocean, resulted in the creation of vapors which alternately rose and fell for 28 days. These vapors, falling into the sea, corrupted the water so that the fish died. The sun strove valiantly with these vapors but was not sufficiently powerful to consume them, so they floated over Europe, infecting the air. This learned document then added: "The like will continue, so long as the Sun remains in the sign of Leo . . . if the inhabitants of those parts do not employ and adhere to the following, or similar, means and precepts, we announce to them inevitable death—except the grace of Christ preserve their lives."

Then followed the remedies: Everyone should protect himself from the air, especially before and after rain; great fires should be lighted to purify the atmosphere; wormwood and chamomile should be burnt in the marketplaces and densely populated areas; young pork and old beef should not be eaten; to leave the house at night or in the early morning was considered dangerous on account of dew; olive oil as an article of food was considered fatal, and bathing was considered most injurious.

In spite of these "helpful" hints, the rate of mortality increased, for the reason that no one had hit upon the real cause of the ailment. Following the superstitions of very ancient authors, the doctors and scientists were convinced that the plague was carried in the air. The more materialistic accepted a doctrine of "vapors," while the theologically inclined affirmed that the odors were the effluvia emanating from the invisible bodies of infernal spirits.

Several authors attempted to describe the elemental beings responsible for the infection. Old artists and engravers have pictured these descriptions. A good example is to be found in Henry Khunrath's *Amphitheatrum Sapientiae Aeternae* (1609). Here is a gallery of "infernal" bacteria which must have terrified his contemporaries into a condition of susceptibility to almost any disease. Human-headed dragonflies, forked-tailed salamanders, and numerous winged composita are depicted as buzzing about the firmament, spreading disaster.

It remained for later generations to discover the true "demon" of the plague—the rat. It is now well established that the flea was the malicious sprite that moved in the air, and that the bubonic plague was carried by fleas from the bodies of infected rats. When one realizes that the human population of the earth is outnumbered 5 to 1 by these rodents, the true measure of the problem is understandable. Even today the bubonic plague is not dead. If modern laws regulating commerce and sanitation were relaxed for even a few months, the specter of the Black Death would rise again.

The astrologers of the 14th and 15th centuries were convinced that the plague cycles were first announced by celestial configurations. Most of them agreed that the conjunction of Jupiter, Saturn, and Mars in Aquarius on the 24th of March, 1345, was the principal cause of the epidemic. They did not hold that the stars actually created the disease, but rather that they timed the cycles of its recurrence.

The Greeks and Romans had been visited by the plague, but for centuries the disease had not appeared in Europe. By causing certain natural atmospheric and magnetic unrest, the planetary positions created a condition suitable for the spread of the disease. When the planets changed their positions, the virulence of the malady declined.

Modern science still is at a loss to explain the cycles of epidemic disease. Physically speaking, one time is as appropriate as another for the spread of contagion; yet it is well known that pestilences follow definite patterns and, having run their course, decline for some unknown reason. Astrologers maintain that only by consideration of planetary positions can the real secret of these health cycles be discovered.

The Dark Ages conditioned Europe for the plague, which became a devastating force in the late Middle Ages. During the Renaissance, wealth, art, and literature flourished; great princes held their courts and patronized scholarship. Beneath all this glamour, however, was an incredible ignorance of sanitation and cleanliness. Dr. Biagi, in his book, *The Private Life of the Renaissance Florentines*, brings out something of the living conditions of a great city during the early years of the Renaissance. The city streets, for example, were scavenged only by herds of swine, and the family refuse was swept under the beds. Once disease struck these communities, it was almost impossible to cope with its inroads.

Too much cannot be said for the sincerity, devotion, and sacrifice of the physicians of that time. Unequipped to meet the challenge of the Black Death and unable even to protect themselves from the contagion, they still remained at their posts, and often died with those to whom they ministered. Similar credit goes to the religious Orders. These seldom, if ever, shirked their responsibilities. Courageously, if pathetically, they contributed their utmost to the great human need.

The plague doctor was a fearsome spectacle. In addition to certain prescribed habiliments, many evolved their own personal theories for self-protection which, if not effective, were at least impressive. It is recorded that patients died of fright at mere sight of the physician. During the earlier periods, the doctor appeared in the approved cap and gown. He usually carried a small bunch of aromatic herbs, which he held to his nose while diagnosing the plague victims; this was on the assumption that the disease was carried by fumes emanating from the body of the sufferer.

Later, the doctor's regalia took on elaborate proportions. From head to foot he was decked out in protections and medications. Some wore long overcoats that reached to the ground, from which numerous bundles of herbs and powders were suspended. There was a protective covering for the arms and legs; great gauntlet-like gloves often adorned with charms and spells; wide-brimmed, tight-crowned hats, over which various neck and face coverings were draped like curtains, and, most fearsome of all, the plague mask. In some provinces these masks were of glass, and breathing involved a none-too-comfortable process of inhaling through filters of chemicals. The most common of the masks had an immense stalk-like proboscis. This snout or beak was tightly packed with herbs, and the first impression of the doctor upon his patient was that of some inquisitive and ungainly bird approaching its victim. The efficacy of this elaborate custume was due, however, to one important but unsuspected truth: confronted with this weird armament of science, the lowly flea could find no point of ingress!

The plight of human society during the plague years is almost indescribable. Families fled from their homes and spread the contagion over the countryside; infants were deserted in their cribs; the aged and infirm were abandoned to their own resources; the dead were left in their beds. In the poorer homes the staircases to the upper floors were so narrow that the bodies of the victims could not be brought down and were, therefore, thrown from the windows into the streets.

To convicted felons was assigned the task of gathering up the dead. Christian burial was impossible and thousands were thrown into shallow trenches. Cemeteries were not adequate to hold all the bodies, and at Avignon the Pope consecrated the River Rhone to receive the Catholic dead.

Many dwelling in coastal communities sought to escape on ships, only to discover after their vessel was well out to sea that the plague was with them on the boat. Hundreds of these derelicts floated about manned only by the ghosts of the dead. So great was the terror that many cases are recorded where families buried the sick before they were actually dead. Those stricken with the dread malady often sewed themselves up in their own winding sheets to protect their remains from the indignities heaped upon the dead.

Naturally, in such emergency, many forms of religious fanaticism appeared. Groups of Flagellants wandered about the countryside, recruiting members in various communities until they resembled huge armies. A great pilgrimage to

Rome was attempted, but nine out of ten who went on the pilgrimage never returned. Repentant sinners, carrying banners descriptive of their sins, howled in the streets at night. Crime increased. Thieves broke into deserted houses, and were later found dead of the plague with the loot clutched in their hands. Some sought life through the practice of abstinence and austerities, while others lived by the philosophy: "Eat, drink and be merry, for tomorrow we die."

Such is the story of the Black Death—the most terrifying and malignant scourge of the human race. Century after century it returned to exact its appalling toll of human life and happiness; century after century the learned schools of Europe vainly sought a remedy to cope with it. Rows of physicians sat in solemn conclave, searching the old writings, pondering the words of Galen and Avicenna, questing into the traditions of the Arabs, grasping at the slightest hint. Every known remedy was tried; a few succeeded, but most failed.

Nearly two centuries after the first appearance of the plague in Europe, Michel de Nostra-Dame, a young man of good family, entered the School of Medicine at the old University of Montpellier. He was held in more than common esteem by his masters, not only because of his personal aptitudes but because of the distinguished scholarship of his ancestry. It was most unusual for a youth of nineteen to possess knowledge of the dead languages, chemistry, and dialing. Still further amazed were the professors at his knowledge of the elliptical motion of the planets, together with such obscure problems as the mathematics of eclipses and the orbits of comets.

While it was not seemly for gray-bearded scholars to seek knowledge from novices, the faculty nevertheless listened attentively to the young man's opinions, and predicted for him a brilliant future when the ardor of youth should be enriched by the experience of maturity.

The young prodigy from Avignon was not, however, an unqualified delight to his professors. His understanding of pharmacology, while extensive, was decidedly unorthodox. He quoted authors with authority, and possessed the disconcerting habit of advancing opinions that could find no verification in the writings of either Galen or Avicenna. Worst of all was the strange kind of astrology he practiced. It was not the sober astrology of Ptolemy, useful in the practice of medicine, but an intricate cabalism involved with theology rather than science.

Like most advanced medics of their time, the doctors at Montpellier were searching for a panacea for the pest. Epidemics of the Black Death and the sweating sickness were forever breaking out in some part of France. The astrogogues of Montpellier gathered periodically to ponder the acts of Providence. They resented this youth who, expressing himself openly and with conviction, exercised an ever increasing influence over his fellow students. It was considered the privilege of the old to teach, the duty of the young to listen.

Legends persist that this difficult young student had discovered, by his obscure calculations, that a new and exceedingly virulent epidemic of the plague was about to break out. When rumors of his findings reached the faculty, the dean decided the time had come to administer a few sound words of fatherly advice. It is not difficult to reconstruct the substance of his "counsel." Undergraduates should not indulge too freely in extracurricular meditation; it was the wiser course, by far, to contemplate the solid advantages afforded by the great university.

With special emphasis, the learned dean dwelt upon the fact that at Montpellier it was even possible to study dissection. There had been years when as many as four corpses were available. Of course the university was not always so fortunate; there had been lean periods when, crime declining, there were no public executions and hence no supply of cadavers. All the doctors could do was to hope for the best. So, in the sedate atmosphere of such scholastic opportunities, young students were admonished not to dabble in magic, but rather to fit their minds for the useful practices of purging, bleeding, and surgery. Furthermore, there had been no serious outbreak of the plague for several years—probably the scourge was conquered.

A year later the same young man stood alone in the vaulted corridors of the old School of Medicine. From their niches in the walls, the stone faces of dead physicians looked sadly down upon him. The classrooms were empty. The professors in their black robes had departed. The students were gone. The great college was closed.

The plague had come again! It had come just as this young man had known it would come—even at the time he had predicted correctly. He was not yet a doctor. There were years of study ahead. As the plague spread through the countryside, the young man had resolved to try his own remedies with the sick. He did not dare to practice in the larger cities where the physicians would not accept an unlicensed student. He would go into the countryside where doctors were few and the suffering great. If he were cautious and circumspect, there would not likely be any interference. When the plague came, the rules of medicine were relaxed; minor infringements of medical ethics were overlooked. This was his opportunity to prove the virtue of his theories and prescriptions. Descending the steps worn smooth by the feet of countless scholars, the young man left through the broad doorway, shadowed by the tower of a nearby church. A mule—the chosen vehicle of the medical profession—awaited below. Mounting the animal, which was heavily packed with the paraphernalia of the healing arts, this young student rode out alone to fight the plague. He was Michel de Nostra-Dame, the young Christian Jew who became the Saint of the plague, and whom France has honored for four centuries as physician and seer.

The golden age of Jewry in Spain came to an end in 1391. A priest, Fernando Martinez, fired by an unholy zeal, incited a general persecution as the result of his fanatical preachings. There were several massacres of Jews who had earned the dislike of the populace because they had been appointed the King's tax collectors. Many fled the country, and settled in more liberal areas of Italy, France, and Germany. At the time of this exodus, Spanish Jewry had reached a high degree of education and culture. A number of influential Jews had aided Ferdinand III (who died in 1252) in his conquest of Andalusia, and enjoyed his protection and confidence. They were elevated to important positions in the State, and gained eminence as councilors, physicians, and lawyers.

The ancestors of Nostradamus were among those driven out of Andalusia. The family of de Nostra-Donna, or Nostra-Dame, had resided for some time in Italy. The astrologer-physician, Pierre de Nostra-Donna, traveled from Italy to France and established a medical practice in the town of Arles. There he Gallicized the family name, and soon rose to prominence because of the success of his medications. Doctor Pierre had brought with him a number of choice recipes from Italy and Spain, and soon became annoyed with the local apothecaries. They were, he declared, too

ignorant to read his formulas aright and too corrupt to fill
the prescriptions.

The good doctor undertook to prepare his own medications. At odd hours he steeped and brewed and crushed and
pounded ingredients both rare and common. He further aggravated the local chemists by dispensing these drugs direct
to his clientele, thus materially increasing his own income.

The apothecaries of Arles conspired to remove this menace
to their fame and fortune. As is usual under such conditions,
the ultimate fate of the sick received scant consideration.
The "foreign doctor" was subjected to a campaign of slander
and abuse. Not accomplishing their ends by these means, the
druggists appeared in a body before the local magistrates
and accused the Master Pierre de Nostra-Dame of falsifying
his drugs.

A providential circumstance rescued Doctor Pierre from
his difficulties. The Duke of Calabria, who had long admired both the astrological and medical skill of the Italian
savant, retained him as his personal physician. He remained
with the Duke for some years, attaining to the position of
his confidential advisor.

The Duke of Calabria was burdened with an affable, but
irresponsible father, Rene (1409-1480), Count of Provence,
Duke of Anjou, of Lorraine and Bar, Count of Piedmont,
King of Naples and Sicily, and titular King of Jerusalem.
A gentle and scholarly soul, Rene was better fitted for the
life of a cleric than a prince. He was devoted to astrology
and the mystical arts, and a staunch admirer of the Jews.
When Count Rene asked his son for Doctor Nostra-Dame, the
Duke of Calabria was well pleased. He knew that his father
would receive good counsel and faithful service from him.
So Doctor Pierre de Nostra-Dame settled in Saint-Remy
as principal physician to Rene, Count of Provence. A manu-

script in the archives of Aix declared that Rene and Doctor Pierre were often closeted for many hours, and discussed the mysteries of the celestial spheres and other choice secrets of nature. As the years passed, Rene developed a great love for his physician, and bestowed upon him numerous tokens of his esteem.

At the court of King Rene, the Master Pierre de Nostra-Dame met another scholar of his own race, Doctor Jean de Saint-Remy, a proficient in the "humanities," a term which embraced the general field of genteel culture, including the classics, belles-lettres and languages. Doctor Jean had lived long at the court of the kindly Count Rene, and was a person of consequence. When he rode his gaily caparisoned mule down the streets of Saint-Remy, the populace made way for him—he was a great personage.

Doctors Pierre and Jean became close and devoted friends. They had much in common; both were astrologers and chemists, and both were philosophically minded. Through long years of association, their friendship ripened. They grew old together in the service of their amiable prince.

Pierre de Nostra-Dame had a fine son for whom he had recently purchased a notaryship, so that the young man might have an honorable profession against the uncertainties of the time. Jean de Saint-Remy had a beautiful and accomplished daughter whom he had named after his friend and patron of many years, the good King Rene. It was only natural that the two old astrologer-physicians should plot a match that would unite their ancient families. In due course, their hopes were realized. At an auspicious time, astrologically computed, Jacques de Nostra-Dame married Renee de Saint-Remy.

The death of King Rene in 1480 profoundly affected the estate of the Jews in Provence. Rene left his territories to his nephew, Charles, Count of Maine, by his will of 1474. Charles, at his death in 1482, willed Provence to the King of France, Louis XI, but it was not officially annexed until the reign of Charles VIII, in 1486. In 1499, the lands passed to Louis XII. Louis suffered from an affliction common to princes: extravagant tastes and a depleted treasury. He chose a time-honored remedy for his difficulties. On September 26, 1501, he issued his edict against the Jews. According to the terms of this edict, they must become Christian within the space of six months or else forfeit all their lands and possessions and leave Provence forever. For a people who had long enjoyed a tolerant and generous rule, Louis' decree meant the end of everything—hope, future, and fortune. Again, Israel must return to its tents and take up its ageless search for the Promised Land. Many gathered up what they could of their worldly goods and departed; others, especially the learned and the powerful, pondered the matter and finally resolved to accept the Christian faith rather than leave the only homes they had ever known.

Among the families which chose baptism rather than exile were those of Saint-Remy and Nostra-Dame. Thus it happened that Jacques and his young wife became nominal Christians and continued to live at Saint-Remy on the best of terms with their Catholic neighbors. There is nothing to indicate that the natives of Provence ever persecuted the Jews, and many of the more illustrious families of France trace their ancestry to these Jewish converts. With the exception of an occasional tax levied against them, the "new converts" lived on in peace and contentment. It has also been pointed out that because of their superior educational and social opportunities, the Jews of Provence were themselves a tolerant and democratic class, and contributed to the honor and prosperity of the communities in which they dwelt.

Into the cultured home of Jacques de Nostra-Dame, on Thursday, the 14th of December, according to the Julian calendar (23rd of December, according to the Gregorian), 1503, was born Michel de Nostra-Dame. The hour of his birth was near noon, and his horoscope—calculated by the traditional rules of the art—bears witness to the extraordinary qualities of his mind. The Sun is in Capricorn, conferring thoughtfulness, gravity, scholarship, dignity of person, a courtly manner, and a grave, religious spirit.

The ascending sign which, according to astrology, describes the most personal attributes of the native, is Pisces, the constellation of the fishes. This sign has long been associated with mysticism and seership, extraordinary clairvoyant ability, second sight, and such obscure faculties as are associated with oracles and divination. Also ascending is Uranus, the planetary significator of the astrologer, lighting the native with the ray of foreknowledge.

The two grandfathers pondered many hours over the starry portents. Here was a child admirably suited to scholarship and adapted by nature for the mastery of mysterious arts. It is not surprising, then, that guided by the horoscope of their promising grandchild, the two aging physicians appointed themselves his mentors.

The French historians give special emphasis to the tutelage of the maternal grandfather. From their accounts, young Michel may have lived with Doctor Jean for a number of years. In the house of this old physician, the child was brought into early contact with the healing arts. There were herbs and simples, syrups and elixirs, rows of jars neatly labeled and filled with an assortment of prescriptions. There was also the research laboratory. Here Doctor Jean and his alter ego, Doctor Pierre, compounded philters and experimented with the virtues of various waters.

Young Michel absorbed a great deal of medical knowledge during his early years. He observed the ailments of the people, that endless procession of the infirm which passes the doctor's door. Grandfather Jean would stroke his beard and discuss the opinions of Aristotle, and Grandfather Pierre would nod his white head approvingly and balance the conversation with well-chosen comments upon the "humours." Each would vie with the other to explain the mysteries of science and literature to their beloved grandchild. The boy had a quick mind and a retentive memory, and all that he learned from his old teachers was safely stored away for use in later years.

When Grandfather Jean died, Grandfather Pierre officially assumed his duties as guardian of a growing mind. But the old savant realized that Michel must receive a formal education, so arrangements were made for the youth to enter the nearby University of Avignon.

Although Michel de Nostra-Dame was baptized into the Catholic faith and throughout his life exhibited a genuine devotion to the Church, he was not without regard for his Jewish ancestry and tradition. From his doting grandfathers he learned the strange story of the wanderings of Israel after the Diaspora. He was told that his ancestors were of the tribe of Issachar, cabalistically the ninth "son" of Jacob. The people of the land of Issachar had been given to the arts of peace. They were tillers of the fields, and their lands were over against Carmel.

Among the mystical traditions of the Jews it was believed that the people of Issachar possessed the power to prophesy things that were to come in the world. Had it not been written of the sons of Issachar that they were "men of understanding, that knew all times to order what Israel should do, two hundred principal men: and all the rest of the tribe followed their counsel"? (I Chron. 12:32, Douai.) And moreover, was it not from the tribe of Issachar that had come "the wise men which knew the times"? (Esther 1:13.)

When the tribe of Issachar was dispersed after the fall of Jerusalem, they carried with them into exile secret rolls and manuscripts of magical arts which had belonged to the priesthood of that time. The territories of Issachar had included a sacred place of pilgrimage near Mount Tabor. Here dwelt a very learned school of ancient Rabbins, versed in the sacerdotal arts.

For some centuries the people of Issachar had attempted to carry on their agricultural pursuits in other countries, but repeatedly their lands were confiscated, their crops stolen from them, and they were finally forced to migrate to other areas. Because of this persecution, they were compelled to abandon the agrarian life and take up merchandising, especially such trades as lend themselves to frequent removal. Finding Spain hospitable, the Jews availed themselves of the opportunities for scholarship permitted by the tolerance of that country. They studied the sciences in the Moorish universities, and rose to honorable positions among a liberal aristocracy.

In the course of their wanderings, the personal possessions of the Jewish families were, for the most part, lost and scattered. Thus it came about that the sacred knowledge of Israel —the mysteries of the Mischna and the secret learning of the Sod—vanished from the people. Only the elders remembered, and even these memories were dimmd to a kind of legendry.

From his race young Michel de Nostra-Dame inherited two priceless gifts. The first was the prophetic spirit—the spirit of the patriarchs of old. The second was a great box filled with old manuscripts, vellums and papyri. These priceless volumes appear to have descended to him through his mother's family. When the tribes of Israel departed from Egypt, they carried with them valuable records from the Egyptian temples. There were rituals of initiation, books on geometry, cosmogony, and algebra, magic scrolls, and strange works dealing with divination and sorcery.

Then came the Romans. The Temple of Jerusalem was destroyed; the Jews were dispersed. Before the Romans sacked the Temple, however, the magical documents and the sacred treasures had disappeared. The Holy of Holies was empty. (See *Le Secret de Nostradamus*, by Piobb.) Some of the tribe of Issachar, who lived near the Temple of the Kings, are believed to have escaped with the priceless documents. The lost books were never recovered.

This literary heritage included other important treasures. There were ancient Persian scrolls, Hermetic and Arabic writings, and rare manuscripts, both astronomical and astrological. Strange books were these that the world has never seen—secret books of ancient mystery!

In the fullness of time, these rare and hallowed manuscripts—wrapped in ancient cloths, into which were woven the secret names of the Splendours—were placed in the young man's hands. Michel de Nostra-Dame became the last custodian of the magical books of Issachar. The transcendental art of Solomon the King, which, traced in strange symbols and ciphers, he had imparted to his son, Rehoboam; the words of power which could draw forth the spirits from the deep; the formulas for the fumigations and the consecration of wands; the making of talismans and amulets; the designing of pentagrams; the rituals for the binding of demons and angels and creatures of the air; the invocations of wizardry and necromancy—all these were the lore of Issachar.

In addition to these ancient treasures of arcane lore, there were more recent books—valuable treatises collected by Doctors Jean and Pierre during their long lives of scholarship—that had come from Spain and Italy, filled with recipes and prescriptions and all that wide array of information which alone can appease the hunger of a liberal scholarship.

If Michel de Nostra-Dame truly possessed the gift of prophecy, and surely the centuries stand witness to this strange endowment, much of his power came from these ancient books. Like Iroe, the Greek, who discovered the priceless key to the wisdom of the three worlds in the ivory casket buried with King Solomon, so Michel de Nostra-Dame found in the books of Issachar the "lost keys" to the three parts of Time—the past, the present, and the future. By the use of these keys he became the greatest prophet of the modern world.

Michel of Nostra-Dame began his formal education in the old University at Avignon, the city of the Popes. Historians fail to record dates or details. Avignon was not regarded as a particularly good university, but it was cosmopolitan and convenient. Sympathetic biographers insist that Michel was a good student. One writes: "Such was his memory that he could recite his lessons, word for word, having heard them once." Michel was about sixteen years old when he entered Avignon to study his "arts."

University life in the early 16th century consisted chiefly of a tedious excursion into the opinions of classical authors. Michel received a liberal dosage of "gentility" from professors who sat enthroned like emperors, and who talked down to their pupils, both intellectually and literally; in fact, many teachers disdained to humiliate themselves by addressing any remarks directly to the members of their classes. Bundled in their voluminous robes, they sat in dignified silence, while their assistants read the lectures and quizzed the students. According to reports, the citizens of nearby communities were occasionally called in to examine the undergraduates and thereby relieve the professors of this tedious responsibility.

Books were scarce and most of the writing paper was brought by camel caravans from Arabia. Those desirous of advancing rapidly made use of the university libraries where the important texts were stapled to the walls with links of chain. The French schools were largely dominated by the Church; they owed most of their dignity and no small part of their wealth to the benevolences of the Popes.

At Avignon, Michel de Nostra-Dame received instruction in mathematics (which also included geometry and astronomy). Here, also, were imparted Greek, Latin, literature, and history. Nothing was taught that would offend the clergy; however, this sovereign body imposed no serious limitations to nominal education. It often permitted wandering professors to hold classes, and the faculty at Avignon was frequently augmented by teachers who had graduated from the Moorish universities in Spain. The latter brought with them a specialized knowledge of natural history, algebra, and optics.

While at Avignon, Michel announced his intention of becoming an astronomer, but this ambition was frustrated by parental disapproval. Astronomy at that time was a conglomeration of navigation, meteorology, geography, mathematics, surveying, almanac making, and the broad field of prognostics. The last factor was a particularly hazardous one; a few bad predictions and a career could be ruined! To combine this kind of astronomy with young Michel's natural inclination toward the mysterious and the marvelous might well lead to disastrous consequences, it was thought.

Jacques de Nostra-Dame convinced his son that it would be far wiser for him to complete his course in medicine and follow in the footsteps of his illustrious grandfathers. Then, if he wished to dabble a little in magic or the cabala or horoscopy, he could do so under the protection of his doctorate.

Medicine was not taught at Avignon; so in 1521, after securing his basic letters (Master of Arts), Michel de Nostra-Dame removed to Montpellier, where in 1522 he entered the medical college.

Part II

PHYSICIAN OF FRANCE

Montpellier was one of Europe's great universities. In 1181, William VIII, Lord of Montpellier and a celebrated patron of the sciences, proclaimed the medical college to be a free school. He invited physicians and scientists of all countries to give instruction there. In the years that followed, the university increased, many buildings were added, and departments of jurisprudence and theology were created. As a result, Montpellier gained a wide reputation as a center of educational opportunity.

To enter Montpellier it was necessary to be of the male sex, twenty-two years of age, of legitimate birth, of the Catholic faith, not to be a menial worker or a mechanic, and to have studied the arts for at least two years. As a last prerequisite, there was also a delicate financial consideration.

The highlights of the medical course at Montpellier were the dissections. During the time that Michel de Nostra-Dame was a student at Montpellier there were at least two of these momentous occasions. The students sat in high-backed stalls in the dissection theater. Upon the ancient woodwork of their benches were carved skulls in high relief. The moldings were decorated with frieze work in the form of festoons of bones and the internal organs.

Each member of the class wore his scholar's robes, and the general atmosphere was one of extreme gravity. On a high dais at one end of the room sat the Doctor of Medicine, hooded and gowned, girdled with the belt of Hippocrates and carrying in one hand the Aesculapian wand. The latter served not only as a pointer but also occasionally for the less dignified office of prodding the dissectors.

It should be borne in mind that the surgery of that day was hardly a part of the practice of medicine; cutting was still in the hands of the laity. Typical of the practice of that period is an authentic account of a Caesarean section being performed by a hog gelder! Since dissection work was much too "messy" for the distinguished scholar, underlings performed this distasteful task. There was no intention to further surgical knowledge or to examine internal pathology. Its chief purpose was to familiarize students with the approximate location of the vital organs, so that poultices and other external remedies might be applied at points more proximate to the center of distress. A few years later, Vesalius caused quite a stir among the Academicians by performing a dissection, with his students gathered about the table.

At Montpellier, Michel de Nostra-Dame improved his knowledge of chemistry, and, like most chemists of his day, dabbled in alchemy and various Arabic formulas then in vogue. A physician was also required to have wide knowledge of herbs, and most of the large universities had herb gardens where various plants were cultivated for medicinal purposes. In some communities a doctor was not permitted to practice unless his herb garden was of a prescribed size.

The clinical observations of Hippocrates were gravely pondered and, of course, Galen and Avicenna were administered in liberal doses. Important medical schools usually exhibited impressively the "wound" man. This effigy represented the human body transfixed in every direction by swords and daggers. As dueling was of common occurrence, attempted assassinations frequent, and war practically constant, the major part of the medical practice of that day consisted in binding up the wounds caused by public and private strife.

For three years Michel de Nostra-Dame applied himself diligently to the "mysteries" of medicine. As usual, the historians assume that he did well; in fact, they rhapsodize on his precocity. It has been speculated that during these years he had the distinction of meeting the great Rabelais, for whom French biographies tend to exhibit inordinate pride.

A fresh wave of the plague swept over Europe about 1525. For a time the epidemic appeared to be mild and caused little concern. Then, without warning, the mortality increased until the pest had assumed monstrous proportions. To make matters worse, famine followed disease, and panic became general.

The contagious nature of the pestilence made it necessary to close the universities, and most of the professors returned to their native communities. Soaking their gowns in protective oils and clenching a garlic bud between their teeth, they went forth to fight the Black Death. Michel of Nostra-Dame had been three years at Montpellier when the sessions there were discontinued for the duration of the epidemic. Though not yet a licensed doctor, he resolved to experiment with the empiric theories of healing which were already well-organized in his mind. His grandfathers had fought the plague and he knew their formulas.

The pest was especially bad at Carcassonne. The apothecaries there were in despair. They were trying desperately to fill the various prescriptions which the ingenuity and imagination of the doctors had devised. Scientific methods had been largely abandoned because of their inadequacy; prayers and magic remained the only hope. The young medical student mingled with the chemists, observed their methods, and memorized their recipes. He also visited learned Rabbins and Talmudists and gained much useful information from them.

About this time, Michel concocted a pomade from a compound of lapis lazuli, coral, and gold. This he presented to the Bishop of Carcassonne, Monseigneur Ammanien de Fays, which caused this most reverend gentleman to "feel life in his body." In his *Traite des Fardamens*, Michel de Nostra-Dame thus describes the peculiar efficacy of the pomade: "If the person is sad or melancholy, it renders him joyous; if he is a timid man, it renders him audacious; if he is taciturn, it renders him affable; if he is sickly, it renders him sweet, making him as of the age of thirty."

During the plague years, Master Michel (as he was already called) stopped for a time at Narbonne where the mortality was appalling. He later journeyed to Toulouse. Here he consulted with the learned, who followed his suggestions with startling success. He then continued on to Bordeaux, where the death rate was exceedingly high. His reputation had preceded him, and he was met by a delegation that begged him to remain in their city and save them from the Black Death.

About this time, he perfected a large brass pump by which he was able to blow a cloud of fine powder into the infected air. Most of the doctors were groping toward the theory of disinfection. They realized that the atmosphere of the sick room should be purified, and they had recourse to the ancient practice of fumigations. They burned vile-smelling concoctions until the patients were well-nigh asphyxiated. Most of the virtue of the herbs or their compounds was destroyed by the process of burning, but Master Michel's pump released the chemicals in their original condition. The greater part of those he treated with this strange device recovered, and his reputation was permanently established. Because of this pump, Michel de Nostra-Dame is often referred to as the father of antisepsis.

From Bordeaux he carried his pump to Avignon, where he was summoned to the bedside of no less important a person than the Papal Legate, Cardinal de Claremont. Philip de Villiers de L'Isle-Adam, Grand Master of the Knights of Rhodes, was taken gravely ill while stopping at Avignon, and asked that young Master Michel be consulted in preference to the prominent local physicians.

While at Avignon, Master Michel perfected a quince jelly "of such sovereign beauty" that it was greatly admired by his distinguished clients. So good was this jelly that it ultimately found its way to the larder of King Francis I.

In 1528, the pest abated of its own accord. The doctors who survived returned to their classrooms and the University at Montpellier officially reopened its doors. The four years he had worked with the plague-stricken emphasized in the mind of Michel de Nostra-Dame the necessity for immediately completing his medical course. Already, success was leading toward persecution. He could not hope to practice without his degree, and the doctors showed definite signs of jealousy.

He returned to Montpellier and matriculated for the second time on October 23, 1529.

It was not seemly that a man with the reputation which Master Michel had acquired should return to the simple

estate of a student. Important personages visited Montpellier
for the sole purpose of consulting him. He was a popular
idol. The college of medicine was very proud of him, and
assumed, of course, all credit to itself. The four years he
had spent fighting the plague were accepted in lieu of formal
training. About a year after his return to Montpellier, Michel
de Nostra-Dame took his final examinations and attained to
the full privileges of a physician.

Writing in the sarcastic vein of medieval education, a
modern essayist has declared that normally it took eight
years to complete a college education, of which time the last
seven years were devoted to bestowing the degree. The birth
of a new doctor was preceded by a period of intense labor.

First, it was necessary to pass the "Triduanes," or the
examination of the three days. The candidate presented to the
faculty a list of twelve illnesses upon which to be examined.
The chancellor thereupon assigned him three of them, and
the dean three others. The faculty then convened and solemnly questioned him regarding his mode of treatment for each
of the selected ailments. His methods were then debated, the
formulas examined, and his prescriptions analyzed. This
examination was concluded with a session in which he was
examined regarding his knowledge of surgery and amputa-
tion. Having successfully passed all these tests, the candidate
was admitted to the doctorate.

It was customary for students petitioning for their final
degrees to select a patron. Michel de Nostra-Dame chose one
of the most learned doctors of his time, Antoine Romier. It
was the duty of a patron to try in every way to befuddle the
neophyte, although secretly hoping at the same time, of
course, that his protege would succeed. Michel made an ex-
ceptionally brilliant showing, for which he was loudly ap-

plauded by an enthusiastic audience that had gathered for
the occasion.

The final step was the conferring of the full medical
privileges; this was called the *actus triumphalis*. The night
before this event the bells of the cathedral were rung to convey the glad tiding. In the early morning, the faculty, in full
regalia and preceded by musicians, paraded in a body to the
lodgings of the candidate. Having received him into their
midst, the procession, led by the mace-bearer and other digni-
taries and attended by a large part of the citizenry, then entered the Church of Saint-Firmin.

At the church, one of the regents, rising with pomp and
circumstance, then mumbled in his beard "a great Latin discourse" redundant with platitudes and hackneyed phrases
worn meaningless by repetition. The candidate was thereupon invested with the robes of medicine. On his head was
placed a square bonnet with a red pompom. A golden ring
properly inscribed was slipped upon his finger as the symbol
of healing. The golden girdle of the physician was bound
around his waist and the book of Hippocrates solemnly placed
in his hands. He received the "Great Oath," after which he
was seated on the raised platform beside the regent who had
made the formal address. The faculty and student body then
passed before him. One embraced him, one blessed him, and
one said to him: "Vade et occide Caim!" The biographers
quoting this Latin phrase declare that none knew what the
words signified, including themselves. But, regardless of
this uncertainty, Michel de Nostra-Dame was a doctor.

As evidence before the world that he was a scholar, it was
customary for a physician to Latinize his name. In this way,
Jerome Cardan became Hieronymus Cardanus; the simple
English doctor, Robert Fludd, blossomed forth as Roberto

de Fluctibus, and Michel de Nostra-Dame, precocious student and pride of his university, emerged as Michael Nostradamus.

There was a time-honored precedent that extremely brilliant and successful students should accept professorships in
their Alma Mater. In this instance, pressure was so insistent
that Nostradamus accepted a chair and taught for a short time
in the medical college. But the educational technique of the
day was far too dogmatic to satisfy an original thinker.

Nostradamus was forced to teach doctrines which he did
not personally believe, and he was not allowed to interpret
the texts according to his own judgment and experience.
Rather than perpetuate errors and fill the minds of the young
with what he regarded as scholastic absurdities, he resigned
his chair, and in 1531 left the university. He was born of
a wandering people. Like Paracelsus, he believed that learning had its true beginning where schooling had its end. All
his obligations to the prejudices of his time had been fulfilled; he was now free to heal the sick in his own way.

Like the Aesculapians of old, the medieval medic belonged to a race apart, a sanctified society of healers which
enjoyed extraordinary privileges. His diploma was a universal passport, and it was customary for the new medic to
make the grand tour before settling down to the practice of
his art. Not only did travel broaden the mind, but it lent
professional dignity and often resulted in useful contacts.
There was no telling when a community might stand in need
of a new town doctor or some noble family become dissatisfied with its astrological adviser.

As Doctor Nostradamus jogged along the road on his docile
mule, he presented a picture typical of innumerable physicians of his day. His square scholar's hat had been ex-

changed for a broad-brimmed, all-weather headgear. His
doctor's long gown was tucked up around the stirrups. He
rode in the midst of a traveling apothecary shop, the various
parts of which dangled about him in a well-ordered confusion. There were books and bundles, a small portable furnace, bottles, jars, and boxes. A few choice specimens from
the dissecting room also shared space with the customary
mortar and pestle. An elaborate case contained the five surgical instruments, and, should the occasion require, the latter also served as cutlery. They also had other uses. Physicians were known to have defended their lives against
brigandage with their favorite scalpels.

The most difficult piece of equipment to transport was
the birth chair. In Nostradamus' time the presence of this
cumbersome device was the true index of the progressive
general practitioner. While to our present-day mind the good
doctor would have presented a most bizarre appearance, in
the 16th century these trappings lent an aura of professional
consequence. As there were few druggists in the smaller
villages to fill prescriptions, the itinerant doctor must carry
with him everything necessary to his practice.

It was on this same heavy-laden mule that Nostradamus
rode into the life of Julius Caesar Scaliger, one of Europe's
foremost literati. The background of the great Scaliger is
strangely obscure. He claimed to be a scion of the illustrious
La Scala family of Milan, but his right to this distinguished
name has never been proved. He professed to high scholastic
dignities, but in sober fact seems rather to have been educated at the mediocre University of Padua. How the Caesar
got into his name is also a mystery. He appears to have
added this haughty title because of his special admiration
for the literary style of Caesar's Gallic Wars. The only part

of his name that he came by honestly is the Julius—if we are to believe his detractors.

Whatever Scaliger may have lacked in ancestry and formal schooling was more than compensated, however, by a rare combination of genuine ability and shameless audacity. It is still a moot question whether he was really a great man without honors or simply a man *sans honneur*. In any event, Julius Caesar Scaliger possessed a wide reading in philology and the natural sciences, and is recognized still as one of the foremost modern exponents of the physics and metaphysics of Aristotle.

Nostradamus was in Toulouse when he received the letter from Scaliger inviting him to Agen. The philologist was intrigued by the reports he had received of the amazing cures wrought by Nostradamus with his "plague gun" and desired to meet the man who fought the Black Death with clouds of white powder.

At their first meeting, the two physicians were mutually "enchanted." They had many long discussions on philosophy, *la critique*, poetry, and history. Nostradamus was so impressed with the extraordinary accomplishments of his new friend that he likened him in eloquence to Cicero, in poesy to Maro, and in medicine to Galen.

The friendship continued for some time and then ended abruptly. Their relations became strained due to Scaliger's Protestant leanings and the choleric disposition which the stars had bestowed upon the noted philologist. The word philology is composed of two Greek words (philo-logia) which, literally translated, mean "exceeding fondness for speech." In brief, Scaliger talked too much!

The townsfolk of Agen were flattered by the presence in their midst of these two famous men. The city council resolved to petition them to take permanent residence in the community. Agen, it was pointed out, was subject to periodic fevers and there was enough work for several physicians. Convinced that the fevers had some local origin, Nostradamus recommended the draining of a nearby swamp from which at night a damp mist arose and invaded the city. But the day of preventive medicine had not yet dawned; the city fathers compromised by ignoring the doctor's advice.

Weary of arguing the mysteries of health with the local magistrates, Nostradamus and Scaliger intimated that they might depart and seek out a more enlightened community. Sorely distressed at the prospect of losing both of their celebrities, the good people of Agen took heroic measures. They appointed a delegation, armed them with gifts and promises and sent them forth to reason with the local heroes. Though touched by the sincerity of the citizens, the two physicians refused the bribes. They reminded the delegates that if the city of Agen were generously disposed, it could devote the money to its aged and infirm who were eking out a miserable existence.

In the words of a French author, this magnanimous gesture "put the whole town into an enthusiasm." The next time Scaliger and Nostradamus rode into Agen, the populace lined the streets cheering and applauding. When the two doctors tried to get off their mules, they were literally picked up by the crowd and carried through the streets. The swamp, however, was not drained.

In his *Life of Nostradamus*, Boulenger gives a vivid picture of the appearance of the great doctor at this stage of his career: "He was more small than great, more corpulent than lean, and he had a face which could be observed with pleasure. His forehead was wide and high, his cheeks always ruddy, his nose aquiline, his hair a dark chestnut, his beard long and forked, producing the best effect. His face was smiling and open, very pleasing to the younger women, while the older ones were not frightened by it."

Equipped by nature with such devastating charms, it was only natural that the eligible ladies of Agen should set their caps for the young doctor. The town entered into the conspiracy, for if Nostradamus should marry a girl of Agen he would almost certainly settle in the community and be readily available to the sick. Rich farmers with eligible daughters boasted of their farms and hinted at appropriate dowries. With similar motives, merchants showed him the contents of their well-lined cash boxes, while illustrious families hinted at the numerous advantages that would follow from a proper alliance with the aristocracy.

While sojourning at Agen and basking in the light of Scaliger's high mind and ready wit, Nostradamus married, not one of the village belles, but an unknown girl whose very name is not authoritatively recorded. It is only reported that she was of affable disposition and good family, but apparently without means or dower. The only possible clue to the identity of Madame Nostradamus is a reference made by one writer, who calls her Adriete de Loubejac.

When Julius Caesar Scaliger settled at Agen as personal physician to the Bishop, he married Audiette de Roques-Lobejac, a beautiful girl thirty years younger than himself, who appears to have been an orphan. The two names are so similar that it is generally supposed that a mistake has been made. Did some historian by some *lapsus calami* wrongly assign Scaliger's wife to Nostradamus? Or, is it possible that close association with Scaliger's household resulted in a marriage between Nostradamus and some relative of Madame Scaliger?

It is, of course, possible that Audiette and Adriete were not the same person. Precedent for such a deduction may be

found in the case of William Shakespeare. It has never been
proved that Anne Hathaway of Stratford was the same Anne
whose marriage banns to Shakespeare were posted in a nearby town. Unsympathetic investigators have begun to suspect
that there were two Anne's in Shakespeare's life.

Nostradamus continued to share local fame with Scaliger
for several years at Agen. According to the meager records,
Doctor Michael adored his wife and idolized his two children.
His career appeared secure. Distinguished visitors came from
afar to consult him. The town was proud of its doctor and he
was loaded with gifts as he made his periodic visits among
the people in the course of his professional activities.

Then the Black Death struck again. Day and night Nostradamus labored with the sick. The pestilence was especially
severe at Agen. Tirelessly the physician visited the stricken
homes and applied his *nostrum*. To those simple folk the
very word became synonymous with his own name. Those
whom he treated recovered, and their gratitude continued
throughout the years.

Then in the life of this quiet, good man, tragedy struck
an all-but-fatal blow. In a few short hours all that was dear
to him was lost; his wife and children sickened and died of
the plague. Frantically he worked upon them, using all his
skill and knowledge. One by one, the flames of life flickered
out. Others he could help, but, by some unhappy fate, his
own he could not save. When the holy ground of the old
cathedral received unto itself the bodies of his loved ones,
the heartbroken doctor sadly turned his back upon their
graves to resume his life of wandering.

For eight years Nostradamus journeyed on, always driven
by some inner urge. He sought to efface the memory of his
personal sorrow by immersing himself in the study of his
beloved medicine. He stopped at numerous inns along the

way. Everywhere he asked about the doctors. He desired to
know their accomplishments and their remedies. He held
converse only with scientists and apothecaries. He would
establish himself in some wayside hostelry, remain for a few
weeks, then suddenly disappear. His days were spent with
the doctors, his nights with his chemical apparatus which he
always carried with him. He visited Genoa, Venice, and
Milan, ever seeking knowledge, ever desiring to know the
formulas other men were using to combat disease.

While in Italy, Nostradamus made his first recorded prediction. Walking along a village street, the physician met a
group of Franciscan brothers. Among them was Felix Peretti,
a youth of very humble origin who had been a swineherd.
As he passed the young friar, Nostradamus suddenly stopped
and fell on his knees to receive his blessing. The monks,
amazed at this uncalled-for display of deference, inquired
the reason. "Because," replied the prophet, "it is proper that
I should submit myself and bend the knee before His Holiness." The other Franciscans shrugged their shoulders, and
whispered among themselves that he was some strange visionary or mystic whose words could have no meaning. Later,
however, the young monk became Cardinal of Montalte, and
in 1585 was crowned Pope under the name of Sixtus the Fifth.

About 1538, Nostradamus came to the attention of the
Inquisitional Court, an honor which he in no way coveted.
Some time before, he had reproached a monk who had cast
a bronze statue of him. The monk had insisted that only
portraiture was intended, but his technique was so permeated
with Gothic fervor that the result was grotesque in the extreme.

Nostradamus suspected that the image was actually intended for magical purposes, of which he was the proposed
victim. He realized that he had aroused the enmity of this

Portrait of Nostradamus from
the 1656 printing of selected
quatrains from his prophetic
works.

monk, which would stand him in bad stead if his remarks
were misinterpreted. Apparently, the Inquisitors had little
interest in preserving his immortal soul, however, and when
he failed to appear for questioning, they made no further
effort to compel him. Throughout his life Nostradamus was
a devout champion of the Church, and there was very little
tangible evidence, aside from his astrology, which could be
used against him, and that was a subject not officially banned.

In 1539, Nostradamus was at Bordeaux, where he was ex-
perimenting with the properties of black amber, which he
preferred to gray in the preparation of his tinctures. He

spent much time there with the apothecaries. One of them, Leonard Bandon, left a record of the opinions of Nostradamus which related to the qualities of various types of amber.

In the village of Saint-Bonnet de Champsaur, Nostradamus read the horoscope of the young son of Madame de Lesdiguieres. He predicted from the chart that the boy would grow up to be one of the first in the kingdom. Francois was made marshal in 1609, and in 1622 became constable of France, the highest military officer in the kingdom.

Nostradamus then proceeded to Bar-le-Duc, where it is recorded that he made some rather broad remarks against Luther and the Lutherans, whose cause he did not favor. At Bar-le-Duc, he was lodged at the Chateau de Fains, the estate of the Lord of Florinville. While there, he cured Madame de Florinville and his lordship's grandmother from ailments which had been pronounced hopeless by other physicians. It was while at the Chateau de Fains that the astrologer became involved in the highly amusing episode of the two pigs.

Though secretly convinced that Nostradamus possessed an extraordinary prophetic power, Le Seigneur de Florinville insisted that the astrologer could not be right on all occasions, and challenged him to a test of skill. He should set up the horoscopes of two suckling pigs and predict accurately what the future held for each. Nostradamus gravely calculated the hcroscopes and pronounced his findings. He saw only tragedy for the little pigs. The white piglet, he declared, would be devoured by a wolf, and the black one would be served up on his lordship's table.

The astrologer's verdict gave his host a happy idea. The Seigneur secretly summoned his cook and ordered that the white pig should be killed immediately and served up to them that very night. Waiting until the dinner was over, the master of Florinville then turned to Nostradamus and jestingly remarked: "Well, my good doctor, this time your prophetic powers have failed. We have just eaten the white pig."

After a few moments' silence, the doctor quietly replied: "May it please your lordship, but I must doubt your word. Send for the cook."

When the chef entered the room, it did not take long to discover that something was amiss. After considerable pressure from his master, the poor man finally broke down and confessed all. He had killed and dressed the white pig exactly as his lordship had ordered, and had placed it on the spit to broil. Then a most unhappy incident occurred. A half-tamed wolf that ranged about the chateau was often fed by members of the household. The animal ran into the kitchen and ate a hindquarter from the half-cooked pig. So distressed was the chef at the prospect of his master's displeasure that he then secretly killed and dressed the black pig and substituted it for the other.

When the confession was complete, Nostradamus turned to his host with the quiet remark: "The white pig shall be eaten by a wolf, and the black one shall be served at your lordship's table. Is it not so?" The Lord of Florinville was convinced.

Before leaving the Chateau de Fains, Nostradamus made another prediction. Pointing to a thickly wooded mountain not far distant, he declared that a treasure was hidden there. This treasure, he further declared, could never be found by anyone who sought it; it would be discovered only when the ground was being dug for another reason. This proved to be true. Years later, scientists, carrying on excavation work in that area in their search for the ruins of an ancient pagan temple, found pieces of money in the very place indicated by the astrologer.

Nostradamus continued his travels until he finally arrived at the celebrated Abbey of Orval, a religious community of Cistercian monks in the Diocese of Treves. It was the custom at this abbey to receive strangers as though they were messengers sent from God; so, prostrating himself in salutation, the abbot invited Nostradamus to abide with them for a time. The learned doctor did so and joined the monks in their strict observances, which included rising each morning at two o'clock for an early mass.

Historians believe that it was at Orval where Nostradamus first began to feel the overshadowing of the prophetic spirit. Prior to that time he had been a physician of empiric medicine and an astrologer of unusual ability. Now was added the awakening of his mystic seership. Was he a little frightened at the strange power that was unfolding within him? Did he desire to retire for a while into the seclusion of a holy life so that he might "try the spirits"? The historians assume such was the case. They write that while at Orval, Nostradamus was possessed by a "lymphatic" spirit and by the "vehemence of a melancholy passion."

By such terms they imply that Nostradamus had passed through a profound psychological crisis. His spirit had descended into the shadows of a great sorrow. The inevitable reaction had set in. The loss of his wife and children had affected him far more than he had admitted to himself. For years he had sought to escape the hidden hurt within by filling his life and mind with useful activities. But, at last, he could deny the truth no longer. He was a lonely, frightened man struggling with a strange power that he did not understand and could not entirely control.

As Mohammed prayed through the night in the cave of Mount Hira, so Nostradamus performed lonely vigils at Orval. Always a devout man, he besought divine aid in the ordering of his mortal life. He must find inner strength and peace if he was to continue his ministrations.

Several authors maintain that Nostradamus is the true writer of the celebrated *Prophecies of Orval*, whose authorship has been attributed to a mysterious person named Olivarius. These prophecies contain such a remarkable account of the advent of Napoleon I that only a truly great seer could have produced them. The abbot of Orval, instead of destroying the curious document, concealed it in the abbey, where it remained unknown for more than two hundred years.

In 1793, Francois de Metz was appointed by the Secretary of the Commune to compile a list of the books and manuscripts which had been pillaged from palaces, churches, and abbeys during the Revolution. One of these books was entitled *The Prophecies of Philippe Dieudonne Noel Olivarius, Doctor of Medicine, Surgeon and Astrologer*. The manuscript was dated 1542, and it had come from Orval.

De Metz was so intrigued by the *Prophecies* that he copied the manuscript volume and discreetly circulated it among his intimates. Napoleon read the copy and demanded that the original be found. After considerable difficulty, the book was discovered and presented to the Emperor. Napoleon kept the manuscript with him, but it was not found among his effects. Its present whereabouts is a mystery as great as its origin.

A few extracts from the *Olivarius Prophecies* will suffice to prove their extraordinary accuracy. "France-Italy will see a supernatural being, born not far from its bosom. This man will emerge from the sea . . . While still a young man, will open out for himself, in face of thousands of obstacles, a pathway in the ranks of the soldiers and become their first leader . . . He will thus gain a name, not as a king but as Emperor—a title coming to him after a while out of the great popular enthusiasm evoked. He will battle everywhere throughout his kingdom: he will drive from their lands princes, lords, kings . . . He will be seen with a mighty array of forty-nine times twenty thousand men on foot in arms, and they will carry arms and trumpets of steel . . . He will carry in his right hand an eagle . . . He will have two wives and only one son . . . Kept in restraint in exile, in the sea from which he started in his young days, close to his birthplace, he will remain for eleven moons . . . Then chased away once more by a triple alliance of European populations after three moons and one-third of a moon, back in his place will be set the King of the old blood of the Cape[t]."

It is certainly a strange coincidence that two prophecies— one by the mysterious Olivarius, the other by Nostradamus, and both compiled at approximately the same time—should describe with equal accuracy the story of the first empire. There may well be grounds for the growing conviction that Olivarius was but a pseudonym and that Nostradamus himself is the author of *The Prevision Out of the Solitudes.*

Nostradamus left Orval about 1543, and resolved to establish himself at Marseilles, a rich and populous center, where he could mingle with scholars of repute. His stay at Marseilles was an unhappy one. He found the physicians there corrupt and the apothecaries worse than uninformed. His criticism brought on the animosity of his colleagues and one of them accused him of magic. His astronomical knowledge they also belittled, and instituted a systematic campaign of vilification.

In 1546 the plague broke out at Aix. It raged from May to January of the following year, and a delegation from the town committee besought him to come and save their community. Two thirds of the population was already dead and none would survive unless better remedies were employed. Doctor Nostradamus prepared a goodly supply of his favorite powders, gathered the implements of his profession, harnessed his mule, and set out for Aix.

After acquainting himself with conditions in the new community, Nostradamus was convinced that the contagion was being spread in the air. He therefore devised a smelling-powder, a compound of medicine and magic, consisting of finely powdered cypress wood, iris, cloves, sweet-flag and woody aloes, and prepared under favorable planetary aspects. The powder could also be made into troches by mixing it with fresh rose petals.

Nostradamus was fortunate in securing the assistance of a "pure and sincere" apothecary, one Joseph Turel Mercurin. Those who used this strange powder were preserved from the plague; the others died almost without exception. After being showered with gifts and blessings by the grateful citizens of Aix, Nostradamus answered the call of the government of Salon, where he also successfully fought the pest.

Soon afterwards he was called to Lyons. Here he had serious difficulties with the leading physicians. Nostradamus made no effort to force his methods upon the people, but, after much wrangling and numerous interferences, he requested the townfolk to choose between himself and another physician, Doctor Antoine Sarasin. Nostradamus issued his ultimatum in the following words: "I wish very much to help you, but you must permit me to experiment in my own way. I greatly honor the celebrated doctor, Antoine Sarasin, my colleague. But as my remedies differ from his, I desire that you choose who should remain physician of your town, and that you adopt immediately for yourself one or the other, myself or Sarasin." The delegation at once cried out: "We choose Doctor Nostradamus, the liberator of Aix!"

So successful were the experiments carried on by Nostradamus that the epidemic was conquered in a month, and the astrologer-physician returned triumphantly to Salon. Here, in 1547, he married for a second time. His wife, Anne Ponsart Gemelle, was described as a charming and intelligent woman of wealthy and respectable family. For Nostradamus, the years of lonely wandering were over. The years of prophetic genius were at hand.

Part III

THE SEER

Another magical device mentioned by Nostradamus was the consecrated basin. Examples of these bowls may still be seen in old museums side by side with unicorn horns and dragon teeth. Bowls made of crudely baked clay, their inner surfaces ornamented with complicated formulas and strange symbols, and intended for purposes of divination, have been discovered in the ruins of Sumerian cities. These bowls were filled with water and, when properly consecrated according to the rituals of transcendental magic, the surface of the water was strangely agitated by the presence of familiar spirits.

Hydromancy was practiced by the ancient Greek philosopher Pythagoras, and on the testimony of his disciples he had the power to cause rivers and streams to speak. Comte Cagliostro, the last of the magicians, foretold future events by causing a mesmerized child to gaze into the surface of a basin of water. The consecrated bowl with its shining contents, the magic mirror with its burnished surface, the crystal ball with its luminous depths, and the glittering particles of sand

used by the Oriental fakir are all part and parcel of the same
magical procedure.

Also, there was the wand, that indispensable symbol of
metaphysical authority. The conjurer's stick is as old as human history. It could be of the purest gold or ivory set with
jewels, or only a twig plucked at a crossroad on All Soul's
Eve. The wand was the scepter of the Mysteries, carried by
the hierophant of pagan rites when he descended into the
abyss of enchantments. With this rod of authority, the
magician, like Prospero in *The Tempest*, controls sidereal
spirits and submundane sprites.

The wand of Nostradamus was a laurel branch, and possessed the properties of a divining rod. When a spirit appeared, the end of the wand inclined itself in a manner
similar to the Water Witch of New England farm lore. The
leafy head of the wand was used to sprinkle the consecrated
waters upon the paraphernalia of the magic arts.

Following the rules set forth in his secret manuscripts,
Nostradamus applied his mystic machinery to the problem
of foreknowledge. Robed in sanctified raiment, he touched
his laurel wand to the waters in the basin and anointed his
robe and his foot. As enchantments must be wrought at
night, the flickering light of his solitary candle was reflected from the brazen legs of the tripod. The Delphic table
moved and the agitation was conveyed to the basin of water
that stood on its polished top. Eddies and ripples swirled
in the bowl; then from the midst of the water came forth
the shrill cry of the captured spirit.

Nostradamus describes the manner in which the strange
agitation which moved the waters in the brazen bowl was
communicated to his own body. His arms shook, he declared, and could scarcely hold the pen; the room was filled
with an eerie mist; phantom shapes moved to and fro in the

heavy air; vapors floated upon the surface of the magical sea; a light shone from the waters. In the midst of an airy turmoil, the spirit appeared, girdled about with a magical circle of pentagrams.

As Nostradamus leaned forward to listen, a small faint voice spoke from across the void, and, shaking in his sleeves, the prophet wrote down the words that were given to him. The Greeks taught that prose was the speech of men, and verse the language of gods and spirits. The Delphic oracles were revealed in obscure hexameter, and when Nostradamus published his *Prophecies* in quatrains and sextrains, he but followed the precedent established by the priests of Apollo.

As the revelations continued night after night, terror accompanied them, for the spirit told Nostradamus of the grievous afflictions that should burden the ages as yet unborn. Hour after hour the voice from the waters foretold plagues, famines, wars, and crimes. The great would conspire against the weak; despots would afflict their peoples; corruption would shake the foundations of both Church and State, and the world would be full of crimes and seditions. Year after year would bring pain; generation after generation would see misery.

Ingenious men, the voice predicted, would devise new means for their common destruction. There would be wars in the air, birds of death screaming in the night; there would be battles under the sea for dominion of the land; forts would move upon wheels; death would come like lightning, and poisons in the air would suffocate the living; cities would be destroyed by fire falling from the clouds, and the helpless would take refuge under the earth; whole nations would be utterly wiped out, and art and science would languish as men devoted themselves wholly to destruction.

Throughout many nights the shrill voice of the spirit proclaimed the doom of an afflicted world. The fullness of the
revelation will never be known, for Nostradamus declared
that so terrifying was the import of the words spoken to
him that he dared not reveal them, lest all the hopes of
humanity be crushed. He pleaded with the spirit to bring
him kindlier tidings. The form, floating in the luminous
mist, complied. Despite wars and rumors of wars, sorrow
and desolation, it affirmed that in the end truth should yet
prevail; for, through its own "self-inflicted pains," mankind would eventually learn the lessons of its survival.

At last the period of revelation came to an end. For the
final time, the spectral shape slowly faded away; the spark-
ling vapors grew dim; the waters in the basin subsided; the
strange agitation ceased. Nostradamus stood alone in his
study, and silently contemplated that strange future which
he would not live to see. How great was the problem of this
kindly man! He yearned to give some warning which would
incline human beings to a wiser course of action.

Like all great idealists, Doctor Michael longed to change
the shape of the inevitable. He had the power to write the
history of tomorrow, yet it was no part of his intention—
as he observed in his letter to King Henry II—merely to
depress men with the terrors of the unborn future.

Out of Nostradamus' meditations was evolved the obscure
style which has been the torment of his interpreters these
four hundred years. It was his purpose to reveal—and yet
conceal—by a cipher of words. The result has been what his
enemies have characterized as a jargon, a meaningless mass
of words. Needless to state, their verdict would have greatly
pleased the object of their detractions, whose firm belief
it was that those who lacked the wisdom to understand should
also lack the power to discover.

Yet another problem remained to be disposed of by Nostradamus. Suppose another person should follow in his footsteps and perform the same conjurations he had used. The spirit might be evoked to speak again. If it did, would that other prophet also have the wisdom and the patience to hide, with the veil of obscurity, the meaning of its fate-laden words? Would he reveal too much and thus add to the sorrows of an already burdened mortal kind? If another Prometheus of prevision should bring to a future generation the sacred fire of prophecy, would he likewise take the precaution to hide it in some hollow reed?

Out of these meditations the wise doctor came to a high resolution. One night, in the quietude of his cabinet he lit the flame of his alchemical furnace and with the bellows blew it to white heat. Then, to this purifying flame he consigned his secret books of magic. He burned them all—the scrolls, the parchments, and the papyri. Gone forever were the priestly books of Issachar and the magical pentacles of King Solomon. According to his own account, the rolls and parchments blazed up with an unearthly splendor. The room was alive with invisible powers as the flaming fingers of the salamanders clutched at the ancient books.

In a little while only ashes were left behind, and Nostradamus remained the last man who would ever know their contents. It was his responsibility to perpetuate, according to his own judgment, the unknown lore. The prophetic *Centuries and Presages* are the product of his decision. He compiled more than a thousand verses covering two thousand years of the world's history, dedicated them to his king, and left them to far places and distant times.

One day a young man presented himself at the door of Doctor Michael's house. His name was Jean-Aymes de Cha-

vigny, and he had come from the village of Beaune. Chavigny had been attracted to Nostradamus through the influence of Jean Dorat, with whom he had studied Greek.
The fame of the prophet had induced Chavigny to present
himself as a disciple, so strong was his desire to devote his
life to the understanding of the mystical arts of foreknowledge.

Convinced of the youth's sincerity and in need of an
amanuensis, Nostradamus accepted him into his confidence.
Though the seer could not communicate to his new pupil
that strange enthusiasm with which he himself was filled,
he could and did supply Chavigny with important keys for
interpretation of the prophetic writings. As far as is known,
this one sincere follower is the only living person whom
Nostradamus made party to his secret methods. The intimacy
between these two continued throughout the life of Nostradamus and was broken only by his death.

If the prophet was veiled and obscure in his writings, he
was frank and open with his student. Chavigny became his
spiritual son, the heir to his mystic writings. It is quite
possible that he dictated part of his prophetic verses to his
young secretary.

After the death of his master, Chavigny published some
interpretations of the *Prophecies*. In 1562, Nostradamus
dedicated an almanac to Pope Pius IV. This dedication was
accepted by His Holiness, and Nostradamus was shown much
respect and consideration by the Church. In 1566, Brother
Jean Vallier, a Franciscan attached to the monastery at
Salon, which was named Des Mineurs Conventules de Saint
Francois, reprinted the *Prophecies* with ecclesiastical permission.

In August 1554, an ominous event took place in Provence.
Two monsters had been born, and the countryside was in an

uproar over the event. It is noteworthy that early scientific books are remarkable for the details with which such prodigious events are recorded. While to ordinary matters only scanty attention might be given, the birth of a monster was so portentous as to be rivaled in importance only by comets and fiery apparitions.

In this case, an infant with two heads, each with a complete set of organs, had arrived unexpectedly at the village of Senas, to the consternation of its parents and the distress of the community. Furthermore, in confirmation of the saying that disasters never come singly, there was born in the town of Aurens near Salon a lamb also with an extra head. These prodigies undoubtedly portended some dire calamity, and both the Church and State were troubled.

There was but one thing to do: Nostradamus must be consulted. So the monsters were brought to him, and in the presence of the Governor of Provence, the astrologer interpreted the omens. These two-headed creatures, he declared, portended a division in the power of France. There would be domestic wounds that only centuries could heal; the long struggle between Catholicism and Protestantism was about to begin, and this religious strife would divide the nation into two warring camps. The assembled elders were duly impressed, and the incident found permanent record in the *Histoire Chronologique de Provence* by Honore Bouche.

Chavigny records another interesting episode of the curious power exhibited by Nostradamus on numerous occasions. While deep in his reveries one night, the prophet was suddenly disturbed by a persistent knocking at the front door. A page of the illustrious family of de Beauveau had been given a beautiful and valuable dog to guard. In some manner the animal had broken loose and had run away, and the lackey in his desperation had turned to the astrologer as a last resort.

Before his visitor could offer any explanation for his errand at that unseemly hour of the night—in fact, without asking the stranger his business—the doctor responded by crying in a voice loud enough to be heard outside: "What is it, page of the King? You make a deal of noise for a lost dog. Go out on the road to Orleans. You will find it led on a leash."

Too astonished to speak, the page hastened to a fork where the roads met, and in a little while found the dog held by a valet, just as he had been told. This story was widely circulated, and was followed by a deluge of requests for Nostradamus to discover missing persons as well as lost articles.

Trone de Condoulet, a rich burgher of Salon, was witness to an important prediction made by Nostradamus on the occasion of his meeting the young Prince de Bearn. The astrologer turned to those accompanying the youth with the pronouncement: "This young prince will sit on the throne of France and the title of 'Great' will be added to his name." The attendants dismissed the remark with a smile, since such a contingency appeared to them unlikely in the extreme. It took the Prince de Bearn ten years of strife to win his kingdom, but he was eventually crowned Henry IV, and, due to his immense popularity, he has always been known as "Henry the Great."

In 1560, the strife between Catholic and Protestant factions became general and, reaching Salon, put the city in an uproar. There were riots in the streets and many suffered violence for their religious differences.

Although Nostradamus' only desire was to be left alone and continue his scholarly pursuits in peace, his neutrality was not sufficient to protect him from attack. He was a man of wealth and importance, well known for his strong Catholic leanings. All this was a source of considerable annoyance to the Protestant faction, in whose persecutions of the doctor both religious fanaticism and personal jealousy were often joined.

On the other hand, the doctors and apothecaries had stirred up the Catholic faction by accusing Nostradamus of the practice of sorcery, and insisted that his pious mien was but a cloak to conceal his heretical and devilish inclinations. So bitter did the persecution become that Nostradamus dared not appear on the public streets for fear of bodily harm.

To make matters worse, the Ordinance of Orleans, published on January 31, 1560, included the following: "And because those who prognosticate things that are to come, publishing their Almanacs and Prognostications, using the terms of astrology, against the express commandment of God, a thing which ought not to be tolerated by any Christian Prince, we prohibit all publishers and libraries of publishing, from exposing for sale any Almanacs or Prognostications that first have not been seen by the Archbishop, the Bishop, or such as they may appoint. And against him who will have composed such Almanacs will be prosecution by our extraordinary judges and corporeal punishment."

Especially dangerous to Nostradamus was the edict because of the false editions of the *Prophecies* attributed to him, which were being circulated under his name and for which he could be held personally responsible under this ordinance.

Just when it seemed that disaster was inevitable for Nostradamus, the course of fate suddenly changed and the prophet emerged triumphant from a period of grave anxiety. His *Prophecies* began to be fulfilled with such startling rapidity that one government official wrote to the King, recommending that Nostradamus should be duly punished for the misfortunes being suffered by France, as though he (Nostradamus) had been the actual cause of them!

This is reminiscent of the experience of William Lilly, the English astrologer, who a hundred years later foretold the date of the Great Fire of London. When his prediction came true, Lilly was summoned to appear before Parliament to prove that he himself had not personally burned the city. Lilly states that he was treated quite decently and dismissed with honors, having convinced his peers that he was no incendiarist.

In France, the quatrains of Nostradamus were on everyone's lips. Henry II had died exactly according to verse 35, "Century I." The conspiracy of Amboise was clearly indicated in verse 13, "Century I;" also the conspiracy of Lyon, verse 59, "Century X." On November 17, 1560, while at Orleans, François II swooned in the midst of a religious ceremony. On December 5, of the same year, he died unexpectedly from an abscess in the ear. On this occasion the Venetian Ambassador, Michele, wrote to the Doge that everyone recalled the 39th verse of the "Xth Century," and commented on it in a low voice.

A man's success, however, only makes his personal enemies more embittered. Each time one of his predictions met with fulfillment was a fresh excuse for charging Nostradamus with sorcery. Never had such a prophet appeared in the modern world. It was obvious that no man who had not sold his immortal soul to the Prince of Hell could possibly know so much about the future. A God-fearing man might occasionally utter a prophetic line, but Nostradamus' uncanny accuracy outraged religious decency!

Part IV

Death—In a Golden Cage

Daughter of Italy's most powerful family, niece of a Pope, wife of Europe's most puissant ruler and mother of three kings, Catherine de' Medici was a woman to be reckoned with. Her indomitable spirit overshadowed France for half a century.

As Lord Bacon observes in his celebrated *Essay on Prophecy*, the Queen Mother "was given to curious arts." She had brought with her to France a veneration for things occult, a predilection for which the de' Medicis had long been famous. Modern writers pass lightly over the Queen's "superstitions," but there is considerable evidence that Catherine herself possessed the gift of second sight and a clairvoyant awareness of occurrences taking place in distant parts.

During the religious wars which burdened the latter years of her life, Catherine described in detail the death of Louis, Prince de Conde, although the incident occurred several days journey from Metz, where the Queen was lying dangerously ill. After the death of the old Cardinal de Lorraine, whose passing was revealed to her in a dream, she declared that his spirit visited her at night, disturbed her rest, and caused terror to her none-too-comfortable conscience.

Catherine's attitude toward sorcery is indicated by several fragments of contemporary history. She was party to a conspiracy to dispose of various important Huguenot leaders by devious methods of enchantment. Typical of such methods are the images which were made of their intended victims, the joints of which were filled with screws of various sizes.

By tightening these screws according to a mathematical pattern or formula, it was hoped that the persons whom the figures represented would be brought to speedy dissolution.

When the great necromancer, Cosimo Ruggieri, was charged with wizardry against her son's life, Catherine accused him of diabolic intent and caused him to be thoroughly tortured. Like the old Roman emperors, Catherine held the practice of the occult arts to be a royal prerogative, and indulgence therein by those of lesser station to constitute lese majesty.

During the early years of her reign, Catherine included among her counselors the celebrated mathematician-astrologer, Lucas Gauricus, Bishop of Civitate. She placed implicit confidence in the opinions of this learned man, and had him calculate not only her own nativity but also that of her husband, Henry II, King of France.

However, the King, an energetic and extroverted man, placed small reliance upon the pronouncements of his wife's soothsayers. Even when Gauricus made the solemn prediction that Henry would die from a duel near the forty-first year of his life, Henry failed to be impressed. Catherine, who had premonitions of her own, was deeply affected.

Years later when Nostradamus published the first part of his celebrated *Centuries*, Catherine at once recalled the fateful words of Gauricus. In the 35th quatrain of the "First Century," Nostradamus describes the circumstances under which the death of Henry II would occur. Catherine communicated with Claude de Savoie, of Provence, ordering him to make arrangements for the immediate presentation of Nostradamus at the court.

When he arrived in Paris on August 15, 1556, by royal post, after a month's hard travel, Nostradamus was met by the Constable of France and conducted to the royal palace, where the excitement caused by his appearance was rivaled only by the visit of some ruling monarch. The assembled courtiers, however, were permitted only a brief glimpse of the famous doctor. In response to Catherine's orders, he was conducted immediately to her private cabinet, where he was received by the King. Their Majesties then demanded that he explain the meaning of the mysterious quatrain; they also commissioned him to read the nativities of their three sons.

Nostradamus assured the Queen that her husband would perish in combat with a lone adversary, and that her three sons would all become kings. Catherine, a devoted if unfaithful wife, was visibly affected by both predictions. She pondered the strange verse which contained the sinister warnings of Henry's impending death:

> "The young lion will overcome the old one,
> In a field of battle by an extraordinary duel:
> In a golden cage he will pierce his eye,
> Two loppings one, then to die, cruel death."

The King's reaction was one of anxiety mingled with amusement. But Catherine reminded him of the earlier prophecy of Gauricus, two warnings, both by men of proved scholarship, could not be entirely dismissed. The defense mechanism in Henry's mind, however, was simple and apparently conclusive. As King, he could not be challenged by any private gentleman. The only man in Europe with whom he could fight a duel was the King of Spain, and such a challenge was beyond credibility. If ever fate should bring about the possibility of such a combat, he would bear the prediction in mind.

Henry then placed the two predictions — the first by Gauricus and the second by Nostradamus — in a special casket near his person. On rare occasions he would take out the prophecies and puzzle over their meaning. Though Catherine tried to explain to Nostradamus the unreasonableness of his prediction, the astrologer refused to revise his verdict.

On July 1, 1599, Henry proclaimed a tournament in honor of the marriage of his daughter, Elizabeth of France, with Philip II of Spain. The place selected was in the Rue Saint Antoine, then well beyond the limits of the city. Later the Bastille was built upon this site. Henry de Valois, a man of great personal courage, was also quite an exhibitionist. His favorite sport was jousting, and on this gala occasion of his daughter's marriage, he listed himself as prepared to meet all contestants.

The King's skill with the lance was well known throughout France, and an enormous crowd had gathered to witness the contest. As a young man Henry had often tilted with his father, Francis I, and carried to his grave the scars of these early tournaments.

In the course of the day's festivities, the King broke a lance with the Duke of Savoy and another with the Duke of Guise. His third course was with young Gabriel de Montgomery, Comte de Lorges, a nobleman with estates in Normandy and captain of the King's Scottish Guards. The young Comte took his tilting seriously and the two met at the barrier with a terrific shock. Their lances were splintered, the King lost his stirrup, and the impact was so great that Henry was visibly shaken in his saddle.

Unaccustomed to so doughty an adversary, Henry was both astonished and somewhat annoyed at not making a better showing before so illustrious a gallery. He immediately challenged Montgomery to another course. When the latter tried to excuse himself, the King commanded.

Catherine, who had dreamed of her husband's death the night before, waited anxiously for the day to end. She sent a message from the ladies' gallery, begging her husband not to ride again. The Duke of Savoy also reminded the King that the hour was late and recommended a postponement. But Henry was obstinate—he would ride once more against the young Norman lion!

Thus it came to pass that the incredible predictions made by both Gauricus and Nostradamus were fulfilled. The King, in his haste or carelessness, neglected to properly fasten the gilded beaver of his helmet. Taking their positions in the lists, the riders balanced their lances, spurred their horses, and the tilt was on.

Montgomery's lance struck the King's helmet, tearing away part of the plumage and crest. The shaft was shattered and the truncheon of his splintered lance crashed full into the King's visor. The half-fastened catch came loose, and several long splinters pierced Henry's eye and penetrated the brain. With a scream, Catherine fainted.

Assisted from his horse, Henry tried to make light of the accident and attempted to walk up the palace staircase with the aid of the Duke de Guise and the Cardinal de Lorraine. The best physicians of the day were immediately summoned, and they removed a splinter of wood four inches long from the wound, also several smaller pieces.

The King stood the pain with the greatest fortitude, and it was hoped that he might survive with the loss of an eye. After the painful operation he was in excellent spirits and commanded the Comte de Montgomery to be brought to his bedside. He assured the young man that he fully realized the mishap was accidental and bore him no unkindness.

After several days, symptoms of blood poisoning set in and it became obvious that the injury would prove mortal. At the deathbed of Henry II, the two greatest scientists of the 16th century met—Andreas Vesalius, the first modern anatomist, and Ambroise Paré, known as "the father of French surgery."

Every effort was made to determine the nature of the injury caused by the splinters. Similar pieces of wood were driven into the skulls of executed criminals in an effort to discover the probable courses that the sharp sticks might have taken. But the scientific knowledge of the time was inadequate, and on the eleventh day after the accident, days of excruciating pain, Henry II died in the 41st year of his life.

Thus was brought to complete fulfillment the cryptic quatrain of Nostradamus. What Henry had ridiculed as impossible or improbable had finally come to pass. The "field of battle" was the tournament; the "extraordinary duel" was the joust; the splinters had pierced the King's "eye;" "the golden cage" was his gilded visor; and, finally, he had died "a cruel death." Even the psychological factor was also intimated. Henry would probably never have ridden the second time had not the youth of his opponent challenged his own advancing years; "The young lion will overcome the old one," the quatrain said.

The fate of the Comte de Montgomery has been variously commented upon by later historians. Though Henry absolved him of all blame, there were those who maintained that Montgomery's failure to cast up the handle of his broken lance was deliberate. Granting such a charge to be true, then the combat becomes an "extraordinary duel" in actuality rather than a mere joust.

The 30th quatrain of the "3rd Century" has been interpreted to predict the fate that would befall Montgomery.
The words of Nostradamus read:

"He who in battle and sword with bellicose deed,
Will have carried the prize greater than he,
By night to the bed six will put the pike to him,
Nude, without armor suddenly will be overcome."

Nostradamus had other things to say about the fate of his
royal patrons. The 55th quatrain of the "3rd Century" contains a cryptic account of that which was to follow. It opens
with the lines:

"In the year that an eye will reign in France,
The court will be in very awkward trouble."

Most interpreters agree that the phrase "that an eye"
means "one-eyed" or some person with a single eye. The
ten days during which Henry II lay dying from the lance
wound is the only time in history that a one-eyed king ever
ruled in France. Henry's successor, Francis II, a delicate
boy of sixteen, died the following year. His younger brother,
Charles IX, ascended the throne in his tenth year, and lived
only to the age of 24.

Catherine's third son, Henry III, then became king, thus
fulfilling the other prediction made by Nostradamus, for he
had told Catherine that her three sons would each ascend
the throne. She had hoped to see them kings of Europe—
she did not suspect that for all three it would be the same
throne.

Henry III was the last of the Valois. The second "lop-
ping" mentioned by the seer certainly implied the assassi-

nation of Catherine's third son. Nostradamus correctly described the circumstances of the death of Henry III in the following prophetic line from one of his *Presages*:

> "*The King-King will be no more, of the Gentle one destroyed.*"

Henry III was the "King-King," for he had been crowned King of Poland just prior to becoming King of France. He was, therefore, twice a king. Henry III was corrupt, useless, and weak. He moved in an atmosphere of plots and counterplots. The evil that he schemed for others finally overwhelmed him.

One morning the King's attendants informed him that a monk named Clement brought news from Paris. Begging permission to whisper important tidings in the royal ear, the little monk came close to the King and drove a dagger through his body. Again, the tenure of Henry's rule—fifteen years— came to a violent end as Nostradamus had foretold.

The riddle of Nostradamus' curious words, "of the Gentle one destroyed," is thus explained. Not only does the term "Gentle one" apply to a religious recluse normally given to the works of God, but the assassin's name (Clement) means "clemency" or "gentleness."

This points up another problem in the interpretation of the famous quatrains. In the arrangement of the words themselves are hidden subtle meanings, which are revealed in their true sense only upon fulfillment of the prophecies. This is but another striking confirmation of the belief that it was Nostradamus' deliberate intention so to word his predictions that their significance could not be fully understood until the incident had actually taken place.

In 1560, Catherine de' Medici again commanded Nostradamus to attend her in Paris. The summons was probably welcome to the astrologer-physician. He was passing through a period of almost constant persecution at Salon. The physicians and apothecaries, jealous of his fame, had spread the rumor that Nostradamus was in league with Beelzebub. Aroused against Nostradamus, the townsfolk burned his effigy on the steps of the cathedral. They then paraded through the streets and threatened to burn the prophet himself if he could be found.

To a man threatened with the possibility of being dragged before the Inquisitional Court, Catherine's summons came as a miraculous intervention. The local tide turned immediately in his favor. The people of Salon, when they learned that their physician had been called to the Court as an advisor to the Queen, found their bitterness had been sweetened to a justifiable pride. The community was honored that one of its illustrious residents should have the royal ear.

Mounted on his favorite mule and attended by the Queen's pages, Nostradamus rode out of Salon amidst the cheers of his erstwhile persecutors. His reputation as a prophet and as a diviner of the mysteries of futurity had preceded him. The rich, in the communities through which he passed, implored him to examine their nativities; the sick begged the privilege of an audience in the hope of securing some of his infallible prescriptions.

Reaching Paris, Nostradamus was immediately conducted to the Queen, who received him in the presence of her sons. Catherine had changed much since those other days when Nostradamus first predicted for her the future of France. After the death of Henry II, the Queen had put on the deepest mourning and continued to dress in black throughout the rest of her life. Never a beautiful woman, she became less prepossessing with age. The intrigues in her soul etched deep lines upon her face. Her hollow cheeks revealed the shadows upon her conscience. Her deep-set eyes blazed with a fanatical light. She was as proud as Lucifer and, like this fallen angel, was resolved to be ruler over all the kingdoms of the earth.

After her husband's tragic end as the result of the tournament at St. Antoine, she gave herself up completely to the fulfillment of personal ambitions. These ambitions were centered largely in her three sons, for each of whom she plotted a kingdom. It was not so much Catherine's desire to be the mother of kings as to dominate, through them, the States that they should govern.

She relaxed her ambitions sufficiently to wage war upon the obstinate Huguenots. There can be no doubt that she was directly responsible for the Massacre of St. Bartholomew's Eve. Her religious piety was exceeded only by her addiction to political intrigue.

Nostradamus himself, though but fifty-seven years of age, was beginning to show the effects of a life devoted to ceaseless toil. Wearied with fighting the plague, and saddened by the bitterness in his professional life, the astrologer-physician was old before his time. Already his back was bent, his long beard was quite gray, his step less firm. He leaned upon his staff as a man clings to one of life's rare certainties.

Catherine had built a chateau at Chaumont-sur-Loire. It was a fantastic place, combining her love of glory with the strange superstitions of her Italian soul. Her new palace included a great room set aside for occult experiments. Here she assembled the elaborate paraphernalia of ceremonial magic, and to this laboratory of sorcery she invited the best magicians of the day. To Catherine, prayer was not sufficient to her purposes. She constantly implored divine assistance, but in order to be doubly sure that her plots worked out, she would not scorn to use the Devil's aid.

The Queen regarded Nostradamus as possessed of infinite supernatural powers. She led the astrologer to the great laboratory and commissioned him to practice there whatever arts might further her intrigues. Too wise a man not to realize the precariousness of his position, Nostradamus did the only thing possible under the circumstances; he refused to have any dealings with political concerns, and took refuge behind his prophetic abilities. Knowing what had happened to the Italian thaumaturgist, Cosimo Ruggieri, Nostradamus did not wish to end his life on the rack as had this unfortunate Florentine.

Nostradamus spent most of his life fighting the plague and the physicians, and it is an open question which he regarded as the greater evil. The "big-wigs" of medicine never have been kindly to the practitioner who departs from traditional methods. The astrologer-physician continued to practice according to his own convictions, and the more vigorously his methods were attacked, the more resolutely he defended them. Nostradamus returned to Salon after his interviews with Catherine de' Medici and resumed his private practice. His reputation was now enhanced by several almanacs he had already published, but to further complicate his affairs, his verses were pirated by unscrupulous publishers and charlatans who printed nonsense under his name. Every effort to discover the perpetrators of these impostures was in vain.

Then, in 1563, the Black Death returned; this time at Salon. For a while the astrologer found one evil substituted for another. The primary problem of survival thrust prejudice into the background. Men soon found themselves too busy trying to preserve their own physical lives to have any time or thought for personal or public quarrels.

As usual, in their emergency, they turned to the one and only man who had never failed them, although they, in turn, had often failed him—Doctor Nostradamus. To the victims of the plague, it made little difference whether God or the Devil had brewed the medicine; their only desire was to recover! This last encounter of Nostradamus with his ancient enemy, the Black Death, wrought its havoc in the old man's life. He was never stricken with the disease, but his aging body no longer was strong enough to support him during his long vigils with the sick.

While the plague was at its height, word came that the boy King, Charles IX, accompanied by the Queen Mother, was on his way to Salon to consult Nostradamus. The stricken city was in no condition to receive the royal guests. The citizens had scattered to the countryside to escape the plague, and only after considerable effort was it possible to assemble a representative group of prominent personages to receive their majesties.

When the royal party arrived, the city fathers who could be found put on their best manners and attempted to appear impressive. The boy King looked them over and with not even a pretense of acknowledgment of their greeting, bluntly announced: "I want to see Doctor Nostradamus." The astrologer was among the delegates, and he was immediately advanced and presented to the King. There and then Charles IX bestowed upon Nostradamus the title, "Physician and Counsellor in Ordinary to His Majesty." After this royal gesture, Nostradamus enjoyed considerably more of the community's respect.

A strange life was drawing rapidly to its end. Men did not live so long in those days. Though a few attained ripe years, there were too many hazards against health, and, measured by 16th-century standards, Nostradamus was an old man. Today he would have had many good years before him, but then only the benevolence of Providence could preserve even princes to their sixtieth year. Those not killed by the plague died of their physicians; and if they escaped the smallpox, the apothecaries poisoned them.

The gout, which had bothered Nostradamus for some years, had now turned to an arthritic dropsy, and each day the disease grew worse. At first, the doctor resolutely opposed his infirmities and outlined his usual habits. As the months passed by, however, it became increasingly difficult for him to go abroad. At last he was confined to his room. He would sit at his bench for a little time, and when the weariness grew too great would take to his bed and rest. The last months of his life—to use his own words—were spent between "bed and bench."

Like all thoughtful men, he made his will. He divided his monies among his wife and daughters, and to his "dear Anne" he left the "furnitures" of her house. His books, together with his letters, manuscripts and miscellaneous papers, he left to that one of his sons who would profit the most from the study of them. He made no inventory of his effects, but instructed that his papers should be put in baskets and locked in one of the rooms of his house until his sons should be of age. It was then to be decided which son should receive them.

He next bequeathed some monies to chapels and holy orders with consideration for the poor. His three sons were his residuary heirs. The executors of the will were Palamede Mark, Lord of Chateauneuf, and Jacques de Suffren, Escuper. In the will is an unusual section giving a detailed account

RARE PORTRAIT OF NOSTRADAMUS AS A YOUNG MAN

of 3,444 pieces of money. This description is believed to be a key to the numerical ciphers used in his predictions.

As might be expected, Nostradamus predicted his own death. On the bench beside him was the almanac of Jean Stadius, and opposite the date June 30 he had written "Hic prope mors est" (Here is death at hand). Earlier he had described the circumstance in one of his *Prophetic Presages*:

> "Upon returning from a mission, gift of the King, back
>   to place,
> Nothing more will occur, I shall have gone to God;
> Near ones, friends, brothers of my blood
> Will find me dead, near to the bed and the bench."

Chavigny, his faithful disciple, who visited Nostradamus on the evening of July 1, 1566, found the sick man in good spirits. He gives the following record of his last meeting with Nostradamus: "The day before he exchanged this life for a better, after I had spent many hours with him, and late at night was taking leave of him until the following morning, he said, 'You will not see me alive at sunrise.'" This, the prophet's last prediction, was fulfilled. In the morning he was found dead at his bench, an open book before him. Like the old Greek scholar, he was a student to the end.

Some fanatics once approached Nostradamus and accused him of being a sorcerer, warning him that on his death the Devil would surely come and drag him away by his feet. To which Nostradamus replied: "Go on with you, wicked, dusty feet. Never will you walk on my throat, neither during my life nor after my death."

By historians, this incident is regarded as the basis for his express desire to be buried in an upright position. So, in accordance with his wishes, Nostradamus was buried in the wall of the Chapel of Saint Martha, in the Franciscan Church of Les Cordeliers at Salon.

The 17th-century citizens of Salon had a legend to the effect that, like the British Merlin, Nostradamus lived on in his tomb surrounded by his papers, pens, and books, and wrote more prophecies by the light of his ever-burning lamp. And whoever should lift the lid of the tomb, they believed, would perish on the spot. One remarkable account relates that when his tomb was opened, a loose stone fell and killed the man responsible for breaking into the sepulchre. A manuscript was found buried with the body stating that the man who broke into the tomb should die. By the 18th century, however, this legend had lost its terror, for in 1791 the Church of Les Cordeliers was destroyed by the Revolutionists. The remains of Nostradamus, together with those of his son, were carried to Saint Laurent and there re-interred.

His son, Caesar, placed a bust of his father above the tomb, and his widow composed the following epitaph: "Here rest the bones of the most illustrious MICHAEL NOSTRA-DAMUS, alone in the judgment of mortals worthy to record the future events of the entire world under the influence of the stars. He lived sixty-two years, six months and seventeen days. He died at Salon in the year 1566. Let not posterity disturb his peace. Anne Ponsart Jumelle (Gemelle) hopes for her husband true felicity."

Gradually, through the alchemy of time, the baser metals of jealousy and intolerance are transmuted into the mellow gold of human charity.

The doctors who had hated Nostradamus alive now honored Nostradamus dead. The apothecaries now remembered him only as a conscientious practitioner whose scruples were not without justification. The religionists, both Catholic and Protestant, now found predictions in the prophet's verses favorable to their causes and decided that he had moments of true vision.

For the citizenry, however, it remained to bestow the final mark of approbation. There was already a fountain enriched by one of his quotations; but this was not deemed enough. In extraordinary session it was decreed that hereafter, and unto perpetuity, the street on which he had lived should be known as Rue Nostradamus.

The prophet lives on, not in his tomb, but in the deathless memory of time which is the final resting-place of the great.

And so it came to pass that a prophet was found at last who was *not* without honor to his own country!

The prophetic spirit, as Nostradamus calls it, began to emerge through him, but being a scientifically trained man, he was not interested in the vagaries of visions and dreams, so he set to work to organize these things mathematically. Some say this was done astrologically; others say, geomantically; but he reduced all these visions and dreams to names, times, and places, being quite disinterested in abstruse, obscure, or indefinite types of material.

Nostradamus gives us an interesting and amazing slant on the shape of things that are to come, and we cannot but realize that there must be some laws operating in Nature by which such phenomena can be produced. If it is possible for any human being, by any means whatsoever, to anticipate the future, then there must be laws governing this; there must be some image or pattern of the future for anyone to be able to tune it in, or discover it, or become sensitive to it.

Let us consider, for example, the Nostradamus prophecy about Napoleon, previously mentioned. Napoleon had not yet been born. There was nothing available to the normal mind of man that could have told anyone that a man would be born near France, become emperor, marry twice, have one son, and die on a rock. That does not fit into the things we regard as possible, but we are beginning to realize more and more that the possible and the impossible as terms are merely limitations which we ourselves place upon things we do not know very much about; and we know so little about so much that it does not pay us to be too dogmatic about that which is possible and that which is not.

Nostradamus says that after he had completed his prophetic "Centuries" he saw a pattern or picture of world events so complicated and so awe-inspiring, so enormous in terms of human suffering and human misfortune, so horrible in the terms of the things that human beings would do to each other in the name of civilization and progress, that he wondered whether it was wise to reveal to the world the misfortunes that lay ahead. Would man's initiative, his hopes, and his dreams be shattered if he realized the terrible things that he would have to go through in order to find the peace and security that he was seeking?

Nostradamus came to the conclusion that it was not good to reveal too clearly these things that might too profoundly influence the course of human living. So he rewrote the prophecies, obscuring them, veiling them, so that only scholarship could reveal the meaning. He said: "In many instances it will be impossible to interpret my prophecy until the event itself occurs. Then you will discover that I have placed within the prophecy somewhere a key, a peculiar, limiting circumstance by which it is possible to perceive that this event, and this event only, is the fulfillment of it." Here is an example of it.

Nostradamus wrote, "The French shall advance toward Montgolfier and a man under the hole shall give the warning." Studious checking did not disclose any place in France, or in the French Empire, called "Montgolfier." What happened was this. Nearly 200 years afterward, the Montgolfier brothers invented the hot-air balloon. The first use of this balloon was for military observation; therefore, the line is explained and we can see exactly what he meant when he said "the man under the hole will give the warning," because the old hot-air balloon had a large hole directly over the basket.

That was the way in which he prepared his predictions, obscure and difficult to interpret until the event had fulfilled itself. Not only did he anticipate exact details, but he described a great number of inventions and devices unknown to his own day. He described accurately tanks, airplanes, submarines, aerial warfare. He even described "the globes that will drop from the skies and will lie hidden in the earth for days while the fire burns in them, and will then explode;" they are what we call time bombs.

If you believe this to be an easy accident, try to figure out what is going to happen 100 years from now with all our perspective on the subject. Then realize that a little French doctor, living in a small town 400 years ago, who, in describing the future of America, said that in time to come the American eagle would fly against the Rising Sun. Nostradamus referred to certain things that would happen in Great Britain. In his time there was no Great Britain. He wrote in 1560, and it was not until 1604 that James I announced the Confederation of Great Britain.

He then goes on to tell us, in his veiled language, that between now and the end of the century we are not going to have too much peace in the world. He regrets it, but with the detached attitude of the scholar he says: "It is all very sad and very terrible, but what can we do about it so long as human nature remains the same?" Wars are not caused by the gods, he says, but by the ignorance, stupidity, and short-sightedness of human beings. So long as that attitude remains there will be no peace, regardless of legislation, world courts, or anything else on earth.

Nostradamus says that the great arc is moving gradually and inevitably toward the year 1997. He is very specific about that date which will be the time of a great war between the East and the West. That is when a united and consolidated Asia, including the Japanese islands, China, India, Siberia, and Mongolia, will form one great empire.

Then it is that the great King of the East will rise and go to war in the air. And in this war, flying machines will be so numerous and will move so continuously across the sky that the sun will be darkened as though by the flight of locusts, and death and destruction shall fall upon the earth. This war will determine the rulership of the whole earth. 1997 is the date. I imagine that most of us will be a little weary of life by that time.

However, Nostradamus does not say that there is no possibility of avoiding this war, but he declares the avoidance of it demands and depends upon basic changes in human nature. Without those changes this great event cannot be prevented. He does not tell us the outcome of that war, except by indirection, but he goes on to say that after that war the great prophet will arise in Christendom. The presbyter, or new priest, will reform and revitalize the entire structure of the Christian faith.

We are led to assume from these statements that Western civilization will not be destroyed, because Nostradamus goes on to describe happenings in the West which imply that Asia does not conquer the Occident, although she would struggle greatly to accomplish this.

Nostradamus describes very accurately and definitely such phenomena as radio, the sending of words and thought and pictures through the air, pictures that move, and innumerable inventions and discoveries that are to come. Being not only a scholarly man, but a philosophical-minded man with a great dream of the common good in the background of his nature, he also dreams forward to consequences of the things we are passing through. He tells us that these experiences are the inevitable result of the immaturity, the childishness of human beings; that only through undergoing these experiences can we grow up, and that only when we grow up can our world mature.

Nostradamus tells us that there is no possible hope for the Golden Age, where we will live together in peace and security, until human beings have experienced and suffered enough to realize that this security is more important to them than the small, selfish actions they perform which destroy that security. In other words, peace must be earned. It must be earned, not only in the relationship of nations, but also in the relationship of individuals.

As long as we do not want to talk to our own relatives, as long as we squabble with our children and fight with our neighbors, there can be no hope of international peace, because the international unit is nothing more or less than the enlarged reflection of our daily living cast upon the affairs of State.

Nostradamus describes the twenty-one democratic powers that would unite against the great league of Berlin and Rome. He says that these and other nations would dream the dream of a great commonwealth of peoples, that they would attempt to establish a great common civilization based upon the basic principles of civilization; that is, that weakness is something to protect—not exploit. He declares that all of these dreams would be dreamed, but that we would not be able to live up to them; we would accomplish a little each time, but we would fall back a little each time.

We would go on in this crab-like manner until, finally, after the fullness of experience, we should become rich enough in values to be able to plan and dream of a world in which we should so greatly desire peace and security that we would work for those things with the same enthusiasm that we now have for personal gain. Only when the common good means more to the average citizen than his own profits, can the common good be expected in the world. That is the substance and burden of the moral philosophy of Nostradamus.

Nostradamus says that he sees ships going forth to war, the sides of the ships painted in curious designs and colors to deceive the enemy. He sees men making ships out of iron that will float, and steel fish that swim under the sea and shoot death out of their mouths. He describes the advent of Oliver Cromwell in England. (He doesn't call him Cromwell, he calls him Old Noll, which, curiously enough, is exactly what the English nicknamed Cromwell when he did come along.) He describes the red beard that would plague Europe. The red beards that plagued Europe in the century when Nostradamus lived belonged to the great family of North

NOSTRADAMUS   83

African pirates—the Barbarossas. He refers to the Spanish people as the stuttering race because of the impediment in Philip II's speech, which resulted in the soft "th" of the Spanish language; it was copied from the lisping of the King.

This event occurred later but Nostradamus picks it up just to indicate that he doesn't miss small details in passing. He describes how the Pope would lose temporal power when the great black beard came to Italy, but that the papal State would emerge as a free country. He describes the development of the Panama Canal—"the great ditch that would unite the oceans"—and of the Suez Canal under the premiership of Disraeli.

Nostradamus describes the Great Fire of London and dates it exactly. He writes much that has to do with America, which he usually calls the Hesperic Isles. On one occasion, however, he definitely calls it Amerique. This is when he says that the child shall leave his parents' house and take up his own abode as a sovereign State. He describes the modern Russians, calling them the Reds, and he predicts the rise of the Slav.

He predicts revolutions of various kinds affecting countries of the Near East; the terrific sorrow that comes to Greece and the flight of the Greek king. He calls Victor Emmanuel of Italy the French king upon the Italian throne, which is correct because the House of Savoy, the Italian ruling house, is a French house. Nostradamus says that the little king would lose his throne as a result of the fall of the duke. All of these things he brings to us step by step.

In all, Nostradamus wrote 1,000 verses which involve 2,500 predictions. Of these about 800 have already been fulfilled, and the others relate either to the future or to events which cannot be checked. For instance, Nostradamus says that the young Dauphin of France, the son of Louis XVI, would not die in prison. According to history, he died in prison. But a statement issued by the Dutch government about 50 years later states that he did not die in prison.

We do not know. Nostradamus may have been right, but history is not detailed enough regarding certain events to tell us whether a certain king was murdered by a certain man. However, over 800 of Nostradamus' predictions have been identified and clearly related to the events indicated—those which relate to the future can only be looked forward to.

Beyond and greater than the entire problem of Nostradamus as a universal genius—and he was that—is another problem; that is, what is the principle in Nature by which Nostradamus' predictions were made possible? They contradict everything that we have regarded as reasonable and practical. How is it possible to read the future if the future does not exist? Regardless of powers, how are we going to see something that is not there?

There is only one answer and that is that the future cannot be so abstract or unformed as we generally regard it. Most scientists can make some predictions. A doctor can make a prediction about the probable course of a disease, but there is no known method for predicting what an unborn person is going to be named or what he will do in his lifetime. We do not know how it is done, but Nostradamus did it.

Nostradamus said that after he had learned how to prognosticate, he was so frightened by the magnitude of his discovery that he burned the documents, the books, and manuscripts which had belonged to his family for centuries and which contained the secret formula for making predictions, for fear that they would be passed on to us.

The whole issue is far more than an issue in prophecy; it concerns our conclusions and convictions about reality and unreality, the known and the unknown. It is a terrific challenge, if we wish to consider it, but most people follow the method of deciding that it is too much of a challenge, and that it is better to ignore it than to worry about it. We cannot *disprove* it; we have no inclination to accept it, so a dignified ignoring is the selected path of procedure.

Now and then thoughtful people accept these problems for what they are worth, study them, and then discoveries are made. Things are worked out by which progress in the race is achieved. To me, the basic interest of Nostradamus is not in his prophecies at all, but in the mechanics of universal Nature by means of which it is possible to predict accurately the tomorrow. To do this, there is only one possible answer— somewhere, some way, tomorrow exists *now*, or nobody could find it and predict from it.

There is something about time and space that we do not understand, and it is a very optimistic person who will deny the possibility of there being much that we do not understand. We are little beings isolated in space, cast away on a little island which we call earth, about which we know almost nothing—and about the larger space we know less. Therefore, we must recognize the possibility of the presence of laws and forces in Nature which, while unfamiliar and unbelievable to us, may be perfectly real and may be the normal acceptance of tomorrow. Surely, were George Washington to be born again today with the memory of his own time, he would be vastly amazed at the things we are doing now—it would seem nothing less than miraculous.

EPILOGUE

The townsfolk of Salon named a street in honor of their distinguished citizen, Nostradamus, and a public fountain was also dedicated to his memory. With the passing of years, legends multiplied, and they grew with the telling. Many of these myths unquestionably originated in actual occurrences, but others are obviously fabrications. Possibly the most interesting of the semi-historical legends are those involved in the story of "The man who could keep a secret"—and did.

In the month of April, 1597, thirty-one years after the death of Nostradamus, an artisan of Salon, whose name unfortunately is not recorded, returned to his home after a long day at his bench; and after a substantial meal, retired to rest. He was a man of small imagination and not given to any special interest in the supernatural. At the midnight hour, he was awakened by a strange chilliness that seemed to fill the entire house. As he sat up in his bed, terrified, the walls of his room appeared to open, and the spirit of Michael Nostradamus, surrounded by an aura of flickering lights, came out of space and stood at the foot of his bed.

The occult physician-magician appeared exactly as in life; he wore the black robe of a scholar, and his long gray beard shone with a silvery fire.

The spectre addressed the artisan, ordering him to go to the Intendant of the province and demand letters to King Louis XIV. These letters should provide for a private audience with the monarch.

"What thou art to say to the King," declared the spectre, "thou wilt not be informed of until the day of thy being at court, when I shall appear to thee again, and give thee full instructions; but remember thy life depends on absolute secrecy towards everyone save the Intendant."

After repeated warnings that, on pain of death, must no person be told of the apparition or the purpose of its coming, the ghost returned to space, and the walls of the little room closed again.

The artisan was terrified; for several minutes he lay in his bed moaning and praying, beside himself with fear. His good wife, disturbed by the commotion, hastened to his side and pleaded with him to tell her the cause of his fear. At last, desperate at the plight in which he found himself, the artisan bound the woman to secrecy and told her the story.

As he finished speaking, the room was violently shaken and a voice said, "I wanted you to tell no one, on pain of death." At the same instant a blinding flash of light filled the room, and the artisan was stricken dead in his bed.

This extraordinary incident caused great commotion in the little French town. There were many private discussions and several public meetings among the burghers. Soon others were visited by the ghost, and each in turn was bound to secrecy. And each in some way and from some cause betrayed the trust, and died.

The epidemic of mysterious deaths became a principal subject of conversation not only at Salon, but throughout France; for the fame of the great departed seer was known in every district and province.

In Salon was a blacksmith named Francois Michel. Included among his neighbors were two brothers, one of whom had recently died as the result of informing his brother of Nostradamus' ghostly visit. One night Nostradamus came to Michel the farrier under conditions exactly the same as they were on his first appearance. A happy man was Francois Michel, and he had a great desire to live a normal ex-

pectancy of his years. He agreed to fulfill the demands of
the spirit, and fortified the decision with the resolve that
not even torture should cause him to betray the trust.

He went immediately to the Intendant, but had considerable difficulty in securing an interview, for the official believed the poor blacksmith to be of unsound mind. But in
time he secured the ear of the officer, and told him of the
letters to the King that must be prepared exactly as Nostradamus had required. The farrier, a practical and direct man,
closed his interview with the words, "I can readily conceive,
your Excellency, that I must seem to you to be playing an
exceedingly ridiculous part; but if you will be pleased to
order your officials to examine into the late sudden deaths
in our town, I flatter myself that your Excellency will again
send for me."

The Intendant made a thorough search into all the circumstances of the deaths and, convinced that some strange
supernatural force was at work, decided on his own responsibility to send Francois Michel to Versailles with the
special dispatches to M. de Baobefieux, the Minister of
State. The Intendant went so far as to supply funds for the
journey, and wished the bewildered blacksmith success in
his strange mission.

Francois Michel arrived at Versailles by coach without
the slightest idea as to what he should say to the Minister
of State when he presented his letters. As he arrived late in
the day, after a long journey, he decided to rest in a local
inn for the night.

At low twelve, the witching hour of spirits, the curtain
of the great canopied bed parted, and the ghost of Nostradamus stood beside the blacksmith. The shade of the dead
sorcerer dictated to Francois, word by word, the message
he was to deliver to M. de Baobefieux. At this time also,

Nostradamus revealed the secret message that was to be given to the King.

"Many difficulties will be laid in your way," concluded the spectre, "in obtaining this private audience; but beware of desisting from your purpose, and of letting your secret be drawn from you by the Minister or anyone else, under pain of instant death."

The Minister of State tried in every possible way to force Francois to reveal his message for the King, but the farrier was not moved, and maintained absolute silence respecting the dreadful message which he could confide solely to the King.

M. de Baobefieux finally intimated that without more explanation he could not request for an unknown blacksmith a private audience with His Majesty. Francois solved this dilemma with the following words: "That your Excellency may not think that what I am instructed to tell the King is all a mere farce, be pleased to say to His Majesty that at the last hunting party at Fontainebleau, His Majesty himself saw the apparition, that his horse took fright at it, and started aside, and that His Majesty, as the appearance was only momentary, took it for a deception of sight, and therefore abstained from mentioning it to anyone."

The Minister of State, gathering his courage, reported to Louis XIV the incident of Francois' arrival and the extraordinary story he had related. To his surprise, the King commanded that the farrier be brought to the palace at the first possible moment. King Louis admitted that he had seen the apparition in the forest in Fontainebleau.

So it came about that the farrier had private audience with the King. He remained at the court of the Grande Monarque for three days, and much of this time he spent in the private cabinet of the King. At the end of the strange visit, Francois took public leave of the King, whose manner on the occasion was most gracious and appreciative. At the time of the parting, the Duc de Duras, who was Captain of the King's guards, remarked apologetically to the King, "Sire, if your Majesty had not expressly ordered me to bring this man to your presence, I should never have done it, for most assuredly he is only a fool!"

Louis answered this with a strange smile, murmuring, "My dear Duras, thus it is that men frequently judge falsely of others; Francois is a more sensible man than you and your friends imagine."

Through the devious ways of court life, the visit of the blacksmith of Salon to Louis le Grande came to general public knowledge. Every effort was made to discover the nature of the message he had brought; but even those who knew the deepest mysteries of the State were unable to find out what transpired between Francois Michel and Louis XIV.

Speculations were innumerable, and for some years every move that Louis made was examined in the effort to discover if his actions were influenced by some supernatural counsel. The most common explanation was that the message in some way involved the program of French influence in Spain by which the grandson of Louis gained the Spanish throne.

Francois the farrier received a handsome present from the Minister of State and returned to Salon, with strict injunctions that he should never mention to any living soul what had transpired between himself and the King.

The good blacksmith had but one weakness of interest to our story. He would occasionally join his cronies in a local tavern and tipple with them far into the night. On these occasions, he would become quite garrulous, and frequently the subject of their conversation was his great journey to the King. One of his companions would ask laughingly, "Come Francois, tell us your secret, if you have one." But even when the farrier's tongue was well loosened, he never forgot the warnings of the ghost of Nostradamus, and his lips were sealed. One writer has pointed out that his silence was as intense and complete as that of the celebrated Count Von Moltke, of whom it has been well said, "He was able to hold his tongue in seven languages."

Further fame came to the blacksmith of Salon; his portrait was painted by M. de Roullet, the outstanding artist of his day. The picture was extensively engraved and copies are still to be seen in collections of old French prints. They depict Francois Michel as a grave and intelligent-looking man of about forty, with a strange somewhat mystical look in his face. In his painting, the artist caught the stubborn silence of a man who had seen something from the other world, and had the wit and courage to take his secret with him to the grave.

FRANCIS BACON
THE CONCEALED POET

The true authorship of the dramatic works attributed to William Shakspere is the greatest mystery of literature. It has been apparent to many scholars that the Stratfordshire actor lacked the intellectual equipment to produce the histories, comedies, and tragedies associated with his name. The universal law of cause and effect demands that a great accomplishment should proceed from an adequate cause. When this law appears to be broken, the subject generally requires further examination.

Who was William Shakspere? What was his background? What were his opportunities? How did it happen that an obscure apprentice to a village butcher suddenly and without apparent justification emerged into the light of fame as the greatest dramatist of all time?

William Shakspere was born in the little village of Stratford-on-Avon in 1564. Of his early life little is known. The humble estate of his forebears is suggested by the fact that the family home bordered on the village dumping grounds.

There is nothing to indicate that his ancestry had been burdened by any touch of genius, nor is there any intimation that his parents were even literate.

While poverty is no disgrace, and greatness frequently arises from humble origin, it is generally possible to trace the circumstances which lift a man to an heroic estate. But there is no record, contemporary or otherwise, that Willy Shakspere possessed great ambitions or extraordinary personal qualifications.

The glowing descriptions of Willy Shakspere's dreamy childhood and poetic adolescence belong to a sphere of wishful thinking. Only three reasonably established facts emerge from the obscurity which shrouds Shakspere's younger years. He poached on a rich man's game preserves, and for this he was haled into court for what his biographers have called an "amusing" episode.

Also, the townsfolk of Stratford remembered the day when the young poet-to-be fell face down in the village horse-trough in a state of complete inebriation. He was dragged out and left to dry on the adjacent green. This incident also is passed over lightly as a shadow across the path of greatness.

More creditable is the record of his apprenticeship to the Stratford butcher. While this may have been the beginning of his career as a respectable citizen, it held little promise of outstanding literary ability.

The educational opportunities of Stratford require consideration. Every effort has been made to prove the cultural opportunities of the community. There was a primary school at Stratford, historians solemnly avow. Here Master William learned the three R's. By this fact, the whole mystery of his life is explained. It is even "supposed" that the school-master took an interest in the youthful prodigy, tutoring him generously in the fine arts.

Literally and factually, it is exceedingly doubtful that any school existed in Stratford until after Shakspere's death, and the genial schoolmaster retreats to the state of hypothesis. There is no proof of any kind that William Shakspere learned to read or write while in Stratford, or, for that matter, anywhere else. Literacy was not regarded as essential to success among tradesmen during the Elizabethan Period. In fact, education as a whole was regarded with suspicion. Even princes were ashamed to acknowledge that they could write more than their own names. There were professional scriveners employed by the gentry, and these were regarded as little better than lackeys.

Sixteenth-century Stratford was an isolated community connected with London by an irregular coach system. There was little travel and almost no contact between the smaller shires and the great metropolitan centers. When the English raised their armies to fight Spain, the militia from the shires had to bring interpreters with them because the local dialects were so involved and obscure that the men could not understand each other's speech.

Later, we are induced to believe that William Shakspere, enjoying at best a most inadequate local education and speaking a meaningless jargon, was already on his way to literary immortality while still serving his time with the local meat-chopper.

It must occur to the thoughtful reader that something is wrong with this picture. Allowing that Shakspere possessed a prodigious capacity for learning, how did he satisfy his thirst for knowledge? Even his most enthusiastic biographers are at a loss to explain this mystery. They can only advance the opinion that in some way he did educate himself, and in the process accumulated so vast an erudition that he excelled the ages.

During this process of external self-improvement, Willy Shakspere had time for the oft sung romantic interlude with Anne Hathaway. The two families got together and decided that in deference to local tradition, it would be appropriate for Willy and Anne to marry before the birth of their first child. Shakspere was a grudging party to this plan, and at the first opportunity deserted kith and kin. Leaving his wife and children without support, he hied himself off to London to become an immortal.

This domestic irresponsibility is passed over lightly by historians as a classic example of artistic temperament.

Having arrived in London, our young hero passed through a period of starving and struggling that would have gladdened the heart of Horatio Alger. His earliest association with the theater is unanimously agreed upon by his biographers— he held horses' heads at the theater doors and eked out his economic survival from the gratuities resulting therefrom. Soon after this menial apprenticeship he emerges as a playwright. There are no records to show how this came about, but some delightful myths have been fabricated about Master William burning the midnight oil. He dabbled a bit in acting, but never achieved any prominence as a thespian; even the most optimistic and devoted Shakespeareans cannot advance any evidence that he ever enjoyed top billing.

His private life in London is a complete blank historically. There is no record that he ever traveled or studied, or that he enjoyed the patronage of the truly learned. The account of Shakspere reading his plays to Queen Elizabeth is apocryphal, but there is a statement to the effect that the members of the theatrical troupe to which he belonged received an allotment of scarlet cloth so that they could make

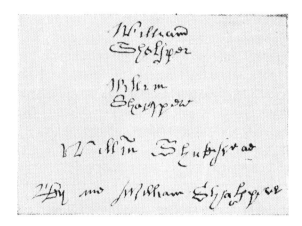

THE SIGNATURES OF WILLIAM SHAKESPEARE

These scrawls are the only original autographs of the immortal bard. Can such writings be reconciled with the statement in the *First Folio* that the original manuscript of the plays was "without blot or blemish"? Consider well the structure of the letters. There is not even uniformity of style, nor is the spelling better than the penmanship. Are we to believe that the world's greatest poet could not decide upon the spelling of his own name? Are these signatures the product of a man whose mind conceived the greatest soliloquies of literature? It appears much more likely, as some have suggested, that Shakspere's hand was guided when he wrote, and that these poor tracings represent the extent of of his literacy.

new cloaks with which to take part in a parade through the streets of London. This appears to have been a high point in the great man's career.

By 1598 the great plays were being published with some regularity. They were decently printed in octavo pamphlets, some anonymously, some with the name William Shakespeare variously spelled fixed to the titles, and some initialed W. S. There is no record to indicate the financial returns from these literary productions, and their extreme rarity today would indicate that the editions were not large. It never has been proved that Shakspere received any royalties from his literary efforts.

As actors and playwrights of the 16th and early 17th centuries enjoyed no reputation unless it was bestowed upon them by powerful patronage, there is little to sustain the belief that Shakspere could have accumulated any great wealth from these activities. He finally acquired a small interest in some theatrical projects which may have provided him with a modest pittance and supplied the ink which he is said to have used "without blot or blemish."

After a number of years in London, years which historians have tried desperately but futilely to account for, the great man returned to Stratford and the bosom of his family. He returned as a financial giant, bought one of the best houses in Stratford, and set himself up as a pillar of local respectability.

To exhibit the versatility of his genius, the poet then became the practical business man. It is pointed out with pardonable pride that even in this respect he was original in the extreme. There is a contemporary document to indicate that he entered the brewing business for which, on one occasion, he made a considerable purchase of hops. The letter relating to this purchase is now one of the priceless Shaksperean documents.

As an avocation, the bard took up money-lending. To demonstrate his refined sense of business propriety he pressed a loan for two shillings, and when the debtor could not pay, sued his surety. This is touchingly reminiscent of Shakespeare's philosophy of economics as expressed in the character of Shylock.

Having become truly a man of world affairs and a leading citizen of his community, the great poet took time to prepare his will. With touching domesticity he bequeathed his second-best bed and his "broad silver gilt bowl." He neglected, however, to make any disposition, or even to make mention, of his literary productions. The will is not in his own handwriting, but was prepared by a notary, and there is question as to whether the actual signatures are his own.

The closing years of his life were uneventful except for mild participation in local politics. The circumstances surrounding his death were somewhat mysterious. It would seem that the immediate cause of his decease was a barroom brawl. His great and noble heart could not stand the strain and stopped abruptly.

He was buried quietly, presumably at Stratford Church. Some years later a half-length figure of him with the hands resting on a sack of malt was erected to his memory. The epitaph, supposed to have been prepared by his own hand, enriched his tomb. The depth and sublimity of the lines have been noted many times.

> "GOOD FREND FOR IESUS SAKE FORBEARE,
> TO DIG THE DUST ENCLOASED HEARE:
> BLESE BE YE MAN TY SPARES THES STONES,
> AND CURST BE HE TY MOVES MY BONES."

So passed the crowning glory of the literary world, the glorious Apollo of poesy, the mind that enriched the English language, whose artistry elevated drama to its highest pinnacle, the beloved son of the muses.

Was there ever a more incredible state of affairs? Did ever Nature more completely contradict herself? An author, not one scrap of whose manuscript is known to exist, a literateur who never wrote a letter and received but one as far as is known; a man who presented himself with family arms without benefit of the college of heraldry; a man learned above other mortals whose daughter Judith, being of sound mind and body, and being of mature years, could not write her own name, but merely made her mark.

This is the historical William Shakspere of whom not even an authentic picture survives. Is it any wonder then that the best thing that Ben Jonson could say of him was that he "knew small Latin and less Greek?" Is it greatly to be wondered at that there has dawned slowly on sincere scholars the subtle conviction that it is quite possible William Shakspere was not the sole and entire author of the plays that bear his name?

THE PROBLEM OF AUTHORSHIP

If William Shakspere did not write the plays attributed to him, the problem is to discover the true author or authors thereof and the reasons for the imposture. There is nothing in the life of William Shakspere known that could have fitted or qualified him as a great literary genius. Nothing short of the miraculous can explain the discrepancies between his life and his supposed works. Before resorting to a doctrine of miracles, we should be wiser to search for reasonable solutions.

To summarize certain somewhat outstanding and obvious points:

The author of the Shakespeare plays must have possessed a superlative education. Shakspere had little, if any.

The author required a broad scholarship in languages, both classical and contemporary. Shakspere had no opportunity to acquire such learning.

The author traveled widely and was familiar with the customs, social conditions, political structure, and geographical particulars of numerous countries. There is no *record* that Shakspere ever left England.

The author had a profound knowledge of academic law, both theoretical and practical. There is nothing to indicate that Shakspere received such training.

The author possessed an intimate knowledge of the court of England, court usage, and the psychology of the aristocracy. It is extremely unlikely that the Stratford actor would enjoy such intimate contact with a sphere so far from his own.

The author had an exceptional grasp of the great systems of world philosophy, including the Platonic and the Aristotelian, and was himself proficient in the interpretation of philosophical formulas. There is nothing to intimate that Shakspere was so trained.

The author must have possessed a considerable library, or, at least, have had constant access to such material with a knowledge of its use. We do not know that William Shakspere ever owned a book.

The author had definite revolutionary opinions concerning governmental and political reforms, and the larger problems of statecraft. Such considerations were far beyond the ken of a humble playwright or actor.

These points are typical of a great many others which arise and reveal themselves in a critical analysis of the Shakespearean plays. The search for an author or compiler must be directed toward some person possessing these external qualifications. It is most unlikely that such a man could have remained obscure during his own time. He should, therefore, be sought among the outstanding intellects of his day.

An examination of the plays of other 17th-century playwrights quickly reveals the towering superiority of the Shakespearean productions. Beaumont and Fletcher wrote great plays, as did likewise Ben Jonson and William Devenant. But the transcendent genius of the Shakespearean dramas is absent; the immense grasp of human emotion is not there; the profound knowledge of human nature is missing. The superlative skill which discovers drama in everything and the great erudition which plumbs the depth of human purpose belong not to the playwright alone, but to some far greater type of mind.

At various times, students of the controversy have advanced a variety of solutions. Some are of the opinion that the plays were the work of no single man, but of a group, each member supplying a specialized type of knowledge. Robert Devere, Earl of Oxford, has been suggested as a possible author. But he resembles William Shakspere in one particular; it is necessary to build a great part of the case for him upon implication and intimation.

During the last century, the attention of the thoughtful has been fixed largely on the person of Francis Bacon as the logical claimant to the distinction of authorship. He is the only man of his time of whom it is positively known that he possessed every quality required of the unknown author. He was the one man in England whose learning was encyclopedic and whose station and personal tastes fitted him for so complicated a labor. As investigation proceeds, the case for Francis Bacon unfolds naturally and reasonably; and most important of all, the purpose of the plays becomes apparent.

Let us, therefore, now consider briefly the life of this remarkable man who justly has been called the "wonder of the ages."

THE LIFE OF FRANCIS BACON

Sir Francis Bacon, Kt., Baron of Verulam, Viscount of St. Albans, Lord High Chancellor of England, was born in York House, London, January 22, 1561.

According to history, he was the son of Sir Nicholas Bacon, Lord Keeper of the Great Seal of England, and Lady Anne Bacon, a woman distinguished for her scholarship in classical languages. From his earliest years, Bacon was in frequent contact with the Elizabethan Court. The Queen herself was especially fond of the child whom she affectionately called her "little Lord Keeper." As a young boy, Bacon exhibited unusual precocity of mind. He made profound and learned remarks which greatly amused his elders, and in his early teens evinced an interest in the drama and the stage. A masque which he had written was performed before the Queen and her court by a company of youthful players under Bacon's leadership.

It is noteworthy that several portraits of Bacon were painted while he was still a child. Such honor was reserved for the truly great and indicates the estimation in which his family and person were held.

Bacon was educated at Oxford. By his sixteenth year he became so dissatisfied with the scholastic doctrines of this institution that he asked to be removed on the grounds that there was nothing further that the university could teach him. He was a source of constant bewilderment and embarrassment to his instructors, who found it impossible to cope with his brilliant intellect.

Almost immediately thereafter, he was attached to the suite of the ambassador to France and resided for some time on the continent. There is a persistent rumor, but rather well supported, that during this time he developed an infatuation for the Princess Marguerite of Navarre. The policies of state prevented the marriage, and Bacon, brokenhearted, returned to England. Though he later married, Marguerite remained to the end the one great love of his life.

Possessed of an independent spirit and finding the life of a courtier unbearable, Bacon established himself at Gray's Inn at London, setting himself up as a lawyer. Years of struggle followed. Although his legal brilliance was recognized early, he had the greatest difficulty in securing patronage and recognition. It seemed that fate conspired to force obscurity upon him. For some reason, Elizabeth, who had idolized the child, ignored the man. And it was not until her death in 1603 that his fortunes improved.

During his years of comparative obscurity, Bacon had not only continued his study of law, in which field he became a recognized but unhonored authority, but found time to publish a number of tracts, most of them of a legal nature. His first printed work, the *Essays,* is now regarded as one of his finest achievements and one of the great books of the English language.

The ascent of James I brought Bacon the advancement which he so justly deserved. Referring to the debt which he owed his King, Bacon said: "His Majesty eleven times advanced me, eight times by preferments and three times by estate." He was first knighted, then given the Barony of Verulam with its houses and lands, and finally created Viscount St. Albans. His public career reached its peak when he was named Chancellor of England, the highest honor that could be conferred upon him by the King. As Lord Chancellor, Bacon became the virtual ruler of England and the most powerful man in the realm.

During these years of political advancement, the scholarship of Bacon was ripening. Many learned works flowed

FRANCIS BACON, VISCOUNT ST. ALBANS, HIGH
CHANCELLOR OF ENGLAND

from his pen, including the *De Augmentis Scientiarum* or
the Advancement of Learning, and his great masterpiece, the
Novum Organum or the new instrument of human reason.
These works revolutionized the whole theory of scholarship
and have won for Bacon the added title of "the father of

modern science." Nor was he less in the field of philosophy; even in his own time he was regarded as a reborn Plato in whom all learning was complete. The excellence of his literary style was little less remarkable than the brilliance of his erudition. Even the records of his pleadings before the court and his miscellaneous legal papers have been described as possessing a matchless elegance. His prose is a kind of poetry, each word carefully chosen, each phrase beautifully rounded. Possibly it was in tribute to his literary skill that the manuscript of the great King James translation of the Bible was entrusted to him for editorial revision.

Among his numerous activities, Lord Bacon was responsible for the distribution of land grants in the new world of America. It was his task to divide this territory among certain noble families of England. The *New Atlantis*, one of the most idealistic fragments of his writings, is believed to have been inspired by his vision of the opportunities of the New World. Here the Platonic empire of the philosophic elect could be re-established and men could live together in a camaraderie of knowledge.

Seldom has history produced a man of so diversified accomplishments. He did many things, and the wonder is that he did them all superbly. It is rare to find a great politician who is a great philosopher. But, when we add to these talents the fact that he was likewise a great scientist and an acknowledged master of the English language, we know why he has been termed "the noblest birth of time."

It is inevitable that so brilliant a man should have had enemies. It is the fate of greatness to be envied. In a day given to treasons and stratagems, it would not have been possible for such brilliance to have escaped persecution. The result was the famous bribery trial in which the Lord

Chancellor's power was broken. He was found guilty by a jury of his peers, or, correctly, by a jury of jealous men who feared his power. The most recent edition of the *Encyclopedia Britannica,* in summing up the case, states definitely that a review of Bacon's entire legal career does not indicate that any decision which he ever handed down was influenced by personal motives or personal advantage. The article further notes that his decisions would be sustained by any modern court of law as just and equitable, and brilliantly arrived at.

The court that convicted Bacon stripped him of his estates and honors, but these were restored to him by the King himself, and the fines imposed upon him were forgiven by the Crown. It has been said that he never again sat in Parliament, but this is disputed. In the closing years of his life, he was called back on at least one occasion when his judgment and knowledge were necessary to the preservation of the State.

Secure in the respect of his King and honored throughout Europe for his scholarship, Bacon retired to his estate at Gorhambury to devote the remainder of his life to literary and scientific pursuits. In a letter to Bacon, King James declares that great as Bacon's services have been to the State, his services to mankind have been still greater. It were better for posterity that his Lordship should devote his declining years to completing his priceless contributions to human knowledge than that he should continue his political activities.

If we are to believe the historical records, Francis Bacon departed from this life in the sixty-sixth year of his age. The immediate cause was quinsy of the throat resulting from a curious and somewhat unbelievable accident—his Lordship caught cold while plucking a frozen chicken. There are contradictory statements as to where he died. Three locations are given. A monument to him stands in the church at St. Albans and this has been supposed to mark his tomb. The epitaph when translated reads: "Let compounds be dissolved." His secretary is buried at the base of the statue.

As Bacon died without issue, the estates of Verulam reverted to the Crown and the present Lord of Verulam is not a descendant of Bacon. The old Gorhambury house stands a bleak and deserted ruin a short distance from the town of St. Albans.

In his will, Bacon returned his soul to God and his good name he left to other nations and other times, and to his own nation after a certain time had passed.

The Mystery of Francis Bacon

Modern Baconians have assembled a quantity of important information relating to Lord Bacon which does not appear in the published histories of the man. While Baconians are not in common agreement on all points, a survey of the substance of their conclusions is necessary to an understanding of the claims which they present for Bacon.

Our present space permits only a brief outline of these findings, and those wishing to enlarge their knowledge of the subject or to verify the particulars of this digest are referred to such standard texts as *The Bi-Literal Cipher* by Mrs. Elizabeth Wells Gallup, *Francis Bacon and His Secret Society* by Mrs. Henry Potts, *Bacon is Shakespeare* by Sir Edward Durning-Lawrence, the several works by W. F. C. Wigston, and the first half of the monumental volume by Ignatius Donnelly, his *Great Cryptogram*, which is most informative. The work of Dr. Orville W. Owens entitled *Sir*

The Ruins of Bacon's Home at Gorhambury

Francis Bacon's Cipher Story reflects the most painstaking research.

The substance of these findings is as follows:

Francis Bacon was the legitimate offspring of the secret marriage of Queen Elizabeth and her favorite, Robert Dudley, Earl of Leicester. Robert Devereux, the ill-fated Earl of Essex, was Francis Bacon's younger brother, whose ambitions to the crown were founded upon much better grounds than optimism. The Earl of Leicester was poisoned, if not with the consent, at least with the knowledge of Queen Elizabeth. Francis Bacon, therefore, was Francis Tudor, Prince of Wales, and the legitimate heir to the crown of England.

It had been the intention of the Queen to dispose of the child, but she was deflected from this course by the entreaties of her most faithful councilor, Sir Nicholas Bacon. At about the time of Francis' birth, Lady Anne Bacon was also confined, but her child was born dead. Francis was substituted for Lady Anne's dead son and was reared without knowledge of his true parentage.

It was my privilege a few years ago to see a photostat of an engraving in the British Museum depicting the confinement of Queen Elizabeth. It was customary at a royal birth for the entire court to be present. Therefore, a great number of persons were privy to the event, but all were bound to secrecy on pain of death.

Queen Elizabeth had a violent temper and in one of her fits of rage she inadvertently revealed to Bacon the truth concerning his parentage, the knowledge of which changed the entire course of his life. He believed that before her death Elizabeth would acknowledge him. It was with this hope that he aspired to the hand of Marguerite of Navarre.

When Bacon discovered the conspiracy that had been wrought against him and his father, his respect for Elizabeth was destroyed, and her regard for him turned to a bitter hatred. It was for this reason that she refused to recognize his abilities at any time during her reign.

The personal temperament of Bacon must be considered at this point. He is described as of small stature and with an unhealthful constitution. His youthful mind, saddened and outraged by the injustice of which he was the victim, took on a certain bitterness and melancholy. He resolved to dedicate his life to several purposes grounded in his own affairs. First, if he could not gain his crown, he would build an empire of his own, an empire of secret learning that should ultimately confound the corruptions of the great. Second, the true story of his life should not perish, but should be preserved to posterity as a human document and as a witness to his real estate. Third, he would discover devious means to prick the consciences of those responsible for the murder of his father and the tragedy which overshadowed his own life.

He was too great a man, however, to be lost in bitterness. For the preservation of his own existence, he turned to philosophy where he found reasons and solutions. His learning was designed first as a comfort to himself, but as his character mellowed with mature years, humanitarian instincts within led him to plan for the general improvement of mankind. His own sadness brought him a realization of the sorrows of others, and he became the champion of numerous virtues which were failing due to the corruption of the times.

He was a quiet and reserved man, given to no dissipations and dedicated to what he believed to be a calling worthy of his true estate. He was a king and as a king he would live and die, honored not by birth but by merit, remembered not for family but for personal accomplishment, and possessed of those qualities which to him represented true leadership. He plunged into the sea of learning; he sailed his little ship of thought out between the intellectual pillars of Hercules into the great sea of the unknown.

The complex internal life of Bacon is the true parent of his genius. His introversion resulted in an almost fanatical intensity of purpose. He fashioned himself into a living repository of learning. He saw himself as a man of destiny. In creating his kingdom upon Mount Parnassus, Bacon drew about himself many of the most brilliant minds of his time. These men, knowing the truth, were his willing servants and instruments, not only because they respected his birth, but because they respected even more his exceptional qualities. Thus even at Gray's Inn, he held court, and here he later laid the plans for his secret society and his philosophical empire, an empire of dreamers, creators, artists, poets, and scholars. He corresponded with the best thinkers of his day in other countries, and everywhere he was acknowledged as a natural leader who had been endowed by providence with the qualities of immortality.

Bacon As The Author Of The
Shakespearean Plays

From the foregoing it is obvious that Francis Bacon possessed in abundance the qualifications required to produce the dramatic works attributed to William Shakspere. The evidence may be only circumstantial, but it is convincing enough to justify further examination. The objections which arise naturally in those accustomed to accept Shaksperean authorship can be met with a broad array of additional evidence.

The first problem to be considered is: Was Bacon a poet? Did he enjoy the reputation for the production of poetic works during his own lifetime or immediately thereafter?

The acknowledged writings of Bacon include a poetic paraphrase of some of the Psalms. He also is known to have been the author of a poem entitled *The World's a Bubble*. But the poetic works generally attributed to him would not justify his ranking among the major poets. Yet in a letter written in 1603 and published in his *Resuscitatio*, Bacon beseeches his honored friend, a Mr. Davis, "to be good, to *concealed Poets*." Howes in his appendix to Stow's *Annals* lists in order of prominence the poets that flourished in the lifetime of Queen Elizabeth. In this list, Bacon's name is given preference over that of William Shakespeare. George Wither calls Bacon Chancellor of Parnassus, the mountain of the muses. *Manes Veruliamiani*, a collection of posthumous tributes to Bacon's memory by the great of his own time, includes references to his Lordship's poetic abilities.

It is curious that a man ranked as a poet above Shakspere by a contemporary historian should have left no important poetic remains. The only reasonable answer is that his poems must have been published anonymously or under a pseudonym. The solution to the problem involves an examination of the Shakespearean plays themselves. A man is known by his works. The signature of true greatness is not to be found upon the title pages of books, but in the quality of their content. We are reminded of the phrase by Ben Jonson which faces the title page of the early *Shakespeare Folios*:

" .   .   .   .   . Reader, looke
Not on his Picture, but his booke."

Among the grist that came to Bacon's mill was a certain country bumpkin, one Willy Shakspere. This ambitious lad from the shires arrived in London penniless and unknown, but with an obliging temper. Such qualities suited Bacon's plans to a nicety. Here was a youth who longed for fame and lacked the qualities of greatness, a would-be actor whose opinion no one would take too seriously, an obscure mouthpiece not worthy of being tried for treason even if guilty of something which resembled it. Always it has been the privilege of mountebanks to laugh at kings; but for courtiers, such hilarity is fatal.

So Willy Shakspere emerged in print as William Shakespeare. He became the symbol of Pallas Athena, the goddess of wisdom who brandished her spear against the dark creatures of the world of ignorance and fear.

It is quite improbable that Francis Bacon alone and unaided produced all of the plays published under the name of William Shakespeare or later attributed to him. They were the product of Bacon's Parnassian empire, gathered, arranged, and vitalized by his personality, and each directly related to some problem in Bacon's complex mental nature. Many of the plays were drawn from older sources or compiled from fragments of contemporary dramas, but each was reclothed and repurposed, and each contained the secret story of Bacon's life and tragedy.

But Francis Bacon had no intention of being lost beneath his own pseudonym. He was determined that future ages should discover the truth. Hence he had recourse to cryptograms, ciphers, and acrostics which were an important part of the statesmanship of his time. Each prince and petty noble had a private cipher to be used in the administration of his devious politics. In *The Advancement of Learning*, Bacon not only acknowledges his own interest in ciphers, but sets forth one of the most complicated ever devised, which he himself developed and perfected while yet a lad of sixteen. Ciphers should be his weapon. With them he would reveal and yet conceal. Sometime, those who should follow after him would have the patience to decode his secret writings.

THE TITLE PAGE OF THE 1695 EDITION
OF FRANCIS BACON's *History of the
Reign of King Henry VIII.*

Fortune stands upon the "Globe"
Theater, turning the wheel adorned with
various symbols, including the grave-dig-
ger's spade and the crown of England.
The actor, in his stage boots, and with
his sword on backwards, represents
Shakspere. The title of the work is hung
upon a theater curtain. This plate, when
deeply studied, reveals much of Francis
Bacon's secret symbolism.

And to insure this, he filled his books and the plays with hints, indications, and arcane references to secret meanings. It requires only a careful reading and a moderate ingenuity to discover that something is concealed, but it requires a great learning to decode all.

Bacon extended his use of cryptograms beyond his personal affairs into the broader scope of his philosophical and scientific knowledge. His mind discovered things which he dared not repeat. He realized the danger of telling men more than they could hope to understand. Some of his choicest discoveries and the rarest gems of his learning he concealed from the profane. Time would reveal all and time would justify him; time would discover him and he was satisfied to rest his case with time.

It may seem to us that this was a difficult, circuitous procedure, involving a vast expenditure of energy when it would have been much easier and simpler to have stated the truths outright. But we are not living in the Elizabethan period; we are not surrounded by jealous courtiers and ambitious knaves; and we are not burdened by the momentous secret which he carried, the secret which hung over his head like a sword of Damocles, threatening his life and liberty, from the day of his birth to the day of his death.

Surrounded constantly by spies, the prize an empire, ends which to the ambitious would justify any means, it was necessary for Bacon to advance cautiously if his dreams were to be accomplished. Not only his own life, but the liberty and fortunes of his friends were closely involved. The death of Sir Walter Raleigh, who was hanged, drawn, and quartered after an appropriate prologue of torture, indicated the fate that any day might befall Bacon himself. Raleigh was not executed because of his depredations against the King of Spain, but because he was a member of Bacon's secret society. Every effort was made to torture him into naming the mysterious power that was rising in England, but he died without speaking.

The celebrated case of treason brought by the Crown against the Earl of Essex becomes much more understandable when we realize that Queen Elizabeth, out of sheer hatred, forced Francis Bacon to prosecute his own brother. He never would have consented to do this had he not been given the most solemn assurance that Essex would be pardoned at the end. Bacon added this perfidy to his list of injuries and incorporated the record of it in his ciphers.

Imagine the moral force of an invisible, intangible organization which could not be discovered, but which constantly was active beneath the surface of what appeared to be a placid state of affairs. The ciphers appeared in numerous books by reputable and conservative writers. Nothing could be proved against any of them, but they came to be a mysterious band of avengers who knew they could not be tried for their knowledge without exposing too many persons close to the throne.

There is extant a curious 17th-century engraving which I have seen, but of which I have not as yet been able to secure a copy. The engraving represents a cellar along the wall of which are ranged seven barrels apparently filled with wine. A man is broaching one of the casks which bears the date 1623. The significance of this engraving is profound. The seven barrels or casks represent ciphers used by Lord Bacon, and the seven keys to the interpretation of his riddle. The opened barrel dated 1623 from which the wine is pouring represents the *First Folio* edition of the Shakespearean plays which was published in that year.

The year following the publication of the *Great Shakespearean Folio*, the most important book of ciphers ever compiled was published. This was the *Cryptomenytices et Cryptographiae* by Gustavus Selenus, Lunaberg, 1624; it is generally attributed to Augustus, Duke of Brunswick. According to the fable on the title and colophon, it was written by a "moon-man," and published at Lunaberg or "moon-town," by the "Star Brothers." The work contains an explanation of thousands of varieties of ciphers and includes all of the information necessary to decode the cryptograms and acrostics used in the *First Shakespearean Folio* published the year before.

From such circumstances as these we can gain some insight into the thoroughness of Lord Bacon's strategy.

According to the various ciphers, Lord Bacon did not die at the time nor under the circumstances historically recorded. It is remarkable, to say the least, that the funeral of so great a man should have been marked by such complete obscurity. There is no record that his Lordship lay in state, or that his remains were accorded any of the dignities which his position and honors deserved. The confused and contradictory accounts of his last illness and the uncertainty surrounding even the place of his death are significant.

Feeling that his usefulness in England had ended and that his enemies ultimately must discover his secret and attempt to thwart his purposes, his Lordship resolved to retire to the continent under the protection of a mock funeral. There is in the British Museum a small woodblock print, of crude execution, depicting Lord Bacon with his well-known beard, hat, and ruff, but otherwise arrayed in the costume of a fashionable court lady, stepping mincingly in high-heeled slippers from the map of England onto the map of Europe.

Bacon's life after his mock funeral in 1626 is exceedingly difficult to reconstruct. He moved under a series of aliases that defy ready penetration. The consensus of research to date indicates that he lived for some twenty years, working with his secret society as its hidden master. The place of his actual decease may have been Holland.

The clearing up of the entire Baconian riddle requires a broad and exhaustive survey of the literature of his time; books in many languages by a number of authors are marked as containing his secret cipher. No wonder, then, that the Bacon-Shakespeare controversy is regarded by many as the greatest literary riddle of all time.

SOLVING THE SHAKESPEARE RIDDLE

The first known published statement questioning the authorship of the Shakespearean plays appeared in the *Life and Adventures of Common Sense* by Herbert Lawrence, London, 1769.

"At the Time of my Imprisonment in *Florence*, it seems my Father, GENIUS and HUMOUR, made a Trip to *London*, where, upon their Arrival, they made an Acquaintance with a Person belonging to the Playhouse; this Man was a profligate in his Youth, and, as some say, had been a Deer-stealer, others deny it; but be that as it will, he certainly was a Thief from the Time he was capable of distinguishing any Thing; and therefore it is immaterial what Articles he dealt in. I say, my Father and his Friends made a sudden and violent Intimacy with this Man, who, seeing that they were a negligent careless People, took the first opportunity that presented itself, to rob them of every Thing he could lay his Hands on, and the better to conceal his Theft, he told them, with an affected Concern, that one Misfortune never comes alone—that they had been actually informed against, as Persons concerned in an assassination Plot, now secretly carrying on by *Mary* Queen of *Scots* against the Queen of *England*, that he knew their Innocence, but they must not depend upon that—nothing but quitting the Country could save them. They took his Word and marched off forthwith for *Holland* . . . . . "

* * * * *

"With these Materials [the stolen goods], and with good Parts of his own, he commenced Play-Writer, how he succeeded is needless to say, when I tell the Reader that his name was Shakespear."

The extreme rarity of the first edition of the Shakespearean *Folio* limited research until the development of photo-engraving. With the appearance of accurate facsimiles, the work became accessible and was subjected to critical examination. Many interesting discoveries followed.

On the title page of the *First Folio* occurs the only portrait of William Shakespeare that merits any serious consideration as a possible likeness of the "author." This portrait is signed by Martin Droeshout. It is a crude, disproportioned figure, the head much too large for the body. It presents a mask-like face with an abnormally high, bulging forehead, and the sparse hair arranged in a manner suggesting a Dutch bob. A mustache and goatee are suggested by a few scraggly hairs.

This noble face rests upon a fantastically shaped ruff, but there is no indication of any neck. This important isthmus between brain and body is totally lacking. The shoulders which support the weight have been strangely deformed by the artist; the engraving shows a coat with two left shoulders, one front and the other back. The left shoulder is correctly drawn, but where the right shoulder should be there has been substituted a rear view of the left shoulder.

We are reminded of Mark Twain's description of the celebrated Stratford bust:

"The precious bust, the priceless bust, the calm bust, the serene bust, the emotionless bust, with the dandy moustache, and the putty face, unseamed of care— that face which has looked passionlessly down upon the awed pilgrim for a hundred and fifty years and will still look down upon the awed pilgrim three hundred more, with the deep, deep, deep, subtle, subtle, subtle, expression of a bladder."

There is nothing to prove that the Droeshout portrait was actually taken from life. Shakspere had been dead for seven years when the *First Folio* appeared, and he had been away from London for a number of years prior to his death. In fact, it is improbable that any true likeness of Shakspere has survived. There are two death masks, obviously of different persons, reverently exposed at Stratford. The recent X-raying of the valuable and supposedly authentic portraits of Shakspere in the Folger collection indicates that they are retouched and revised portraits of Edward De Vere, Earl of Oxford. Other famous portraits of the bard would bear similar examination.

Likenesses of Francis Bacon usually depict his Lordship wearing a broad-brimmed, high-crowned hat jauntily tilted. The exception is a painting by Vertue depicting his Lordship in his robes as Lord Chancellor. One is immediately attracted to the massive domed forehead and the prominent aquiline nose. It is the same forehead represented by the Droeshout caricature. A careful checking of the measurements of Lord Bacon's face supports this point admirably. In fact, if the engravings of Bacon by Passe and Watts be enlarged and laid upon the Droeshout Shakespeare, every

part of the features agree exactly, even the eyeballs register-
ing perfectly. It requires no technical knowledge of the Ber-
tillon method of identification to see that the Droeshout
portrait is a doctored and thinly veiled mask of Francis
Bacon.

Indicative of the reason why it is necessary to have an
exact photographic copy of the *First Folio* is the curious
example of type-setting which occurs in the dedicatory leaves.
A poem of considerable length but of no great merit is inscribed to "The Author Mr. William Shakespeare." There
appears to be nothing unusual in this wording, but consider
the typesetter's taste when the letters are arranged thus:

THE AUTHOR   Mr. William Shakespeare

It would seem a trifle irregular that the name of the great
poet should be in very small letters and the words "THE
AUTHOR" in such massive characters. Ben Jonson evidently
admired the author much more than he did the man. It has
been pointed out that this might well indicate that they were
not the same.

The opening play of the *Folio* is *The Tempest*. The first
letter is a nicely engraved initial B artistically entwined and
with numerous flourishes. Miss Annette Covington of Cin-
cinnati noticed that the curlicues had a certain sense about
them. Examining the letter under a magnifying glass, she
saw that the name Francis is obvious at the top and bottom,
and that the initial itself with the flourishes to the right spell
the name of Bacon. This "coincidence" is sufficiently obvious and convincing to be mentioned in the April 18, 1931,
issue of *The Literary Digest*.

The text of the *First Folio* is enriched with numerous
references that are irrelevant to the action of the plays and
which frequently are omitted when the dramas are performed.

A Section from the Engraved Title Page of *The Essays* of Michel De Montaigne.

This is an example of the method used by Bacon to conceal and yet reveal his identity in the frontispieces and vignettes of contemporary printed books. The shaded area of the center background shows a reversed letter "F" formed by the broken arch, with a capital "B," lying on its side, formed by the double arch beyond. To the discerning, the initials "F" "B" are associated with the name Francis Bacon. Also present are his two columns which later appeared in Freemasonic symbolism.

These interpolations are not bright shafts of poetic genius, but loggy and often clumsy bits of superfluous verbiage. There is no reason why the author should have included them. But they become significant parts of the secret story if we assume that Lord Bacon intended both to conceal and at the same time to reveal his own identity in the text.

Consider the line from *The Merry Wives of Windsor*: "Hang-hog is latten for Bacon, I warrant you." In the first place, the statement is untrue. In the second place, it is unnecessary. There is no glitter of greatness in the composition. The line evidently refers to a humorous occurrence in the life of Sir Nicholas Bacon. That worthy jurist once condemned a malefactor by the name of Hog to public execution. The criminal pleaded for leniency on the grounds of relationship. When the surprised Sir Nicholas inquired as to what kinship the man claimed, Hog replied: "The kinship of name. My name is Hog and yours is Bacon." With the quick humor for which Sir Nicholas was justly famed, the Lord Keeper retorted: "A Hog is not Bacon until it be well hanged."

Sir Francis Bacon includes that incident in his apothegms as an example of the wit of his day, thus pointing up an important part of the symbolism which he employed. The name Bacon offers many possibilities to a creative imagination. It is a name that can be played upon. During his school years, the diminutive Sir Francis was greatly plagued with nicknames, among which was one he especially disliked—Hamlet, or the little ham.

From the same *Merry Wives of Windsor* can be gleaned another poetic pearl: "What is AB backwards with a horn on its forehead?" Here, indeed, is a riddle! AB backwards is BA; and horn in Latin is *cornu*. Combine them and you have Bacornu. This is evidently a phonetic play on Bacon's name.

King Henry the Fourth contains an example of literary grandeur with thirty-three repetitions of the name Francis, which we quote in part:

"*Prin.* Anon *Francis?* No *Francis,* but tomorrow *Francis;* or *Francis,* on Thursday: or indeed *Francis* when thou wilt. But *Francis.*"

This quotation sounds as though the author had been writing on the modern basis of two cents a word. This Steinesque gem born out of time repeats the word *Francis* thirty-three times, an example of Bacon's simplest numerical cipher based upon his own name. If the letters of the alphabet, I and J considered as identical, are numbered consecutively, A equals 1, B equals 2, and so forth, the sum of the name Bacon is thirty-three, a number rich in religious and masonic implication. Thus the thirty-three repetitions of Francis give us the name of Francis Bacon.

The plays are enriched also with numerous acrostics. The simplest form of an acrostic is that employing the first letter or letters of lines read downwards instead of from left to right. A good example of the acrostic occurs in the following lines from the *Tempest*:

> "Begun to tell me what I am, but stop
> And left me to a bootless Inquisition,
> CONcluding, stay: not yet."

By reading the capitalized letters at the left from above downward, we have the name BACON. Nor is the acrostic merely a signature; it is used as a means of emphasis. Consider the content of the lines. The author intimates that he intends to reveal an identity, and then decides that the revelation is premature.

I have examined more than a hundred such acrostics in the *First Folio*. In many cases the playwright had to resort to elaborate complications of his text to bring about the required word-patterns. Nor is the acrostic frequently met with by accident. Whole books may be read without this arrangement once occurring by coincidence. While such acrostics may not be regarded as proof positive of authorship, they certainly strengthen the case in favor of the man whose name has been so ingeniously included throughout the text in so many different ways.

The Tragedy of Hamlet presents an entirely different type of concealed writing. *Hamlet* is a play on the name of Bacon, one which he is known to have been problemed with in his younger life. Here the secret meaning requires no special cipher expert to reveal it. Hamlet is Bacon, whose father was foully murdered and who has been deprived of his rightful crown. Inspired by the ghost, the memory of his father, he hits upon the device of the theater as a means of accomplishing his revenge. He hires struggling actors and prepares the play depicting the details of his father's murder and causes it to be performed before his mother and his uncle.

The reason for the whole Shakespearean cycle is summed up in the words: "The play, the play's the thing with which I'll catch the conscience of the king." How rich and clear the meanings become when purpose is added to the tragedy!

In the limited space of a brief summary it is not possible to elaborate upon the more involved aspects of Bacon's numerical acrostic and bi-literal ciphers. Suffice it to say that beneath the surface of the more obvious and apparent indications is a wealth of further information. There is scarcely a line that is not enriched with some hidden meaning.

In *The History of King Henry VIII* occurs an outstanding example of Bacon's ingeniousness. *Henry VIII* is one of the plays that appeared for the first time in the *Folio Edition*

of 1623. At that time the historical William Shakspere had
been dead for seven years. In 1621, five years after Shakspere's death, Lord Bacon passed through his celebrated
bribery trial. As the result of this trial, he was removed from
the chancellorship and deprived of the custody of the Great
Seal.

Kenneth Guthrie in his brochure *Shakespearean Authorship Divulged*, 1936, comments as follows: ". . . in *Henry
VIII* we find the King disgracing Cardinal Wolsey as Chancellor, by sending to him three nobles to retrieve the Great
Seal of England, of which he was the caretaker, which was
his chief badge of office, and which is seen suspended by
a gold chain around the neck of Bacon in most of the current pictures. This is historic; but judge of our surprise in
discovering in the play the names of those nobles, the Dukes
of Norfolk, Suffolk and Surrey who came to Bacon himself
to relieve him also of the Great Seal. This could not have
been done by any but Bacon himself, especially as the play
appeared long after the actor's death. Would the ignorant
actor, long since dead, have known enough to do this?"

This circumstance in itself proves at the very least that the
plays have been tampered with. If they were merely literary
productions, what justification could there be for such a
mutilation of the text. If, however, we acknowledge with the
Baconians that the entire cycle of plays was devised to reveal historical, psychological, and scientific knowledge concerning the life and works of Francis Bacon, then the errors
in the text become obvious clues to the purpose which Wolsey
is made to play in the drama.

Confronted with this increasing body of evidence, and
apparently impressed thereby, The Cambridge Press, in 1922,
published a limited edition of *The Comedy of Errors*. In

this edition no author's name appears upon the title page, but facing the title is inserted the portrait of Lord Bacon. *The Comedy of Errors* is one of the earliest of the Shakespearean plays. It must have been written either before William Shakspere reached London, or almost immediately thereafter. Was Cambridge impressed by the obvious fact that William Shakspere was ill qualified at that time to be the author of such a work?

Thus, seeking for clues to the discovery of the man whose genius inspired the *Great Shakespearean Folio*, we shall do well to remember that his Lordship's epitaph may reasonably apply to the systems of ciphers contained in his plays:

"Let compounds be dissolved."

THE MYSTICAL FIGURES OF
JAKOB BOEHME

There is a very important message in the story of the life and teachings of the great German mystic Jakob Boehme, for certain of his mystical investigations, if not original or new, are extremely unusual.

He was born about the year 1575; detailed birth data is not available. A cobbler by trade, he lived to the age of forty-nine years. Boehme was a comparatively young man when in his kitchen the sun struck a pewter plate and he was blinded by the light. From that time on, he has said, he was able at will to see the beings of the invisible universe.

It is obvious that Boehme had been previously endowed with clairvoyance; that he came into this life with it; and it was through this curious accident that he achieved his illumination. Being clairvoyant in the 16th century, when it was not at all orthodox, he brought down on his head the animosity of both the Lutheran and the Roman Church.

These churches, particularly the Lutheran, persecuted him unmercifully, and were the ultimate cause of his death.

During a comparatively short lifetime, while cobbling shoes and raising a family, Boehme authored more than twenty-five mystical books. He found it necessary to reprint re-statements of certain of the documents, to write them in a new language, in order to clarify them. He used a jargon created out of the alchemical, metaphysical, and scientific works of his time, and to each word he gave a special meaning. This makes it difficult for the average person to read Boehme; his words are not those used commonly, but are a coined vocabulary to explain metaphysical truths he alone perceived.

During the years of his so-called ministry, which was the period of his writing, he was on at least one occasion forbidden by the State to produce his manuscripts, and for many years he never wrote anything. When the urge again came upon him irresistibly, he moved to another community and continued with his writings. Not until after his death was it appreciated that this simple shoemaker, a man of unpleasing features and harsh voice, had left behind him an exceedingly rich heritage, in the findings of one who had sought long into the mysteries of life. Among his books, the *Mysterium Magnum* and the *Aurora* stand out as very great achievements.

Boehme was a contemporary of some of the mystics of the early 17th century, including the first Rosicrucians. He was contemporary with Dr. Robert Fludd, Michael Maier, Johann Valentine Andreae, and Sir Francis Bacon. An interesting note in Francis Bacon's writings implies that he knew of Boehme, and while he does not mention him as living a contemporary life, they died within a few years of

each other. In the ornamentations of the writings of Francis
Bacon, the early editions of which can be consulted in the
Library of our Society, is a curious device called an orna-
ment or headpiece; it is engraved and goes across the head
of the title page of the book. The heading usually consists of
two capital A's, one black and one white. The device is repeated in a dozen different forms, and it occurs in the First
Quarto Edition of Shakespeare's plays. These two A's, the
light and dark A, have never been explained in connection
with Bacon's writings. They have been noticed and commented upon, but no one seems to know where they came
from. It appears they were derived from Boehme; the light
A signifies the Redeemed Man, and the dark A signifies
the Fallen Man. Bacon's mysticism led him to the writings
of Boehme, which conceived the Kingdom of Heaven reproduced on earth for the benefit of relapsed mankind. Also,
the capital A stood for the spiritual man, the Redeemed Man
who abode again in heaven, represented by means of a double
capital. "A," shaded and light, symbolized the Fall and the
Redemption. This keynote to Bacon's writings seems definite,
for Bacon's writings were as much concerned with the redemption of man through knowledge as Boehme's were
through mysticism.

Boehme's philosophy is intensely human, relating closely
to the mystery of man's own salvation. He sensed the Biblical
story to be allegorical, not literal. His *Mysterium Magnum*,
which is curiously compiled, is largely devoted to proving
there is a great and deep mystery behind the story contained
in the Bible itself.

It would be very good, I think, if we could cross the centuries and try to get the feeling of Boehme's philosophy,
not as 20th-century thinkers, but as 20th-century participants
in his ideals and in him, trying to feel as he felt, to think

as he thought, to see as he saw the vision of a great spiritual renaissance.

The mystical doctrines of Jakob Boehme, surnamed "the Teutonic Theosopher," are remarkable for the profundity of their concepts and for the obscurity and complexity of the terminology in which these concepts are set forth. This celebrated German mystic was comparatively unlettered; certainly he was unlettered in the classical languages, and even inadequate in the subtleties of his own language. His parents instructed him sufficiently so that he could read the Bible slowly and laboriously.

In attempting to write out his own material, Boehme was forced to grope for words, and frequently his final selection of a term was unfortunate. Figures of speech suggested by his friends were not always appropriate, and usually obscured more meaning than they clarified. In all probability, Boehme's writings were entirely clear to him, and possibly were not too difficult for those who had the privilege of discussing the subject matter with the master himself. But after the lapse of centuries, a world far removed from both the ideas and the idioms, has been troubled by both.

Boehme drew considerably upon the terminology of contemporary cabalists and students of medieval Jewish esoteric doctrines. But the use he makes of the terms is entirely his own and the accepted cabalistic definitions are of little help when applied to his text. Astronomical and astrological symbols are sprinkled generously through the tracts, but the student of astrology is also at a loss when confronted with Boehme's applications and interpretations of the astrological glyphs. Alchemy is represented through his writings by a number of choice aphorisms, figures of speech, and emblems, but Boehme had nothing in common with the cult of the

PORTRAIT OF BOEHME SURROUNDED BY SYMBOLICAL FIGURES

In this remarkable 17th-century engraving, the entire mystical philosophy of the German seer is unfolded by means of the emblems appearing in early editions of his writings.

gold-makers, as this is represented in historical and literary remains.

Boehme was not using words as formal, intellectual instruments, nor was he building a concept based upon the pyramiding of philosophical terms. His illumination came to him as an internal impact. The spiritual experiences and extensions of consciousness which inspired his writings were by their very nature outside the natural boundaries of the written word. His thoughts transcended the inevitable limitations imposed by language upon the communication of ideas.

In his effort to name the Nameless and define the Undefinable, Boehme sought desperately for terms that could bridge the interval of consciousness which existed between himself and his disciples. Had he been more skilled in rhetorical forms, his doctrines would have attained a much wider sphere of influence. As it was, his teachings were so completely unfamiliar, both inwardly as to content and outwardly as to form, that they discouraged and confused the majority of his followers.

The teaching of Boehme was essentially a Christian mysticism, founded in personal piety and devotion, and extending outward from the gentle sincerity of the man's personal beliefs. In this Christian mystical concept, Boehme discovered a sufficient and sustaining internal extension of consciousness, moving irresistibly toward the substance of the Universal Reality.

There can be no doubt that the experiences of this humble German shoemaker were in part psychological, but certainly they transcended the boundaries of the psychological concepts of today. The revelation was peculiar to the man himself, and actually could have no existence apart from the man. The same mystical intensity occurring to another person would have produced an entirely different pattern of ideas.

For this reason, we must continue to identify men with the messages which they bring. These messages cannot exist independent of the men, for the human being is a positive equation in any mental or emotional concept which emerges through his personality.

The mystical experience remains formless and has no definition or distinction apart from the mystic himself. He is the interpreter of a series of vibratory impacts, and the interpretation must always be consistent with the mental and emotional personality pattern of the seer. Because of this equation, mystics of many races and many religions, experiencing certain definite extensions of consciousness, still remain within the natural boundaries of time, place, and personality. By natural boundaries I mean the racial tradition, the national pattern, and the personal religious or spiritual beliefs of these mystics. Illumination extends or unfolds a belief, but does not exchange one basic pattern for another. Illumination, therefore, may be said to enlarge our concept of that which is already held to be fundamentally true.

In Boehme's own words, and the words of others who have had the experience of enlightenment, it was something like this: Whenever Boehme felt the spirit move him, he would lay aside the shoemaker's hammer and go into a little room back of his shop; and there he would sit down in the quiet and wait. As he waited, practicing only an attitude of piety, which he lived constantly, things would suddenly grow dim about him. According to his own description, he would then see the walls grow dim and then become transparent like glass. The air would become transparent in a new way. Boehme said there is an opaqueness in the air, although men think it is transparent. The air was like a cloud; and slowly, when it cleared, Boehme would find himself in a state exceedingly mystical. He was surrounded by light, but he was not in any place. Great mysterious vistas reached out far beyond his comprehension, and these vistas were the living abodes of Beings. And Boehme would flow through these spaces; he had only to will to move from one place to another. He could look upon himself, and his features, hands, and face were different; they seemed to be made of semi-transparent glass. He was out of his physical body, and was in one of his etheric bodies, for he would look back and see himself sitting in his room back of the shop.

And so he learned again in the School of the Angels; discoursed and discovered. What was taught, he perceived. No one spoke; but he could hear words. He could also read thoughts. Then, after a certain period of study, a voice would say, "Jakob, return to your house," and he would see himself back in his little room; and as the walls turned gray again, he would suddenly find himself sitting in his chair.

On paper, he would then write down carefully the secrets told to him; for now, as he expressed it, he no longer saw through a veil dimly, but beheld face to face. He no longer had to depend on the words of men; he was fortified by the inner experience he knew to be true. For he knew it came from no evil source, but from some great good within himself. It was thus he began the preparation of the *Mysterium Magnum*, a great mystical document of interpretation of the true meaning of Creation.

When it was completed, it received favorable local consideration from a number of the nobility, and through the assistance of influential friends, Boehme was able to have the manuscript published. Then the storm broke. He was called up before one religious council after another. He was ordered to recant. He was ordered to admit that the book was the work of the Devil. He was ordered to say what he had written was a lie; that he did not see these things.

Boehme made a discovery. It was that he could not tell anyone else what he had seen, although he knew it to be true with all the conviction of his soul. For when he told them what he saw, they laughed at him. He explained everything he had seen in minute detail, every experience, and they laughed. Like Plato's Idiot, he had seen more than the rest, and was therefore a fool. This realization came to Boehme as a great shock. To him it seemed incredible that anyone should either intentionally misdirect, or fail to see. He wanted Light so sincerely, and so passionately wanted other men to have the Light, he could not understand why they would doubt.

What Havelock Ellis has called "the mystical experience" may produce a marked change in the life of an individual; but this is because his conduct prior to his enlightenment was inconsistent with his own deepest and most devout convictions, as revealed through those testimonies which converge to produce what we call conscience. Even though a man's early life may be dissolute, as in the case of St. Francis of Assisi, this unreasonable pattern of conduct was contrary to the conscience of the man himself, and his illumination actually restated values already present but submerged in his personality.

To make this point more clear, we can say that the religious experience of the average human being prior to his twelfth year becomes an enduring and comparatively unalterable level of internal convictions. In the course of life, the individual may drift away from the early impressions and even reject them completely. Later, however, some spiritual, mental, or emotional crisis may impel him to the restatement of religious convictions. When this occurs, the earlier impressions are released through the subconscious, and play an important part in the formation of a mature philosophy or code of action. The old convictions and concepts may reappear in a much more highly refined and sophisticated arrangement, but they are an inevitable part of the psychcchemistry of the human personality.

In the case of Boehme, we have a man brought up in a devoutly religious home by simple, orthodox parents, who practiced their Lutheran persuasions with gentleness, humility, and sincerity. By personal experience, he knew of no other religion or doctrine except that in which he was raised. Comparative religion was an unknown department of learning in those days in little cities like Gorlitz.

Boehme must have been aware that other religious sects existed, but they all departed, in some degree at least, from the infallible footings laid down by Martin Luther. At the same time, Boehme himself was a sensitive, kindly, and lofty-souled man. Regardless of the creed to which he belonged, he was pious by nature—that is, by instinct and impulse. No matter how strict or dogmatic a faith might be, Boehme would interpret into it the natural benevolence which was an essential ingredient in the compound of his own character.

When the mystical experience came to Boehme, it deepened and clarified the devotion of the man himself, but it did not emancipate him from the inclinations which had already shaped his disposition. It was his own faith—that is, the faith of Martin Luther—that he saw opened and unfolded within him. It was his own conscience that found its final satisfaction in the revealed richness of familiar doctrines. He never transgressed the essential statutes of his childhood beliefs, but he discovered new spiritual treasures, new evidence of

divine love and wisdom in the teachings which had always
been familiar to him.

There is everywhere present in Boehme's writings, therefore, not only a mystical profundity but a mystical orthodoxy, for his dreams and visions were circumscribed by
the dictates of his own theological morality. This in no way
reduces the importance of his revelations, but assists us in
developing instruments of interpretation and of sound perspective on the problems involved.

The faculties by which Jakob Boehme was able to experience his strange participation in the divine mystery of
the world are beyond scientific analysis. Even the light of
modern research into the complicated phenomena of mind
is not sufficient to satisfy the thoughtful investigator.

Boehme reported, and others have added their testimony
also, that illumination produces a real chemical difference
in the life of a person. The first thing it changes is the way
of looking at things. Boehme could look at something and
instantly, by will power, look through it. He was able to look
at a growing plant and suddenly, by willing to do so, to
mingle with that plant. He could be part of the plant, and
feel its small life struggling toward the Light. He was able
to share the simple ambitions of that plant, to rejoice with
the joyously growing leaf. This was not because he loved
the plant—many people do that; not because he loved life—
many people do; but because he was capable, by an actual
scientific adjustment, to feel life with the plant, to sense
life with other living things. It was not that he knew them
through kindness or association with them; his was actual
mystical union with them.

Frequently associated with this mystery is the dog; for
most people love animals. Not to like an animal is regarded
as a bad sign from an esoteric standpoint, because it means

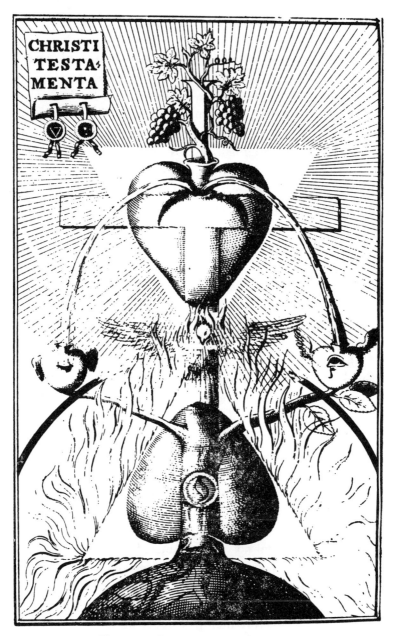

THE HEART OF CHRIST AND THE HEART OF MAN
According to the Mystical Symbols of Jakob Boehme.

that the animal does not like you—not because of tangible thoughts, but because through a peculiar psychical power, the animal senses the motives behind your life. The animal is capable of tuning in on man in a way that few men are capable of tuning in on the animal. You may be a person who will sit up all night with a sick animal, feeling if it passes on you are losing a member of the family; but that is not what Boehme meant. No matter how close you can be to the animal—or, for that matter, to another human being—never can this be related to mystical union. Mystical union is when one person is actually capable, inwardly, mystically, of being one with the other person, so that there are no longer two minds with a single thought, but one mind capable of many thoughts. They are no longer people, each near to the other, but have become one person really capable of identity in ideals. This is the mystical union.

In the story of Pygmalion and Galatea, derived from the Greek mysteries, Pygmalion created a statue out of stone, which he worshipped, and it came to life. He had fashioned it so well that it finally came alive with his life. Galatea represents that phenomenal object outside of itself, the blade of grass, the star, another person, or a so-called inanimate object; Galatea is merely the not-self. Pygmalion, through his art, the art of life, had fashioned out of not-self an idealistic concept.

To explain how this could be done. Suppose we are mystically inclined, but not yet illuminated. We say, "I find God in everything; I find Truth in everything." This is Pygmalion's image, because it is made of stone. We have intellectually found these things, but the statue is not alive, because they are merely qualities which we have intellectually ascribed to the phenomenal universe. We say, "God is in everything," and then we dislike our neighbors because the image of our idealism is still made of stone. But when finally, through mystical union, through mystical at-one-ment, we cease to bestow our minds upon the things of life, and bestow ourselves instead, then suddenly we find that the stone image of our created idealism becomes the living thing. We find the Light we have sought. As we ensoul the idealistic statue we have built, the universe of divine things comes to life in ourselves, and we come to life in it.

That mystical union leaves the world a very different place. We cannot bestow that communion upon others, but through it in ourselves, we can bestow our lives upon others. Although they may not understand, we can literally flow with them and in them. Although the stone cannot understand the mystic, the mystic can find the heart of the stone. Though the blade of grass never knows the sage who meditates upon its mystery, the sage is one with the blade of grass and understands it.

We can bestow, although the thing upon which we bestow can give nothing in return. We can have nothing in return, for the simple reason that the bestowal of life enriches us beyond any possibility of desiring return. This mystical ability, according to Boehme, becomes like a magical eyeglass. Possibly these were the same magical eyeglasses Joseph Smith is supposed to have used in the preparation of his Book of the Mormons, and Mohammed in the preparation of the Koran. Be that as it may, they become a new lens to the eye, a mystical eye by which we perceive the heart of things. Once the heart of things has been perceived, there is nothing else in the universe worth looking after.

Having received this enlightenment, we are capable of putting the universe in order. We no longer say, "Why did the gods not create it a different way?" Rather, we have a new vision of the universe—a vision so perfect, so transcendental, that all things are as nothing in comparison.

There seems no justification for assuming that Boehme was the type of person who would escape to mysticism because of personal frustration or some pressing neurosis. He was a successful and respected citizen prior to the occurrence of his illumination. He was happily married and his children were an ever present source of comfort and security. He was not obsessed by inordinate ambitions, and there is nothing to indicate that his life had been hazarded or his career made difficult until he complicated his affairs for himself by advocating strange doctrines in an extremely orthodox Lutheran community. There is no report that Jakob was hypersensitive or nursed any phobias, complexes, or fixations which might have caused what psychologists like to interpret as escapes from reality.

Boehme did not show any signs of progressive mental disease or of the deterioration of his faculties. He never became a fanatic or made any effort to force his beliefs or revelations upon an unbelieving world. He was content to live in the light of grace from within himself. He was also willing to share with those who desired to understand the mysteries which had been revealed, but he had no ambition whatever to found a religion or to overthrow the dominant faiths of his time. He seemed to accept without doubt or question that his mystical experiences had revealed to him a fuller appreciation and understanding of Lutheran theology. He was not the kind of man about whom a great deal of biographical material is available. The accounts of his life are meager, but in the main sufficient, and it is scarcely possible that he could have had any outstanding characteristic that has not been mentioned.

Nor can we find any grounds for advanced neuroses in the childhood of the seer. From his own report, his family was loving and spiritually worthy, though materially poor. He seems to have been well treated, and raised with a gentle care within the means and possibilities of the parental psychology and the family budget. It is possible for any man to be neurotic, but there appears no reason for assuming that Boehme's life was any more repressed or depressed by environmental circumstances than was true of most of his contemporaries, who in no way experienced the revelations that came to him.

The mystic died in 1624, in the full possession of his faculties, and his last words indicated a complete certainty as to the security of his future state. He lived without fear, and died without fear, accepting all the burdens of his years with a patient humility, obviously entirely sincere. Although the second half of his life was considerably burdened by his sense of responsibility for the preservation of his revelations, he seems to have functioned without unreasonable or unusual pressures from within himself. In substance, Boehme was in most respects normal, and his mystical experiences cannot be rejected as the aberrations of an unbalanced mind.

Boehme found censorship inescapable while he lived; and that would be true today. One who possesses an inner enlightenment becomes an outcast, a pariah; he loses social standing and, as I think most metaphysical students will admit, loses financial standing. It is very difficult to conceive of a wealthy philosopher. One Greek said, "Poverty is the disease of the wise." For it is required of the mind, turning toward greater concerns, that it should be impoverished in lesser matters. And it is also inevitable in the world in which we live that a person who does not make a reasonably good showing in material matters will be regarded as a failure; and who will listen to the words of a failure?

Boehme, trying to get his message to the world, reminds us of Confucius, who spent his life trying to find someone who was wise enough to see what he so well understood. When Boehme failed to find understanding among his contemporaries, he settled down and wrote his books, indifferent to his time. If he could have acquired that indifference ten years earlier, he would have lived twenty years longer. As soon as he became indifferent to the results of his work, his work flourished. In this is a valuable thought. When we begin to detach ourselves from the consequences of what we do, simply doing the best we can and letting the chips fall where they may, we do better. When constantly striving to achieve or help, we generally accomplish neither end. Boehme came in time to a conclusion of great importance: Illumination is an individual matter; it is not to be communicated; it is achieved.

When Boehme died, his various works formed a general pattern of doctrine. During his lifetime, these manuscripts were circulated privately among a small group of enthusiastic followers. Shortly before his death, Boehme prepared a key to his writings. This was a table of principles intended to co-ordinate the terms which he used. Even this, however, was not sufficient to clarify for the average layman his more recondite speculations. Perhaps, had he lived longer, he might have realized the need for a simple summary of his teachings, but he died soon after completing his table of principles.

In all parts of the world, wise, virtuous, and beautiful human souls have experienced extensions of understanding, by which they felt themselves to be in peculiar sympathy with the heart and mind of God. Most of the great sages and prophets have belonged to this class, and the impact of their lives and teachings has advanced civilization far more than the careful plotting and planning of so-called sober intellectuals.

In India, the Yoga and Vedanta schools have led to a mystical state of identity with the divine. In China, the Taoist monk aspires to the same goal. Buddhist and Islamic mystics share the basic belief that a highly spiritualized state of consciousness is possible for man. Many of the canonized saints of Christendom have been honored because of mystical experiences in the forms of visions, illuminations, and the *stigmata*. It is hardly possible that all these accounts preserved among many people over vast periods of time could be entirely psychotic. Perhaps the most natural and reasonable solution to this mystery is that a spiritual extension is possible, but is beyond standardization, at least at the present time.

We may also be asked: What are the practical benefits of advanced mystical experiences? Certainly those benefits are largely personal and internal, but even to those of superficial mind, it is painfully evident that the whole race stands in desperate need of internal enrichment. The weakest part of our life-pattern is the inadequacy of internal power in times of emergency. As nature seemingly never leaves any form of life without the means of attaining its own security, there is nothing remarkable in the concept that buried within the human potential is some faculty or power capable, under specialized development, of supplying the human creature with the means of working out its own salvation.

According to the concept of esoteric physiology, the mystical experience is the result of intensifying the vibratory rate of the pineal gland. The magnetic field of this gland acts as a medium for the transmission of impulses from the over-soul or higher spiritual self. Recent findings indicate that hyperactivity of the pineal gland is not present in cases of psychical delusions. There is glandular imbalance in such cases, but this imbalance is due to mental, emotional, physical, or environmental pressures, and not to an actual increase of spiritual function. Thus, while neurotics often have psychical disturbances accompanied by visions, voices, and a variety of delusions, such psychical phenomena are not evidences of genuine extrasensory growth or unfoldment.

The zones of mental activity recognized by materialistic psychiatrists, are all aspects of mental activity, and the phenomena produced by and within these spheres can be traced to the intensification of various personality compulsions. After these compulsions have been accepted by the mind and have been reinterpreted symbolically by the subtle machinery of the subconscious, we are likely to lose our perspectives concerning them. When these reinterpreted impulses emerge again under stress or pressure, they are often mistakenly accepted as genuine examples of inspirational or intuitive apperception. It requires considerable experience and wisdom to evaluate correctly the importance of such impulses, and those by nature most impulsive are the least likely to develop this discrimination.

The psychologist, by temperament all too often a materialist, is satisfied to limit his concepts to the sphere of mental phenomena. To him the mind is the source of all thought, and all processes that resemble thinking must be explained by reference to the mind and its functions. Naturally, he attempts to interpret the genuine mystical experience according to the limitations which he has imposed upon his own concepts. His first thought is that these experiences must originate somewhere in the sequence of mental-emotional action and reaction. It does not dawn upon him that under certain peculiar states of mental-emotional exhilaration the personality can receive into itself a ray of spiritual light, which originates in a part of man superior to and beyond the limitations of the mental organization.

If a spiritual light, which in this case carries an intense vibratory impression, is projected into the mental organization from above and beyond the mind, it does not necessarily follow that this inspirational energy can be distributed through the objective personality independent of the laws governing human thinking. It is necessary for the mind to interpret inspiration and distribute inspirational force through the faculties by which it is rendered susceptible of recognition and acceptance by the objective mind and brain. Therefore, all inspirational and intuitive energies are more or less confused in the process of transmission, and emerge through our personalities imperfectly. Most genuine mystics have discovered the communication of their inward experiences to be almost impossible because they are forced to use a means of communication inadequate to the transmission of spiritual impulses.

The vibration of the pineal gland is increased in one of two ways. It may be intensified by specialized disciplines, such as the practice of the Yogas, but this is extremely dangerous without the constant supervision of a qualified teacher. It is also possible to increase the vibration of the pineal gland by an intense mystical devotion, by means of which the emotions are refined and regenerated through a devout attitude toward life and the mysteries of God and nature. This devotion may lead to a state of apotheosis, marked by a profound sense of internal spiritual exhilaration. This exhilaration may in turn lead to a state of ecstasy in which the entire personality is transfigured from within itself, and seems to approach a state of cosmic awareness. This ecstasy itself, sometimes described as an elevation or a lifting up toward God, results from stimulating the vibratory rate of the pineal gland. If this stimulation is sufficient, it may result in a temporary attunement with a superior level of consciousness, and the mystic becomes internally aware of a qualitative condition of Being which is beyond his normal experience.

With the intellectual phase of his nature, the mystic may be aware that such a superior state exists, but it is only by an actual attunement that he is able to experience the *fact* of this higher plane of consciousness. As his personality is not naturally adjusted to this higher vibratory polarization, his ecstasy cannot be maintained for any extended length of time, but the impressions transmitted to his objective mind in these moments of exaltation are so powerful that they will endure for an entire lifetime, and change the whole pattern of human conduct.

The mystical experience is the only satisfactory explanation for Boehme's extraordinary revelations. Naturally, he could not convey this experience to others, but those who came under the direct inspiration of the man's life and convictions received definite impressions which intensified their admiration. The disciples in turn attempted, through contemplation and devotional meditations, to discover inwardly the true meanings of his mystical writings. One of the most important of the followers of this great German Illuminist was Johann Georg Gichtel, a man peculiarly equipped by his own consciousness for the task of explaining the obscure teachings of the master.

JOHANN GEORG GICHTEL

In a note published in *Lucifer*, Vol. 3, p. 131, H. P. Blavatsky makes the following reference to the German mystic, Johann Gichtel: "There is an enormous difference between the *Sophia* of the Theosophist Gichtel, an Initiate and Rosicrucian (1638-1710), and the modern Lillies, John Kings, and 'Sympneumatas!' The 'Brides' of the Mediaeval Adepts are an allegory, while those of modern mediums are astral realities of *black magic*. The 'Sophia' of Gichtel was the 'Eternal Bride' (Wisdom and occult science *personified*); the 'Lillies' and others are astral spooks, semi-substantial 'influences,' semi-creations of the surexcited brains of unfortunate *hysteriacs* and 'sensitives.' No purer man ever lived in this world than Gichtel. Let anyone read St. Martin's *Correspondence*, pp, 168-198, and he will see the difference. From Marcus, the Gnostic, down to the last mystic student of the Kabala and Occultism, that which they call their 'Bride' was 'Occult Truth,' personified as a naked maiden, otherwise called Sophia or Wisdom. That 'spouse' revealed to Gichtel all the mysteries of the outward and the inward nature, and forced him to abstain from every earthly enjoyment and desire, and made him sacrifice himself for Humanity. And as long as he remained in that body which represented him on earth, he had to work for the deliverance from ignorance of those who had not yet obtained their inheritance and inward beatitude."

The place of Gichtel in the descent of Boehme's mystical philosophy is not entirely clear. About 1660, Gichtel met Baron Justinius von Weltz, and from this Hungarian nobleman he received the inspiration to attempt the reunion of the sects of Christendom and the conversion of the entire world to a mystical or cosmic Christianity, which was not to be confused with the teachings of the Church. The society which Gichtel promoted was regarded with hostility by the Lutheran clergy, and in 1665 he was banished from Germany and settled in Holland.

According to the life of Gichtel, which appeared in the *Theosophia Practica*, Vol. 7 (Leydon, 1772), it was about eleven o'clock at night on Christmas, 1673, that the mystic received, while in meditation, the vision of the Heavenly Virgin, (Divine Wisdom) whom, though unseen, he had intensely loved for so long a time. Divine Wisdom spoke into the soul of Gichtel ineffable words which cannot be outwardly expressed. These words were spiritual powers, and were preserved unchangeable within his heart.

Wisdom's inner language transcends all physical speech, yet Gichtel understood the message which he received as though it had been in his own mother tongue. To the mystic, these experiences were proof that God looked upon him with kindness, and with an abiding faith he placed himself unreservedly in the hands of his Creator.

After these experiences, much was disclosed to Gichtel about the mystery of the fall of Adam, the regeneration of mankind, and the rebirth of humanity through Christ, but the revelation was so lofty that it could not be revealed by human speech. Divine Wisdom opened to him the treasures of knowledge, both of the inner and outer spheres, and Gichtel was so much affected that it seemed to him that he was living in Paradise rather than in this world.

Gichtel knew that he carried within himself the body of the first Adam. He realized that within himself was a heavenly and sufficient state, although he still had a physical body which laid on him the obligation to strive for his brothers and sisters who had not yet found peace. Thus he attained union with the Virgin of the World, Divine Wisdom, which was lost in Adam and regained in Christ. She was his new heavenly strength, a mystery which no one could understand unless he were united with Jesus.

Gichtel has left us no record of the circumstances which led to his interest in the writings of Jakob Boehme. Apparently this interest did not become a dominant factor in his

life until about 1668. After that date he devoted many years
to an effort to comprehend the obscure terms of Boehme,
which Gichtel regarded as an important key to the Bible.
Gichtel's friends developed such a desire for the writings
of Jakob Boehme that the Mayor of Amsterdam was moved
to donate six thousand guilders for the republication of these
works. This was accomplished in 1682, and the edition was
edited by Gichtel, who contributed notes and a complete
index.

It cannot be said that either Gichtel himself or the Gich-
telians, of whom he was the moving spirit, subscribed completely to Boehme's metaphysical speculations. It has been
pointed out that Boehme had no desire to break with the
existing Church, and all the feuding which burdened his
life originated in the exasperation of the Lutheran clergy.
On the other hand, Gichtel taught at least a moderate sep-
aratism and his followers became Separatists. If Gichtel did
not hold the same convictions as Boehme on many subjects,
we cannot be certain that his symbolical figures were un-
influenced by his own personal beliefs.

We must not forget that Gichtel was a mystical philosopher
in his own right, and should be studied from this premise.
His association with Boehme's works does not indicate that
he was a mere interpreter. He did interpret, but from certain deep and enduring convictions of his own. Thus, in the
edition of Boehme's writings, to which he added figures
and descriptions, Gichtel appears as an independent influence, and we must study the doctrine of two men in
one work.

Johann Gichtel published his *Theosophia Practica* in 1696,
and the complete title of the work freely translated from
the German reads, *A Short Exposition of the Three Principles and Worlds in Man, Set Forth in Clear Figures, Re-*

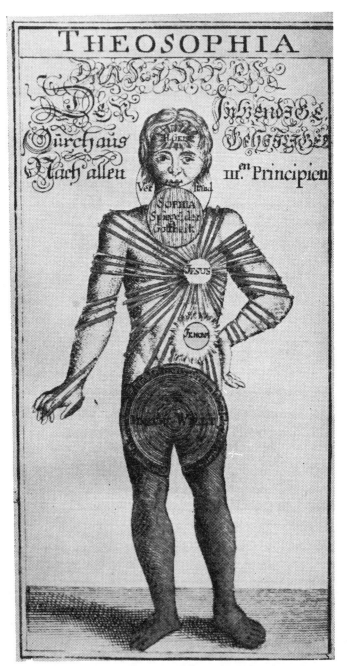

—From Gichtel's *Theosophia Practica**

*vealing How and Where They Have Their Respective Centers
Within the Inner Man as the Author Has Found Them Within
Himself by Godly Contemplation, According as to What he
has Felt, Tasted, and Perceived.*

A faithful reprint of this rare book was issued in Berlin
and Leipzig in 1779 by Christian Ulrich Ringmacher. The
reissue is as difficult to secure as the original imprint. In
one edition of this work, it is stated that the symbolical figures of the human body, which illustrate the text, were not
added until ten years or more after Gichtel's death. A French
translation of the *Theosophia Practica* was sponsored by the
Bibliotheque Chacornac in Paris in 1897.

Charles W. Leadbeater, in his monograph on *The Chakras*,
reproduced one of the Gichtel figures as proof "that at least
some of the mystics of the 17th century knew of the existence
and positions of the seven centers in the human body." It is
not clear, however, that Gichtel, following in the traditional
form established by Boehme, intended the various symbols
imposed upon his human figures to represent the chakras
of Eastern metaphysical tradition. The German mystics were
so arbitrary in their selection of their symbols that we must
suspect that they may have used familiar designs for purposes
entirely different from those of other more conventional
writers.

The Gichtel edition of Boehme's works is illustrated with
a series of extraordinary engravings, highly mystical in content and exceedingly well-drawn. In most cases these plates
are used as frontispieces, but occasionally others are scattered through the text. Usually, the plates are accompanied
by one leaf of descriptive text and a list of references to
books, chapters, and verses relating to the figures. These

*Plate: Symbolical figure of the spiritual world in the human
body.

descriptions, if they can be so referred to, are much in the spirit of the old emblem writers, whose moral remarks bore but slight resemblance to the designs which ornamented them.

The origin of the so-called Gichtel plates has been the subject of considerable unproductive research. It is not certain that Gichtel drew them himself or even supplied the basic design. Many of the figures are extremely dramatic, and they reveal a profound internal apperception of spiritual mysteries. Possibly the engravings were made by one or more of the artists who prepared the curious emblems found in old alchemical and cabalistic books. Some attempts to explain this situation have led to the suspicion that Gichtel may have belonged to some secret order like the Rosicrucians, and merely served as a medium for the dissemination of such esoteric teachings. A more or less careful check seems to indicate, however, that organizations claiming Rosicrucian descent at that time, borrowed, usually without credit, the Gichtel material.

As we have said, the comments accompanying the figures are entirely mystical, and the reader must interpret the inferences and implications to the best of his own ability. The descriptions are not signed, but according to popular belief they were prepared by Gichtel or his group to accompany the symbolical engravings. There is no proof that Boehme himself left any sequential series of symbolic designs to illustrate his principles. There remains the possibility of course that some drawings or sketches of his own or his immediate disciples may have been preserved and inspired the later illustrations. A reprint containing the engravings, slightly larger in format but lacking the description leaves, was issued in 1730. The plates had been modified and recut.

It must have been extremely difficult for Boehme to interpret through any formal medium the formless impressions and feelings which flowed through him on the occasions of his mystical experiences. It is probable that he never actually integrated his experiences into such a system of symbolism, but some of his disciples were able to systematize his doctrine through contributions of their own, and they designed the explanatory emblems. The Christian mysticism of this old German shoemaker certainly carried within it many concepts which antedated the Christian revelation.

As William Law, whose contributions we will consider in detail later in this article, pointed out, there are definite traces of Pythagoreanism and Platonism present in Boehme's writings. In fact, the system can be defined with reasonable accuracy as a Christianized Neoplatonism. There is no doubt, however, that as far as Boehme himself is concerned his system was entirely instinctual. He was not a trained mystic, and he had little if any acquaintance with previous philosophical schools. He shared in their doctrines only to the degree that his own impressions paralleled those of earlier Illuminists. He experienced all things within himself, even though many of his reports had been anticipated by sages and prophets of earlier times.

The modern intellectualist may be antagonized by Boehme's frequent references to such abstractions as God and his angels, or Satan and his legions. The first reading of the curious books may produce only a certain admiration for the vividness of the German mystic's imagination, but a deeper study will transmute this into a profound astonishment at the magnitude of his comprehension and the extent of his self-acquired knowledge.

"I am not collecting my knowledge from letters and books," writes Boehme, "but I have it within my own self; because heaven and earth with all their inhabitants, and moreover God himself, are in man."

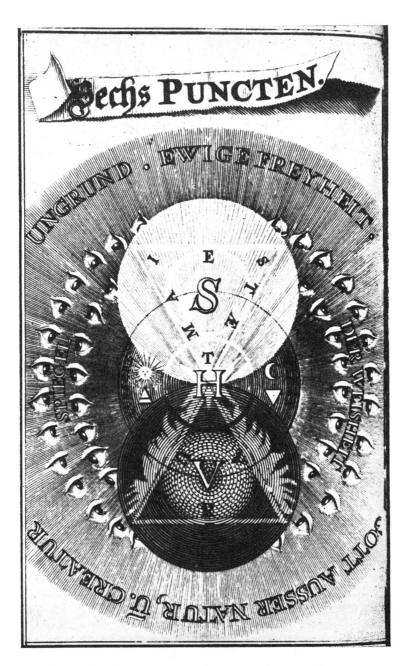

THE EQUILIBRIUM OF LIGHT AND DARKNESS*

The God of Boehme is not the God of the Church, nor is his Christ the Christ of the theologians. As the pagan initiates of antiquity clothed their profound doctrines in fables and myths, so Boehme concealed his mystical revelations under the form and word of the Christian Scriptures. Perhaps it would be more correct to say that Boehme restated a universal doctrine, which for more than fifteen centuries had been locked within the adamantine orthodoxy of Peter's Church.

Boehme's philosophy is established upon a premise that it might profit modern science to examine with great care. Dr. Franz Hartmann, an outstanding Theosophical writer, summarizes the concept in the following well-chosen words: "In the study of man as a cosmic being there are three subjects to consider, although the three are only aspects of one. These three subjects are God, Nature, and Man, and neither one of them can be understood in its inner essence without an understanding of the other two."

Examined apart from God and nature, man is bereft of origin and ultimate, and left as a purposeless accident upon the face of the earth. A recognition of the fundamental identity of God, nature, and man, constituting together a divine equilibrium, is essential to the establishment of a reasonable philosophy of life.

Boehme's God was not apart from man and nature, but within both, expressing Itself through both by what Boehme termed "properties." As he pegged shoes, the seer of Alt-Seidenburg envisioned a universal order, suspended from three principles, themselves resident in and co-eternal with Ab-

---

*Plate: This figure from Gichtel's edition of Boehme's writings, represents the sympathy of the light and dark worlds, with the divine splendor redeeming the creation and the creature from that outer privation which is called "the Wrath."

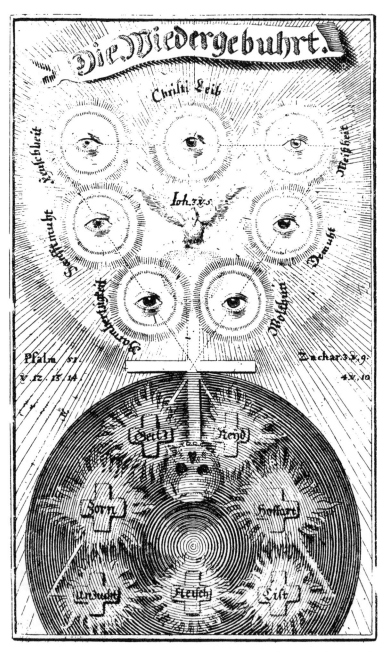

THE HEAVENLY PRINCIPLES REFLECTED IN THE MUNDANE SPHERE*

solute Cause. These principles correspond very closely with the scientific concept of light, matter and mind as uncreated agencies, subsisting throughout time and eternity, and precipitating the whole diversity of existence through their mutual strivings.

Accompanying the frontispiece of the first section of the edition of Boehme's writings edited by Gichtel, there is a brief reference to the design and purpose of the plates. A free translation of these remarks is indicative of the dominant concept: "The diagrams attempt to visualize how the entire Holy Scriptures flow out of the mouth of God through his sanctified teachers, prophets, and apostles, for the primary purpose of teaching and motivating [all men] to repentance and to absorption in divine mysteries. The word of God is almost entirely concealed in figures, in obscure prophetic utterances, in riddles and allegories, in which are actually disclosed the wonders of divine wisdom. That which is past is reported, that which is present is indicated in pictures, and that which is in the future is anticipated and implied. Appeal is made directly to the earth-born, self-centered, human consciousness, which cannot immediately understand and decipher such an approach. To the earth-born man the mystery of divine wisdom does not unveil its dignity, but only stimulates the understanding heart to seek and dig after the causes of wisdom. We must discover and release wisdom just as we must excavate out of the dark and coarse earth that radiant gold, which is the noblest of metals in the body of nature."

Johann Lorenz von Mosheim gives us a few side lights on the rise of Boehmenism. As might be expected from Mosheim's position in the world of letters, he was not sym-

---

*Plate: from the Gichtel figure illustrating the philosophy of Boehme.

pathetic to the mystical point of view. It is only necessary to
read a few lines to conclude that his opinions were strongly
prejudiced. In all fairness, however, it should be admitted
that he accumulated much interesting information on a variety
of subjects.

Mosheim included Boehme among the Lutheran fanatics
of the 17th century, "who in their flights of enthusiasm had
such a high notion of their own abilities as to attempt melt-
ing down the form of religion, and casting a new system of
piety after a model drawn from their wanton and irregular
fancies. At the head of this visionary tribe, we may place
Jacob Behmen, who was remarkable for the multitude of
his patrons and adversaries and whom his admirers commonly called the German Theosophist.

"This man had a natural propensity toward the investigation of mysteries and was fond of abstruse and intricate in-
quiries of every kind; and having partly by books and partly
by conversation with certain physicians, including Tobias
Kober and Balthasar Walther, acquired some knowledge of
Robert Fludd (a native of England and a man of a surprising genius) and the Rosicrucians, which was propagated
in Germany with great ostentation during this century, he
struck out of the element *Fire* by the succours of imagination a species of theology much more obscure than numbers
of Pythagoras or the intricacies of Heraclitus—some have
bestowed high praise on this enthusiast, on account of his
piety, integrity, and sincere love of truth and virtue; but
such as carry their admiration of his doctrine so far as to
honor him with the character of an inspired messenger of
heaven . . . . must be themselves deceived . . for never
did there reign such obscurity and confusion in the writings
of any mortal . . . He entertained the following chimerical
notion: 'The minds of men are purged from their vices and

corruptions in the same way that metals are purified from their dross.' "

The 17th century was remarkable for the quantity of mystical and esoteric publications printed between 1610 and 1690. During this period a number of skillful engravers were producing highly imaginative symbolic plates and emblems, many of which possessed extraordinary artistic merit. This school of engraving upon copper and wood merits more research than has yet been devoted to either the products or the producers thereof.

Doctor Mosheim mentions the English mystic, Robert Fludd, as a possible source of Boehme's speculations. An examination of Fludd's writings does not support the opinion that Boehme was indebted to the English Rosicrucian for his Theosophical doctrines. But the fantastic symbolic figures which illustrate Fludd's treatises and which were cut by Theodore de Bry are imaginative masterpieces and the products of a distinct school of skilled artisans. Fludd remarked that it was more economical and satisfactory to have his writings printed in Germany, especially at Frankfurt, which at that time was actually the printer's city.

One sometimes suspects that the engravers had doctrines of their own, and designed their symbolic plates with more consideration for their own opinions than for the opinions of their authors. In many cases, it appears that any resemblance between the text and the pictures is purely coincidental. The suspicion is increased when we observe that the same engravings are inserted in different works by different authors and to illustrate unrelated material. Fine engravings were a valuable property in themselves, and when no other purpose could be found they were compiled into collections and some writer selected to prepare short verses, epigrammatic observations, or moral platitudes to tie the unrelated pictures into a loose design.

After the great masters of symbolic illustration had been gathered to their fathers, their designs brought great comfort and profit to the numerous pseudo-esoteric societies that emerged from the general cultural confusion. The various elements of the early emblems were rearranged and extended by inferior workmen to lend an air of verisimilitude to the pretensions of impostors. The so-called Gichtel figures were the products of a high degree of originality. They were not copied from previous emblems, but were themselves the source of numerous subsequent devices of inferior ingenuity.

There is little to support von Mosheim's opinion that Boehme derived inspiration from Doctors Kober and Walther. These small-town practitioners left no impress in the mind of their times except as sincere disciples of the German Theosopher. They probably did contribute such assistance as lay within their power, but von Mosheim was merely seeking an easy explanation for that in itself inexplicable. It is usual for the historian to seek to explain away mysteries by any device that comes to hand. The entire tribe of historians resents exceptions to general rules. To them it appears expedient to sacrifice the exception and preserve the rule.

The point I wish to make is that there was a guild of illustrators, the members of which were extremely sensitive to mysticism, alchemy, and cabalism. These engravers must have possessed a profound knowledge of such obscure subjects, and may have been appointed to prepare emblems and figures without supervision and at their own discretion.

When the Duke of Brunswick wished a symbolic frontispiece for one of his books, he explained his requirements in a letter to his publisher. The finished engraving was a masterpiece, but its details were not the result of the Duke's suggestions. The finished product was the work of an independent genius, who was amazingly proficient in the creation of an appropriate and, in a sense, self-sufficient emblem that has piqued the curiosity of scholars for over three hundred years. Perhaps the Gichtel plates had a similar history.

WILLIAM LAW

William Law, a prominent English divine, was the major exponent of the teachings of Jakob Boehme in the 18th century. He appeared in the dual role of translator and editor, and was responsible for the first complete English translation of the writings of the German mystic. Law was a controversialist, a utilitarian religionist, and in the later years of his life, a mystic. It should be mentioned that although he is best known for his interest in the writings of Boehme, he was an outstanding mystic and theologian in his own right. He had the type of mind not commonly found among English intellectuals of his day. He was something of a misfit, both historically and geographically. He would have fitted into the early 17th century much better than the 18th century, and had the mood of southern Germany or central Asia as distinguished from that of the English countryside.

William Law was born in 1686 at King's Cliffe, Northamptonshire, the son of a grocer. In spite of his father's rather humble profession, there seems to have been sufficient means available for the young man's education, for he entered Cambridge University in 1705. He remained there until 1711. When King George I came to the throne, young Law refused, on grounds of conscience, to subscribe to the oath of allegiance then demanded, and, as a result, he lost his fellowship at Cambridge. Thus it appears that at an early age Law was already well established in the simple but strict code of personal piety which regulated his entire life.

In 1727 he accepted the position of tutor in the Gibbon family. He was placed in charge of the father of Edmund Gibbon, who was later to acquire immortal fame as the historian of the decline and fall of the Roman Empire. Law remained for ten years with this family, and upon the death of the senior Gibbon, retired to his native town, where he devoted himself to writing and study. He received financial assistance from the Gibbon family and several of his students, and spent the rest of his life in comparative comfort. As a Jacobite and nonjuror, however, Law's life was plagued with numerous reversals of fortune, and it can scarcely be said that he was entirely addicted to transcendental speculations. He wrote well, and devoted one tract to an attack on the theater, actors, and related subjects, which he described as absolutely unlawful.

Law was drawn to the writings of Boehme about 1735, possibly a little earlier. He admitted that, on first reading, the German mystic put him in complete confusion. Yet, there were certain glimmerings, intimations, and inferences that stirred his eager heart and mind. He therefore continued, combining study and prayer, and was rewarded by a gradually increasing apperception of the secret of Boehme's revelations. He was the author of several works in which he revealed his thorough understanding and enthusiastic admiration of Boehme's profound speculations. Law passed quietly from this life in 1761, and has been described as "a worthy and pious man, who believed all that he professed, and practiced all that he enjoined."

Just as Gichtel had a mind of his own, Law was definitely a person with strong convictions, and a mentality capable of individual initiative. We must assume, therefore, that the various commentaries and descriptions appended by Law to his great edition of Boehme reflected the individual convictions of this learned editor and compiler, and also, to some degree, the religious and political disturbances of the time.

For students of mysticism William Law is especially important for his translations and interpretations of Boehme's writings. Doctor Alexander Whyte summarizes Law's life and work in these words: "The best books of Law's contemporaries are all more or less known to everyone who loves books. *Crusoe, Gulliver, Homer,* and the *Essay on Man, The Spectator, The Tatler, The Vicar of Wakefield, The Analogy,* and the *Sermons,* as well as Southey and Boswell— but many not ill-read men have never read a single line of William Law. And yet it may with perfect safety be said that there are very few authors in English literature, if there is one, whose works will better reward readers of an original and serious cast of mind than just these wholly forgotten works of William Law. In sheer intellectual strength Law is fully abreast of the very foremost of his illustrious contemporaries, while in that fertilizing touch which is the true test of genius Law simply stands alone. And then his truly great and sanctified intellect worked exclusively, intensely, and with unparalleled originality on the most interesting, the most important and the most productive of all subjects— the Divine nature and human nature, sin, prayer, love and eternal life."

The monumental work of William Law still remains as the finest edition of Boehme's writings in the English language. It was published in four volumes of folio size in

1772, under the title, *The Works of Jacob Behmen, the Teutonic Theosopher . . . With Figures, Illustrating his Principles Left by the Reverend William Law, M. A.* In this edition an entirely new series of symbolic designs make their appearance. Some of these are reminiscent of the earlier Gichtel figures; others bear no obvious relation to earlier illustrations.

Due to eccentricities in binding, the plates occur in different places in various copies of the work, but they usually fall at the end of a short section, entitled *Four Tables of Divine Revelation, Signifying what God in Himself is Without Nature; and how Considered in Nature, According to the Three Principles. Also What Heaven, Hell, World, Time, and Eternity, are: Together with all Creatures visible and invisible: And out of what all Things had their Original. By Jacob Behmen, the Teutonic Theosopher.* There are twenty engravings in the series. Of these, two are hand-colored, and thirteen form a series representing the fall of Adam and the human regeneration through Christ. Then follow two independent designs, one including folding parts, and lastly, there are three manikins with many flaps, revealing the spiritual constitution of man and his relationship with the universe. These last three are the most extraordinary examples of such figures known to exist.

Again, the origin of the design is obscure. In his work now referred to as *The Latin Manuscript,* Peter Paul Rubens referred to Boehme as "that blessed instrument in the hands of the Spirit of God." We further learn that this manuscript was appended to Ruben's *Treatise on the Proportion of the Human Figure; Cabalistic Principles; and the Property of Numbers Applied to Chemical Operations, etc.*

There is evidence that Rubens possessed not only a profound admiration for the writings of the German mystic,

THE TRUE PRINCIPLES OF ALL THINGS

Herein are set forth, according to the obscure doctrines of Jakob Boehme, the three principles which, uniting in fire, generate the material universe. (From the William Law edition.)

but also a deep understanding of Boehme's metaphysical speculations. The artistry of the manikin figure in particular is distinctly Rubenesque. The figure of Sophia in the third table is especially reminiscent of Ruben's technique. We should like to hazard the speculation that the manikins either originated directly with Ruben or were inspired by drawings which he prepared.

One thing is certain: the manikins are infinitely superior to the engravings usually found in the occult books of the 17th and 18th centuries. They are more than illustrations; they are works of art. Had William Law actually conceived the pictures, he would certainly have been in a better position to describe them than is apparent from his meager comments. In short, the figures have descended to us with very inadequate keys to their interpretation.

There are many similarities between the designs of the human body which appear in Gichtel's *Theosophia Practica* and the manikins in the William Law edition. The later artist or engraver certainly was aware of the former work.

In his brief introduction to the four tables, we have from Law the following description of the general plan of the enterprise: "It contains four tables with their explanations; wherein may be seen, by a spiritual eye, the ground and foundation of all the author's works, and profound mysteries: Yea, there is also clearly deciphered, that so much sought and so rarely found, secret Cabala of the ancient rabbis. These tables, indeed, contain the sum of all the author's writings; and of all his knowledge; of all in heaven and earth; yea, of all the highest mysteries that man in this life is capable of knowing."

The first table explains and reveals God and how Deity out of Himself continually begets and breathes forth Himself. The mystery of God, concealed within Himself and separate from all nature and creatures, is expounded as a septenary or a seven-fold essential Being, extending downward from *Abyss to Wisdom*. According to Boehme, God, most hidden and entirely without objective manifestation, is properly designated the *Abyss*—the *Nothing* and the *All*. God is *Nothing* in the sense of *no thing*, completely and entirely incomprehensible, and not to be discovered and experienced except by the complete detachment of consciousness from the illusion of nature and creature. Yet this *no thing* is at the same time the *All*, for from it is made manifest every visible, sensible, and attainable nature and condition.

Within the nature of *Nothing* and *All* reposes the *Will of the Abyss*. This *Will* is the secret Father of all beings, for by means of the *Will* the mystery of God is manifest in the creation, which is the extension of the *Abyss*, from center to circumference, according to *Will*.

It is the *Will* that reveals the *Lubet*, the *Delight* or emotional impression of the *Will*. This is the joy of the God that begetteth the God, according to his own pleasure. This begetting is by the breathing forth of God the Son, a revealed expression of the *Delight* of the Father.

From the *Delight* proceeds motion which is science, for all knowledge in the material world is the knowledge of motion. This motion is the *Holy Spirit*, which is the breath or outbreathing of the *Delight*. Herein is concealed the mystery of how the Father of himself begets the Son, and how the *Holy Spirit* proceeds from them both, yet is one Being.

In the next level is God in Trinity, a triune Being, known unto the similitude of the *Will*, the *Mind*, and the *Senses*, wherein together lie the eternal understandings. Thus, are all natures and creatures locked within their own causes, from which they may be unfolded or opened by a divine mystery.

From the One Eternal Understanding and the understandings, which are many and one, there stands forth the *Word*, which is the perception of the *Self*, by which the creature is aware of the Creator. By this awareness the creature discovers God to be the eternal good, and even this discovery itself is an experience which abides eternally in God.

In the last and seventh place stands *Wisdom*. This is the divine contemplation of the creature, which, by use of its own divinity, becomes aware of the universal Divinity. By *Wisdom*, God in himself and to himself becomes intelligible, perceptible, and revealed. These seven conditions or states are within the nature of the Eternal Cause and in fact are that Cause. By these seven virtues, that Cause is in itself complete, and that which is outside of these seven departs from the incomprehensible, and moves inevitably toward that which is comprehensible.

That which is comprehensible is nature and creature, and these two are finally embodied, personified, or symbolized by the *World* and *Man*. The *World* is the sum of nature, and *Man* is the sum of creature. He exists within nature, and nature within him. In his outward parts, he exists in *Time*, but inwardly he exists according to eternity, which is the *Abyss* of *Time*. For *Time*, like God Himself, is *Nothing* and *All*. *Time* in the *Spirit* is *no thing*. *Time* in the *Mind* is past, present, and future, and *Time* in the *World* is *All*, for it measures the duration of both nature and creature.

From this brief excursion into Boehme's principles and terminology the measure of the difficulty of interpreting his writings can be estimated. But if his words are insufficient to clarify his meanings, they are quaintly dramatic and perhaps carry a greater impact than may first appear. The very unfamiliarity of the terms separates them from the common definitions which arise in the mind. It is necessary to accept Boehme's definitions without any recourse to things previously studied or known. This has one great advantage, even though it is burdened with several lesser disadvantages.

The whole of Boehme's mystical idealism is brought to bear upon the subjects of the fall of man, the miseries of his relapsed state, and the secret of his redemption, through a mystical attunement with the spiritual substance of life.

To the state of Deity, which is beyond dimension and is represented by the *Abyss,* Boehme applied the term "the first temperature." Here God in himself is that Eternal Liberty which the vulgar call *chaos.*

Chaos is not lawlessness but law beyond comprehension. This is the *Mysterium Magnum;* that which is without, before, and above nature. This is the first world, the eternal world; that which gives birth to creations without being itself created; that which decrees form without itself being formed, and that which is ever sustaining growth and motion, but which itself neither grows nor is moved. This state is beyond the objective awareness of any thing that is created. Nothing may know it or share in it but itself, but men and angels may consider it by the powers of the heart and mind without the capacity to actually share in its substance, or identify themselves with its purposes.

In this "first temperature" abides the triune Deity in the state of complete subjectivity. This triune Deity is called the Father, the Son, and Holy Ghost by those who have not been initiated into the mystery. But more correctly, the Trinity exists only on the lower planes of creation; whereas, in the "eternal temperature," there is only a triunity of God, which is the divine fire or the mutual love of that in itself beyond separation. This is a love in unity, rather than a love striving for unity.

The "second temperature" is the residence of the brightness of the Father or Glory. It is less than the *Nothing* and the *All* for it is of the nature of the *All*, rather than sharing equally in the nature of the *Nothing*. This *All* is the upper extremity of nature, the apex of an ascending pyramid. Here is all union, all concord, and all harmony. This is the *light world* or the *love fire*, whose root is in the divine *Desire*, and which flows forth out of that triune divine fire Deity, which in the "first temperature" was not an object of our understanding, but only of our consideration.

In an effort to sense a mystical experience apart from an intellectual enlightenment, we may do well to consider Boehme's division of terms, by which he contrasts *understanding* and *consideration*. By *understanding* he means the conscious sharing of the state in which the creature experiences the creator as an internal reality. Naturally in this sense, the word *understanding* has a much larger and deeper meaning than in familiar usage, but undoubtedly it is the familiar usage that is at fault. Things, for example, are not understood because they are seen or described. We cannot understand music, for example, merely by attending concerts. To fully appreciate an art or science, there must be self-participation. A thing must be done or performed in order to be fully known.

According to Boehme, the "first temperature" of God cannot be a direct object of understanding except under extraordinary conditions; in fact, no mortal creature can attain through participation to a complete internal experience of the substance of the *Mysterium Magnum*. A creature like man, who knows only the bondage of creation, cannot experience the *Eternal Liberty* of that which is beyond na-

—From the William Law edition

THE TREE OF THE SOUL

In the teachings of Boehme, the human soul and the world are represented by a tree, which, rising from the material universe, ascends through the four spheres of life, attaining to its flower and fruit in the Light of Majesty.

ture and creature. That which dwells forever in the presence of *some thing* cannot fully experience *no thing* and *All.* The relapsed Adam, living in the heart, blended by the dark, cold fire of nature, cannot understand through participation the brightness of the *love* fire of the *light world,* or the *divine fire* which abides forever in the darkness of the causeless Cause.

Thus, the creation becomes aware of the Creator only by *consideration,* and this term we must understand to represent the contemplation of something or some state, separate and distinct from actual experience. Thus, we may consider the natures of the creatures about us in the *World,* but we cannot know these creatures by internal experience. We can consider the stars, the motions of the year, and the intricate balance of universal laws and forces, in which we have our mundane existence. These things may be observed, noted, and recorded; they may give rise to reflection within us.

Our thoughtfulness, in turn, may lead to the formulation of concepts. We may evolve elaborate explanations for the diversity of natural phenomena, and we may even postulate certain profound conclusions about God and salvation, but these must arise only from *consideration* and not actually from experience.

We understand the world of which we are a part better than we understand space, which is without any familiar landmark to assist us toward a reasonable estimation. The mystical apperceptive powers of the seer differ from the intellectual accomplishments of the scholar in this one particular; namely, the degree of conscious identification with life.

The two columns that support the portico of the Everlasting House are *Wisdom* and *Understanding. Wisdom* is the natural extension of *consideration,* which ultimately leads to the acceptance of certain overtones, or contemplated realities. Devotion leads toward *understanding*, which is a communion or spiritual sympathy, in which the mystic in his ecstasy feels that he is experiencing "a sharing in God and with God," and in this way attains the security of the Divine "temperature."

Out of the descent of the "first temperature" into the "second temperature" there is established the middle part of eternal nature. Here the fire of the first principle becomes the constant, clear, burning and flaming fire of manifested divinity. This is the tabernacle of the Father's omnipotence or All Power. This All Power is symbolized by the sun, but it must be understood that this is not the physical orb in the sky but the cosmic spiritual sun, which bears to the whole of creation the same relationship that our sun bears to its solar system.

Boehme's spiritual sun, or manifested divinity, corresponds with the Paracelsian concept of a God light, which appears upon the surface of the eternal darkness, and corresponds to the *Fiat,* or the *spoken word*. This is the sun whose coming is heralded by the *aurora* or the *dawn light*, which is the promise of the revelation of the *Eternal Splendor*.

Boehme represents the eternal manifestation of Divine Being through temporal nature as a triune mystery of *darkness*, *fire*, and *light*. We must understand that the mystic is now considering creation from the viewpoint of *consideration;* that is, he is meditating upon the nature from the natural substances and essences of matter. The three constituent parts of the inferior universe are heaven (the sphere of light), earth (the sphere of fire), and hell (the sphere of darkness). All natures are bound by the light in themselves to the light of the world, and by the darkness of themselves to the obscuring and crystallizing material elements.

Naturally, Boehme does not use his terms in an orthodox or literal sense, but to represent those moods or states of consciousness which he experienced in the mystical extensions of *understanding*. To him, light symbolized increasing awareness of the spiritual mystery; fire, the intensity by which awareness itself was diminished; and darkness, the obscuration of internal comprehension. Fire was a kind of striving, whereas true illumination was a suspension of all effort in a state of perfect luminous tranquillity.

Having established his principles, Boehme extended them out of the nature of God into the substance of the world, and finally into the constitution of man. He set up analogies by which each sphere interpreted the others, so that man himself might become the interpreter of all secrets, human and divine. Only great time and thoughtfulness can elucidate all phases of this extraordinary mystical revelation, but it does unfold sequentially and with remarkable consistency.

Among the William Law figures is one representing the spiritual life of man growing up through the four great spheres or worlds toward the *Light of Majesty*. In this conception the two forms of *Will*, that is, the Divine Will which leads to Christ, and the Self-Will, which ends in the abode of fire, which is the habitation of Satan, are represented as the branches of a tree. The Divine Will leads toward the spirit, which, passing out through the upper part of the solar world, grows through the sphere of darkness and the sphere of fire to blossom and bear fruit in Paradise. In the symbolism, the tree represents the spiritual life which, planted in the human heart—the seed of an immortal being—grows upward toward the light which is its proper destiny.

From these universal considerations, we come naturally to the three curious manikin figures. These form together what Boehme calls the similitudes of the three worlds. In

each manikin, man is represented as consisting of three parts
—body, soul, and spirit. This three-fold division may not
be at first apparent, because of the numerous sections making up the engravings. Together the three manikins represent
man in three states or conditions—"the first, before his fall,
in purity, dominion, and glory; the second, after his fall,
pollution, and perdition; and the third, in his rising from
the fall, or on the way of regeneration, in sanctification and
tendency to his last perfection."

The three conditions of man represent his imagination
focused upon the three parts of his own nature—i. e. spirit,
soul, and body. Before his fall, he dwelt in a spiritual state.
By the fall, he descended into a bodily state, and by regeneration, he ascends again into the estate of soul.

Once more we should beware of the confusion arising
from the use of a terminology which makes unusual usage of
familiar words. For instance, according to Boehme, God is
"the Will of Eternal Wisdom," and in *The Three Principles*
he writes: "If anyone desires to follow me in the science of
the things whereof I write, let him follow rather the flights
of my soul than those of my pen." Boehme thus sums up
the method by which he is to be understood: "I am often
forced to give terrestrial names to that which is celestial,
so that the reader may form a conception, and by meditating
about it penetrate within the inner foundation."

ALEXANDER WHYTE, D. D.

We should like to introduce at this point the Reverend
Alexander Whyte (1837-1921), a Scottish divine who received the freedom of the city of Edinburgh in 1910. Dr.
Whyte published the life of William Law in 1893, and an
appreciation of Jakob Boehme in 1895. From these circumstances and other details of his life, it appears that

Whyte was much addicted to the biographies and doctrines
of prominent mystics and religionists.

In the Library of the Philosophical Research Society, we
have a curious scrapbook dealing with Jakob Boehme with
the *ex libris* of Dr. Whyte. From the appearance and condition of this manuscript collection, which is a large thin
folio, it does not appear that the material was written by
Whyte but belonged to a somewhat earlier date, probably
18th century. Although no clues are given, it is barely possible from the nature of the fragments that Whyte may have
come into possession of some of the original drawings prepared for William Law, and not included in the printed
edition. The problem is difficult but most interesting.

In addition to several pages of manuscript laid in, there
are thirty symbolical drawings of various sizes in the Whyte
scrapbook. The figures were drawn by expert draftsmen,
and the text worked into the design is variously in English,
German, and Latin. Of special importance are the figures,
obviously belonging to the Boehme cycle, which do not occur in the Gichtel edition or the William Law translation.
These figures include manikins with movable parts, and are
sometimes tied to Boehme by direct quotations from his
books. The drawings are by more than one artist, and I
have not been able to trace anything similar to them in the
British Museum collection of Boehme's works.

Among the curious figures in the Whyte collection is a
fragment evidently a part of a larger work. There is no clue
to the author, but from the appearance of the writing and
the paper the fragment is probably 18th century. The in-
complete text is in German, and serves as a description for
a curious emblem, drawn in line and washed and tipped
onto the margin of the text. Part of the symbol is reproduced
herewith. The figure is oval, and the obverse side consists of

WILLEMINA SOPHIA

From the collection of Boehme's symbols made by Alexander Whyte.

an inscription surrounded by a wreath of leaves and berries. The inscription consists of what appears to be an extravagant summary of the honors and achievements of that most noble, high-born princess, Willemina Sophia, by the Grace of God, Queen of the nations of Europe, Asia, Africa, America, and the Islands of the sea. Next comes a list of her Cabinet ministers and the members of her privy council, with the departments over which they ruled. These great and noble ministers are Saturn, Jupiter, Mars, Mercury, Venus, and the Moon.

In describing this figure, which was inspired by that god-illumined mystic, Jakob Boehme, our unknown author states that by Willemina Sophia is to be understood that worldly wisdom, by which all material achievements are made possible. Looking carefully, we notice that he has written the name of the princess in large capital letters, so arranged that they are spaced in two words, thus: Wille Mina. Boehme frequently used the word *Wille* to represent the internal resolution in man which impels to action. It does not require much exaggeration to consider that *Mina* is the feminine and fondly diminutive suffix. Thus, Willemina can mean the feminine diminutive or negative or lesser form of the will. When combined with Sophia, it can read "the small, feminine will of wisdom."

Our author, with the redundant literary form usual to the mystical writings of the period, explains, after a number of profuse apologies, that he was indulging in a little game of make-believe. He is imagining that the world is ruled by a beautiful princess, who possesses the attributes of reason and knowledge, but is without internal, mystical apperception. She is given rulership over all the arts and sciences, trades and crafts; and because she is ever making men more skillful and more profound, and assisting them in the accumulation of wealth and honor, they regard her with the highest admiration and are proud to be subjects of her empire.

The reverse of the same figure shows a coat of arms with two supporters. The coat is divided into six compartments, in each of which appears the hieroglyphic of one of the planets and various implements illustrative of the attributes of the planet. In the center of the shield is a miniature water-color portrait of Willemina Sophia, with a crown on her head, pearls about her neck, and the royal ermine draped from her shoulders. The artist tells us that she is radiantly beautiful, but evidently his technique was inadequate or he was indulging in sly satire, for the princess has a definitely subnormal appearance.

The shield containing the coat of arms is supported by a female monkey wearing a bonnet, and a fox with an eccentric-appearing helmet. The author explains that the monkey is the symbol of the false appearance of worldly wisdom, like Aristotle's ape of learning. The fox represents shrewdness, deceit, imposture and cunning. Thus, worldly wisdom is supported by stupidity and deceit, for there is no foolishness more dangerous than learned foolishness, and no deceit more dangerous than skilled deceit.

With delightful naivete, our author now recommends that we lift up the little central flap, bearing the miniature likeness of Willemina Sophia, and observe that underneath is another representation of the illustrious princess. Here she is depicted as seen by the internal eye of the seer. She now has the complexion and attributes of a scullery maid, an unlettered, untutored farm wench, wearing the crown, pearls, and ermine with bad grace.

The burden of the writer's opinions is in substance that worldly wisdom and all that knowledge which arises only in the mind, although outwardly beautiful and sufficient, are in fact illusions. There can be no true enlightenment except through the discovery of spiritual truths by meditation, prayer, faith, and good works. Mortal institutions are supported by false knowledge and ulterior motives, until the light of God brings essential wisdom into the heart of man, and he cheerfully exchanges all outward pretensions for inner peace and beauty.

Among the papers assembled by Reverend Whyte is a copy of the last will and testament of a certain Mr. Freeher.*

Unfortunately, the copy is not dated and contains no information about the life or times of the testator. It is quite possible that the whole will is a mystical allegory. In any event, Mr. Freeher distributes his worldly goods by means of five specific bequests, and it would appear that the greater part of his estate consisted of books, manuscripts, and the like.

Item 2 bestows upon Mr. Special the books of Jakob Boehme in High Dutch. Item 3 leaves to Mr. Lichter several volumes by older authors, including "my figures *de uno, puncto, centro*: together with all the manuscripts in the possession of Mr. Watle, and the press wherein they are laid up." It is possible that these figures refer to symbolical drawings dealing with Boehme's writings, some of which may be in the Whyte folio.

Mr. Freeher also bestowed his ring, engraved with the memorandum: "Prepared be to follow me," his hourglass,

---

*Through this article, appearing in our Journal in 1948, the Freeher will came to the attention of Charles H. Muses, who stated that this item "filled an important hiatus in the bibliographical and biographical data of Freher." For the researches of Dr. Muses bearing upon the material in the Library of our Society, see *Illumination on Jacob Boehme, The Work of Dionysius Andreas Freher*, New York, 1951.

weather house, feather bed, and a very fine chimney gate. It is evident that he was a follower of Boehme or Gichtel, for he concludes: "I die in the communion of the Church of Christ; that is, of all them that are living members of his mystical body, wherever they are dispersed in the world; and keep nothing against any human creature: I thank you all, my friends, English and German, for all your love and kindness, your reward you shall find when you come into the *Mysterium*: and I exhort you all to love one another, and to keep up among yourselves union and peace. God bless you all; and I desire an interest in your prayers."

The gradual accumulation of symbolic devices as instruments for the interpretation and dissemination of esoteric philosophies has been practiced by nearly all religious systems. Formal courses of study, by which the concepts of a teacher or a doctrine are transmitted to followers and disciples, have never solved completely one of the most basic problems in the world of learning. Instruction imposes upon the mind of the student certain patterns of knowledge. These he must accept, commit to memory, and apply as best he can to the complications of personal living. His conduct is motivated by ideas not actually his own, and in critical situations, this imposed learning usually proves insufficient. In other words, his studies may extend over a considerable area, but they are limited to surfaces, whereas life itself depends upon penetration. It may not be correct to say that the intellectualist is superficial, but the entire theory of formal education deals with the acquiring of facts considered in themselves separate and apart from the person learning them.

Symbols, by their very structure capable of numerous interpretations, invite the student to draw upon his own resources in an attempt to discover *the* or *a* satisfactory explanation. The symbol, therefore, leads to an experience intensely personal and individual. We discover what we know when we bring our wit and wisdom to bear upon some abstract device. This is especially true when we have every reason to believe that the emblem or figure was devised by a person of unusual spiritual attainment. The unexplained issues a challenge. It demands that we think for ourselves, and soon reveals the degree of our own ability to perform the function of creative thinking.

Nature about us uses the language of symbolism for the unfoldment of the potentials of all its creatures. The mysteries of life do not explain themselves or issue any dogmatic statement about their ways or workings. As Boehme would express it: "The creature must discover the Creator by extending human faculties toward the Divine Mystery."

It naturally follows that symbols are subject to numerous misinterpretations, even as nature itself can be incorrectly estimated. Thus art is necessary to perfect instinct and impulse. If the mind is trained to proceed in an orderly manner, it will not depart from that which is reasonable and probable. If formal knowledge is strong enough to prevent fantasy, the symbol will be explained with the guidance and censorship of judgment.

Symbols also can convey a collective impression usually lost by premature analysis. As a result of meditation upon a sacred emblem, a mood or over-all impression of values is communicated without the limitations imposed by word patterns and word definitions. The written word or even the spoken word is seldom sufficient unless the speaker or writer attains an extraordinary degree of artistry. Even then he accomplishes penetration by pressure of his own personality. As Socrates so well pointed out, understanding must be coaxed or persuaded to come forth out of its hidden retreats within the soul. We never release man by pressing our opinions upon him, even if those opinions are themselves true. We must lure a reluctant consciousness to reveal its own purposes, thus leading the creature to a condition of sufficiency.

The crises which arise in daily living seldom can be solved by formulas, for the incidents are never exactly in line with our preconceived solutions. We prepare for one emergency, and another happens. We then seek advice, only to discover that the experiences of others differ sufficiently from our own to invalidate most of the suggested remedies. Solutions theoretically adequate are practically deficient, and we seek in vain throughout the whole world for the specific device appropriate to our pressing need. In the end we discover that each of us must solve his own problems by drawing upon the reservoir of experience within himself. It is therefore important that inward faculties be stimulated if the external conduct is to be wisely regulated.

One of the disasters of modern civilization is the prevailing tendency to surround the individual with so many external supports, patterns, and techniques that the development of internal resources is largely frustrated. When everything is explained, we are inclined simply to accept and drift with prevailing prejudices.

Once upon a time, most folks met the challenge of a door with a degree of ingenuity. Noting the hinges and the handle, they instinctively recognized the principles involved; and if they desired entry or exit, they took hold of the knob and proceeded accordingly. Today we deny people even this opportunity for personal ingenuity by placing a neat sign above the handle, saying, "Push," or "Pull," or "Entry," or "Exit." The prevailing conviction seems to be that we would languish indefinitely before the portal without these helpful hints.

This eternal restatement of the obvious can and does result in an inferiority complex and mental laziness. The more we are helped in this way, the more helpless we become. In the end, we mail letters in trash boxes, because no one has labeled the container with an appropriate warning. In dismantling a town pump, twenty letters were discovered carefully posted in the slot where the old handle had been. Every few days the fire department is discomfited by a false alarm, resulting from someone mistaking the firebox on the corner for a public telephone. Such conditions will always exist where life is so regimented that the human being loses all thoughtfulness, and drifts about in a false security demanding no thinking of his own.

Our spiritual institutions could be and should be sources of individual security, but even these are dedicated to saving souls rather than to fitting souls to save themselves. It ends with everyone expecting — even demanding — to be saved, protected, and nursed. Then, when our affairs go badly, we resent the institutions which have failed us, completely oblivious to the fact that we have failed ourselves at every step.

The ancients used mathematical, musical, dramatic, artistic, and graphic symbols and emblems to convey abstract truths, because such a method of conveyance advanced the essential growth of the human consciousness. Boehme probably did not rationalize the importance of emblems, but he and his followers made use of them because they offered obvious advantages. Confronted with the almost impossible problem of transmitting formless truths to minds functioning only in form dimension, the symbol became the only possible means of attaining the desired end. All students of advanced mystical or philosophical systems will do well to familiarize themselves with the instruments of symbolism. Only those capable of interpreting correctly the symbolism of God in nature, of nature in man, and of man in the dissemination of his ideas, can hope to discover the secrets of the esoteric tradition.

THE SHEPHERD OF CHILDREN'S MINDS
JOHANN AMOS COMENIUS

The works of men must always be framed in terms of time and place. It often happens that great sincerity of spirit breaks through the boundaries imposed by dates and localities, but in judging the merits of an endeavor, we like to know its author. We want to understand him as a person, and not merely as a name. His humanity is his reality. It may be of little philosophic import whether he be tall or short, dark or fair, but we still want to know. We would like to become acquainted with his family, the house in which he lived, his friends and, for that matter, his enemies. We cannot know whether he was a reactionary, a liberal, or a progressive, unless we know his time and the history which surrounded him. Did he live in days of peace or war? Did he enjoy security, or was his life troubled with those uncertainties which have burdened most ages? The man without a personality, without a date, so to say without a body, is only a fragment of a person—perhaps little more than the long shadow cast by his words and thoughts.

The history of education is long and complicated. There have been alternating periods of fertility and sterility, with sterility predominating. The modern story of man begins with the Renaissance, aided and abetted by the Protestant Reformation. So great a change in the collective thinking of Europe could not fail to move the foundations of educational theory and practice. The relentless drive of humanism was gaining momentum; the old ways could never return, and the new ways were yet ill-fashioned. The Reformation in Germany resulted in the establishment of many universities and schools inspired and sustained by Protestantism. It is evident that these institutions were not founded in the same concepts that had inspired education prior to the Renaissance. A strong spirit of rivalry was introduced, and the Church extended its efforts, calling upon the resources of the Society of Jesus. This was perhaps the little-considered source of the division between the secular and parochial schools.

The troublous era was punctuated by the Treaty of Augsburg, which cleared the way, in 1555, for state domination of the school system. The rulers of the numerous kingdoms and principalities were to decide how the educational programs within their territories were to be administered and sustained. Protestant states therefore emphasized Protestant schools, and it was assumed that the right of individual worship would be preserved. The Treaty of Augsburg, however, had little effect upon private and public convictions, and few of the basic disputes were actually solved. The various states, with their differing policies and strong religious prejudices, not only perpetuated their old animosities, but developed new enmities, and these were finally consummated in the terrible Thirty Years' War, which lasted from 1618 to 1648. It is evident that while this bitter struggle continued, all cultural programs languished. Men were too busy hating each other to make any reasonable plans for the future. Thus the children, so far as their schooling was concerned, became victims of the intemperances of their elders, and noble theories were sacrificed to brutal practices.

In areas not directly ravished by war, Protestant leaders were certainly desirous of rescuing education from the surviving remnants of scholasticism. They were opposed to old methods, but had not yet devised a newer or better methodology. As might be expected where religious prejudices were numerous, the problem of method assumed large proportions. It was not possible to declare that mathematics was either Catholic or Protestant, nor could the sciences and arts be aligned under such banners. The universe continued to move in its eternal course, but there was much philosophizing about the relationship between knowledge and faith. The 17th century has been called "the era of method," and the general drift was from revelation to experience. Authority was giving way to experimentation and research. Infallibilities were sorely shaken, and as they fell, fallibilities became supreme.

The rise of method also had its effects. The learned became so involved in the immediate project of means that ends were almost forgotten. In a world greatly in need of educational facilities, and where illiteracy had long been the rule rather than the exception, it seemed reasonable that there was urgent need for a rapid and efficient method of bringing knowledge to young and old. This laid heavy emphasis upon the selection of those branches of learning most basic and necessary. The trimmings and trappings could well be dispensed with in favor of the enlargement of factual content. School books as such were either unavailable or couched in ponderous Latin beyond the reach of the average reader. There was no systematic program of instruction, and there was special need for books suitable to the mind of the very young. This was long before the coming of the McGuffey

Reader or similar works. The methodologists of the 17th century were, for the most part, sterile thinkers. They were certainly earnest, honorable men, but they totally lacked imagination. They contributed little of lasting value that would entitle them to the grateful remembrance of later times. The one exception that stands out clearly against the drab background was Johann Amos Comenius (1592-1670). It is said of him that his primary interest in education resulted from the badness of his own.

Comenius, born Komensky, was the son of a miller, and his family belonged to a sect of reformed Christians sometimes called The Bohemian Brethren, but better remembered as The Moravian Brethren. Although these Moravians were broadly known as Lutherans, they maintained an organization of their own, claiming ecclesiastical descent from the Bohemian reformer John Hus. Comenius, who shared with other Moravians the simplicity of faith and the belief in the brotherhood of men, was born at Nivnitz in Moravia, and is described as a Slav born within the sovereignty of Austria. He has become a distinguished personality among the Czechoslovakians, and a series of postage stamps featuring his portrait has recently been issued.

The parents of Comenius died while he was still a young child, and his youth and education were entrusted to guardians. Sufficient funds were available for him to enjoy four years of instruction in a local school. This offered only elementary instruction, and was typical of the prevailing situation. It was known as a "people's school," located at Strassnick. These "people's schools" were the direct result of the Reformation, and were usually deeply concerned with the immediate religious problems of the community where they existed. Promising children were encouraged to prepare for the ministry, but this encouragement was sustained only by courses in elementary reading and writing, the memorizing of the catechism, and the barest rudiments of simple arithmetic.

The young orphan has been described as a quiet and gentle soul, rather slow of learning, but thoughtful and observant. About his fifteenth year, he took up his studies at the grammar school of Prerau. He was considerably older than his fellow students, and therefore more critical of the limitations of the prevailing system. Here the young man was condemned to procedures little better than intellectual punishment. Of course, Latin was required, especially as it appeared likely that Comenius would enter the ministry of the Moravian Brethren. Proper lexicons and grammars were unknown, and teaching was mostly by interminable and practically unintelligible formulas and rules distinguished principally by their acceptance. About four years later, when Comenius was twenty, he passed to the College of Herborn, located in the dukedom of Nassau.

While it can be said that he enjoyed good advantages according to the times, and his college was no worse than those in other localities, Comenius later summarized his conclusions about such places of learning in these words: ". . . They are the terror of boys, and the slaughterhouses of minds,— places where a hatred of literature and books is contracted, where ten or more years are spent in learning what might be acquired in one, where what ought to be poured in gently is violently forced in and beaten in, where what ought to be put clearly and perspicuously is presented in a confused and intricate way, as if it were a collection of puzzles,— places where minds are fed on words." While he was still at Herborn, Comenius was attracted by what was called the Ratichian scheme, a proposed reformation of teaching meth-

—From *The Great Didactic*

Portrait of Comenius at the Age of Fifty

ods being favorably considered by the Universities of Jena
and Giessen. This hope of general improvement produced
a lasting effect on his mind.

From Herborn, the young man traveled to the Low
Countries, living for a time in Amsterdam. He also studied
in Germany at Heidelberg. In 1614, he returned to Moravia,
and, being still too young for the ministry, he was made

Rector of the Moravian school at Prerau, where he attempted some of his earliest educational reforms. Two years later, he was ordained to the ministry and became pastor of the most important and influential of the Moravian churches, located at Fulneck. His duties included superintendence of the new school, and he began seriously considering his new concepts of teaching. While at Fulneck, he also married, and it is reported that the three years between 1618 and 1621 were the happiest and most peaceful of his life. As a result of the Thirty Years' War, Bohemia and Moravia were grievously afflicted. In 1621, Fulneck was captured by Spanish troops serving as allies of the German Emperor Ferdinand II. Although the town was captured without resistance, Comenius was the personal victim of the religious feud then raging. His house was pillaged and burned down and his library and all his manuscripts were destroyed. He fled to Bohemia with his family, and shortly afterwards lost his wife and child by death.

From this time on, the sect of Moravian Brethren was under almost constant persecution. In 1627, the Evangelical pastors in Moravia and Bohemia were formally proscribed by the Austrian government. They fled into various distant places, taking refuge when possible under the patronage of some liberal nobleman. Gradually, their living became more precarious, and, in January 1628, several exiles, including Comenius, left Bohemia. Arriving at the Silesian frontier, they knelt together in prayer to God, entreating him not to avert his mercy from their beloved country, nor to allow the seed of his word to perish within it. Comenius never returned to Bohemia.

In February of the same year, Comenius arrived at Lissa, and here he spent a number of years serving as preacher and schoolmaster of the small Bohemian community that had settled there. He married a second time, and had five children—a son and four daughters. In 1632, a synod of the Moravian Brethren at Lissa was convened, and Comenius was selected to succeed his father-in-law as bishop over the scattered members of the faith. Gradually, the fame of this earnest and devout man extended beyond the boundaries of Poland, Bohemia, and Germany. In England, where civil war was also threatening, Samuel Hartlib, the friend of Milton, became interested in the works of the Bohemian pansophist. Hartlib offered financial aid if Comenius would visit England. About this period, also, some dissension arose in the community at Lissa, and Comenius, because he was naturally inclined to an attitude of Christian tolerance, was becoming involved in theological controversies.

After a difficult and perilous sea voyage, Comenius reached London on September 22, 1641, where he learned that in addition to Hartlib's interest, he had received an invitation from the English Parliament. King Charles was absent in Scotland at the time, and Comenius had to wait until a commission of learned men could be appointed. The Parliament went so far as to promise that the revenue and building of a college should be set apart for the study and unfoldment of Comenius' great pansophic plan. The proceedings developed so far that Comenius, who greatly admired Lord Bacon's scheme for the advancement of learning, began to hope that his Lordship's dream would be realized, and that a universal college would be opened which would be devoted solely to the advancement of the sciences. About this time, however, there was a serious rebellion in Ireland, with a massacre of the Protestants, and the entire country was on the verge of revolution. Parliament was forced to direct its attention to the preservation of the country and the

Crown, and was unable to proceed with any educational program in the face of this national disaster.

Comenius left London in June 1642, only a few weeks before the outbreak of civil war in England, and, traveling through Holland and Germany, he reached Sweden in due course. He had been invited to Sweden by the Chancellor, who wished Comenius to prepare a series of school books for use in the Swedish schools. This he consented to do, but he decided not to live in Sweden, settling instead in a small town on the Baltic coast near the border of Sweden. Here he remained until 1648, when he returned to Lissa to accept the highest office of the Moravian Brethren. Shortly thereafter, however, he was invited to Transylvania by its ruler, George Rakoczy, a staunch Calvinist in search of a prominent Protestant educator. In 1654, Comenius returned to Lissa, but a year later war broke out between Poland and Sweden. Lissa was sacked, and Comenius, for a second time, lost his library and manuscripts. He was now sixty-five years old, and a homeless wanderer. His wife had died about 1648. He finally settled in Amsterdam, where he died on November 15, 1670. He was buried on November 22nd, in the Church of the French Protestants at Naarden, near Amsterdam.

In his *Traditio Lampadis*, Comenius solemnly passed the lamp of his method, and the dream which inspired it, to those who were to come after him. The work of his life, he commended to God and to the future, sincerely believing that better schools would become the secure foundation for better conduct. Only a world inspired and disciplined could establish this foundation of peace and good will among men.

The learned speculations of Lord Bacon so fired the imagination of Comenius that he hoped to reduce all essential learning to a systematic or encyclopedic form, perfecting a great pansophic college for the universal study of the whole body of science. Comenius outlined this plan in his most profound, if generally neglected, work, *The Great Didactic*. To attain the perfect end of education, it was necessary that learning should be arranged in a philosophical order, under a broad and inclusive pattern, and thoroughly systematized. All human knowledge should lead to an understanding of God in the heart, and so the new university was to be the temple of Christian pansophy or all knowing, and was to consist of seven parts.

First, the possibility of a total knowledge and the general outline of the entire enterprise were to be justified. Second, the general apparatus of wisdom, and the concept of a total approach to knowing of all things knowable, were to be examined. Third, the resources of visible nature, and all the lessons which could be derived therefrom, should be explored. Fourth, the inner life of man himself, and of the reasoning power within him, should be revealed. Fifth, the essential relationship between free will and responsibility, and the restoration of man's will in Christ as the beginning of a spiritualized existence, should be known and emphasized. Sixth, under the concept of theology, man's complete acceptance of God as the eternal center of eternal life, should be realized. Seventh, the machinery for the dissemination of wisdom should be methodically perfected, so that the whole world might be filled with divine knowledge.

Comenius defined didactic as the art of teaching, and amplified his interpretation of the term as follows: "Let the main object of this, our Didactic, be as follows: To seek and to find a method of instruction, by which teachers may teach less, but learners may learn more; by which schools may be the scene of less noise, aversion, and useless labour, but of more leisure, enjoyment, and solid progress; and through which the Christian community may have less darkness, perplexity, and dissension, but on the other hand more light, orderliness, peace, and rest."

In outlining the aims of his system, Comenius affirmed certain things to be essentially true. Man is the most complete and excellent of living creatures, and though he has a physical existence, his purpose and destiny lie beyond material limitations. Physical life is a proper preparation for an eternal life. The visible world is not man's true home, but is only a "boarding house." In preparation for an eternal continuance, man must know all things; he must have power over all things and himself; and he must submit all things and himself to God, the Eternal Source. Lastly, the seeds of knowledge, virtue, and religion, are within each of us as gifts of Nature, and therefore they should be released and permitted to grow.

Comenius was convinced that a reformation in education was not only possible, but immediately necessary. Proper instruction should make the human being wise, good, and holy. Every individual should receive an adequate education while young, for such preparation is necessary to adult living. Instruction should be without severity or compulsion, and should be made so inviting, pleasant, and obviously productive, that it will be spontaneously accepted by the child. Education is not merely the training of memory, but leads to a solid kind of learning which makes available the internal resources of the student. Teaching should never be laborious, either for the teacher or the pupil. Any normal child can be well educated, if he attends school not over four hours a day. It is the business of the educator either to prolong life or shorten the processes of learning. Most of the mysteries of education are in the keeping of Nature, and if man becomes the servant of natural laws, he will instinctively improve his methods of teaching. Intelligence should be opened, and not burdened, for "Nature begins all its operations from within outward." Furthermore, Nature moves sequentially from step to step, never ceasing a project until it is completed. Education should be advanced and unfolded in the same way.

According to Comenius, words should always be conjoined with ideas and things, so that we advance by realities, and not by terms and definitions alone. Reading and writing should always be taught together, and lessons, even for small children, should have body and substance. For example, the child learning to read should be introduced immediately to ideas which, though simply stated, will remain forever true. Anything which demonstrates itself to be irrelevant or superfluous, or likely to break the simple pattern of unfolding knowledge, should be dropped from the curriculum. There can be no division between education and morality, for unless the eye of the mind is pure, the reason will be contaminated or perverted. Whatever is known to be true must be taught, for the prejudiced teacher betrays his student. Moral harmony within the child depends upon early instruction in the cardinal virtues. Prudence, temperance, fortitude and justice—these should be taught with the ABC's, for they are also beginnings of a superior kind of knowing. There are three sources of true piety—the Holy Scriptures, the world of Nature around us, and our own souls. Comenius believed that children should not be taught for this world alone, but for eternity. In his day, school discipline was hard and cruel, but he believed that punishment should not be retaliation for a transgression, but a remedy against the recurrence of wrong action.

Scene in a 17th-century schoolroom. To make
study more interesting, Comenius built reading
lessons around pictures of familiar scenes. In this
case, the teacher and his class are identified by
numbers, and the persons and objects are associated with words in the text. From the *Orbis Pictus*.
(Illustration by courtesy of the U.S.C. Library.)

In his general outline for a school system, Comenius
said that a complete pattern of instruction should cover the
first twenty-four years of human life. He divided this period
into four sections of six years each, which he called infancy,
childhood, adolescence, and youth. During infancy, the child
should be taught in the Mother School; that is, at home,
where basic orientation must be accomplished. During childhood, the proper place of instruction is the vernacular public
school, where the inner senses, including imagination and
memory, are exercised. During adolescence, training should
be bestowed by the Latin school, or gymnasium, where intellect and judgment are formed and delineated. Having
arrived at the last period, the young person should further
advance his education at the university and by travel. Thus
he would come to learn those things which depend upon the

will of man, including theology, mental philosophy, medicine, and jurisprudence.

On the assumption that all learning must be established on an adequate foundation, Comenius advised that education should proceed from generalities to particulars. Arts and sciences should not be separately cultivated, so that a man learned in one thing might remain ignorant of all other things. Full comprehension of any subject depends upon an understanding of the relationship of that subject to the total body of knowledge.

The simplest way for the small child to approach the world around him, and the mysteries of his own soul, is by means of the Mother School. As our space is limited, we shall devote ourselves principally to this aspect of the teachings of Comenius. He seems to have perceived, with unusual clarity, the importance of the first six years of life. During this period, the child gains its first orientation, and opens its eyes, so to say, to the world in which it is going to live. At this time, also, its habits are established, and as the twig is bent, so will the tree be inclined.

Comenius has long been a controversial figure in the sphere of learning. The theologically minded have resented his emphasis upon natural arts and sciences, and the broad footings which he sought to set down as necessary to enlightened living. The scientifically minded have felt that he was first and last a Moravian preacher. They regarded his constant references to personal piety and humility as incompatible with the dignity of higher learning. None can deny, however, that in his own day, and under the conditions which burdened his labors, Comenius was a practical idealist with profound convictions and broad experience.

In many ways, Comenius was a mystery to those who came after him. Despite having been a victim of miserable educational procedures, he became a distinguished scholar. Although he was perhaps deficient in some parts of philosophy, he read broadly and deeply, and, like Bacon, believed in the importance of the Latin tongue. He collected two considerable libraries and attained standing as a brilliant intellectual. It cannot be said of Comenius that he was ruined by learning. He stands out as proof that scholarship does not conflict with piety and that the well-read man with a prodigious memory need not be lacking in spiritual graces. As his knowledge increased, this Moravian bishop never lost touch with the underprivileged world around him, nor did he ever outgrow his tender sympathy for children and his intuitive perception of their needs. Next only to God, he desired to serve the young, and many generations of boys and girls learned their letters from his picture books.

To be convicted of mystical speculations does not generally endear an educator to his contemporaries, or even those of later times. It has been assumed that dreamers must be impractical or deficient in judgment, or lack immediate contact with their fellow men. Against this broad skepticism, however, there is a strong defense. Comenius lived in a time when Europe was powerfully influenced by an elusive spirit of metaphysics which revealed itself through the writings of the Alchemists, the speculations of the Cabalists, and the manifestoes of the Rosicrucians. Although the prevailing mysticism could not be attributed directly to Martin Luther, it is nevertheless true that the Protestant Reformation released a spirit of inquiry which soon took on a religious coloring and caused a renewed interest in the essential concept of the mystics; namely, the possibility of man's personal experience of God.

Early in his career, Comenius wrote a curious and stimulating little book entitled *The Labyrinth of the World and the Paradise of the Heart.* Although he admitted in later life that certain details of his first conceptions were imperfect, he never departed from the essential theme of this gentle, but somewhat pessimistic, work. In structure, the book is not remarkable or unusual. It is founded on the old symbolic formula that the world is a city, and man a pilgrim exploring the highways and byways of life. There can be no doubt that Comenius identified himself with the pilgrim in his story. Count Lutzow, in his editorial contributions to his translation of *The Labyrinth*, believes that Comenius was acquainted with the famous Table of Cebes, anciently attributed to a disciple of Plato, but possibly of somewhat later origin. In this celebrated relic of antiquity, the world is represented as a kind of mountain, the summit of which is reached by a circuitous road. All manner of people are traveling along this road, but only a few reach the distant cloud-capped summit of the mountain. The 1640 edition of *The Labyrinth* of Comenius contains an engraving representing the Gate of Life leading into a great city. On the various streets of this community, men reside according to their calling, and in the heights above are the dwellings of eternal bliss.

Comenius mentions both More and Campanella by name in this book, but he does not refer to Lord Bacon, with whose writings he apparently was not yet familiar. Later, however, in his *Physica*, Comenius states that Verulamis and Campanella are "the two Hercules that have vanquished the monster Aristotle." The books that seem to have influenced Comenius most, at the time when he was writing *The Labyrinth*, were some of the works of Johann Valentin Andreae. It is certain that he had studied the writings of this Wurttemberg divine during his stay in Brandeis, and knew him personally. The contact with Andreae is interesting and significant because it forms a link, first with Lutheranism, and second, with the

Society of the Rosicrucians. Andreae was certainly a moving spirit behind the Brotherhood of the Rose Cross, and
admitted that he had written the original Manifestoes of
that order. Comenius shows indebtedness to the *Fama Fra-
ternitatis, Roseae Crucis, Peregrini in Patria errores, Civis
Christianus*, and *Republicae Christianopolitanae Descriptio*
—all written by Andreae.

The first chapter of *The Labyrinth* is virtually a paraphrase of the opening part of Andreae's *Peregrini in Patria
errores*, and the pilgrim's visit to the philosophers is largely
founded upon a passage in Andreae's *Mythologia Chris-
tiana*. The pilgrim's experience with the Rosicrucians is main-
ly copied from Andreae's writings concerning that fraternity.
In summary, *The Labyrinth* introduces a pilgrim journey-
ing through the world in search of knowledge and understanding. He sees a city built in the shape of a circle and
divided into countless streets, squares, and houses. There
are six principal streets, named for the main professions,
and here the members of these groups dwell. The purpose of
the symbolism is to prove that all professions are vanity,
beset with hardships and disappointments, and ending in
sorrow and tragedy. In the second part of the work, the
Paradise of the Heart, Comenius gives a version of the
heavenly splendor, much in the spirit of the Apocalypse.
The scene ends on a high note of mysticism, and the work,
though religious, is essentially non-controversial.

Chapter XIII of *The Labyrinth* is entitled "The Pilgrim
Beholds the Rosicrucians." Not much is added to the general
literature on the subject, but it is mentioned that these mysterious persons knew the languages of all nations as well as
everything that happened on the whole sphere of the earth—
even in the new world—and that they were able to discourse

with one another even at a distance of a thousand miles. Comenius then notes: "For Hugo Alverda, their praepositus, was already 562 years old, and his colleagues were not much younger. And though they had hidden themselves for so many hundred years, only working—seven of them—at the amendment of philosophy, yet would they now no longer hide themselves, as they had already brought everything to perfection; and besides this, because they knew that a reformation would shortly befall the whole world; therefore openly showing themselves, they were ready to share their precious secrets with everyone whom they should consider worthy." A curious fable is introduced which tells that the treasures of the Rosicrucian Brotherhood were wrapped in boxes painted in different colors and ornamented with inscriptions derived largely from the titles of books written by Rosicrucian apologists. But when the boxes were opened, the contents were invisible, causing considerable consternation. Comenius seems to have believed that Hugo Alverda was the true founder of the Rosicrucians. It is possible that he had contact with important source material, as Count Lutzow says definitely that Comenius was a pupil of Andreae.

Comenius was fully aware of the practical problems of the Mother School. He knew that the parents might not be so well educated that they could communicate solid instruction to their children. He also recognized that in supporting a family, the adult members might not have adequate leisure time or sufficient freedom from the pressing burden of economic survival. He did not, however, regard these handicaps as completely detrimental. The most important consideration was the general attitude of the parents. If they were sincere, devout persons, conscientious in their desire that their children should grow into honorable citizens, this in itself was a most important object lesson. If the home was

sustained by a spirit of true integrity, the child could recover from other defects as he advanced into the vernacular
school.

In the small world of childhood, nearly all lessons and
experiences have their beginnings. Among the most important
rudiments which should be established and cultivated in the
young are piety, morality, virtue, and unselfishness. To teach
these things, the parents themselves must set the example.
They must convince the child of the importance of right
conduct in all things. Most important is honesty, for it becomes the basis of the total policy by which the individual
will later live. Also commendable is respect for the rights,
convictions, and possessions of others. Honesty, respect, and
patience, help to establish regard for truth in all things,
and this in turn leads to the valuing of honor and a respectable place in human society.

Comenius was convinced that in the simple procedures of
home relationships, the small child could be introduced to
nearly all subjects which would later be more thoroughly
studied and investigated. Without actually realizing that he
was becoming informed, the little one unfolded his five
senses, learned the first words of his language, and discovered the names of many simple objects around him. He
also learned the meaning of certain abstract words, and
could associate them with processes rather than with things.
He discovered the significance of "yes" and "no," like and
unlike, when and where, thus and otherwise, and these discoveries, according to Comenius, became the foundations for
metaphysics. The child should also be encouraged to culti-
vate the capacity for silence, and discover the joy of that
quietude which later would be strengthened into contemplation, meditation, and quiet devotion. He would thus learn

Cornix cornicatur, die Ärähe trechzet,	} a a	A a
Agnus balat, das Schaf blödet,	} bé é è	B b
Cicáda stridet, der Heuschreck zitzschert,	} ci ci	C c
Upupa dicit, der Widhopf ruft,	} du du	D d
Infans ejulat, das Kind wemmert,	} é é é	E e
Ventus flat, der Wind wehet,	} f f	F f
Anser gingrit, die Gans gackert,	} ga ga	G g
Os halat, der Mund hauchet,	} hâh hâh	H h
Mus mintrit, die Maus pfipsert,	} i i i	I i
Anas tetrinnit, die Ente schnackert,	} kha kha	K k
Lupus úlulat, der Wolff heulet,	} lu ulu	L l
Ursus murmurat, der Beer brummet,	} mum mu	M m

An example of the method used by Comenius to correlate
the sounds of the letters of the alphabet with various pictures of familiar creatures and activities. From the *Orbis
Pictus*. (Illustration by courtesy of the U.S.C. Library).

to seek inner resources when presented with external pressures.

Instruction of this kind is positive, not negative. Recommendations should always be toward the right because it is right, and not because there is penalty for doing what is wrong. A child is more resourceful than we imagine, and grows best when it is protected by a sense of security. It cannot live in a world of exceptions, contradictions, and inconsistencies without being morally damaged. Indirectly, Comenius was recommending to the Christian reader that the simple rules of his faith played a vital part in the instruction of his children.

What is learned should, if possible, lead to some kind of action. The child is thrilled by the ability to do things, and if action is properly cultivated, it supports inquiry and stimulates the desire for attainment. Gradually, the demands of action must be supported by knowledge and skill. Thus the child learns that education is not simply an accumulation of facts, but a strengthening of means so that various necessary things can be done more proficiently. It is probably true that a small child's education cannot always follow a fixed pattern, nor can it be so regularly advanced. It can, however, cause the child to grow into good habits of natural seeking, and transform later schooling from a drudgery into an adventure.

The fine arts also have their place in the beginning of instruction. Music is very good, and the child can experience something of it from the hymns which form a part of family devotion. Poetry should be admired as a gentle and inspiring form of literature, through emphasis upon verses and nursery rhymes. Health should also be brought to the attention of the child at an early age. This includes cleanliness, exercise, and regular habits of eating and sleeping. Young children must play, and when they are not engaged in some regular enterprise, they should seek recreation in pleasant but not dangerous games and sports. The child must never be idle, and should learn to recognize his own needs.

It is obvious that all children do not develop at the same rate of progress. Comenius warned against the over-cultivation of precocity. He felt that parents should not force their children or demand of them wisdom or understanding beyond their years. To neglect this point, is to disturb childhood. Some part of general experience must be sacrificed if specialization comes too early. Comenius advised that those of markedly inferior abilities, or of uncertain morals and ethics, should be separated from other children in school, lest they communicate their infirmities to the rest who are still in an age of imitation.

The child should reach the vernacular school with a certain degree of internal poise and adaptability. If he is not able to adjust to association with other children, something has been neglected, or the principles of training have in some way been misdirected. The small child normally does not have fears, hatreds, prejudices or intolerances. These he must acquire, usually through poor example. Most children are by nature friendly, with little consideration for controversial subjects or petty antagonisms. They are too interested in the world around them to pass negative judgment, unless they have been conditioned to do so. Comenius points out that many parents say to their children, "Wait until you go to school. The master will teach you obedience and respect." This is wrong, for it will result in a classroom of incorrigibles. The teacher will be confronted with an unreasonable burden, the students will lack respect, and instruction will proceed with great difficulty. It is in the Mother School, therefore, that the child should be prepared to receive education, to value it, and to cooperate with those who are endeavoring to teach him. As the young person grows up, the virtue of basic learning becomes ever more apparent. In whatever trade he practices, or in the home which he will later build, the lessons of his first six years will remain a powerful foundation for success and happiness.

Failure of the Mother School endangers the world, for it launches upon society a person intellectually informed but morally immature. As knowledge becomes the basis of action, increase of knowledge may result in an enlarged sphere of influence, and a man may become a leader of other men, a great scientist, or a brilliant scholar. First and foremost, however, he must be a good human being. The end achievement of the Mother School is this natural goodness. It comes from a normal and happy childhood, but one that has had proper discipline and clear inducements to self-improvement.

The prayers learned at his mother's knee may serve a man in good stead in later periods of stress. If the mature person can take refuge in the simple dignity of his own childhood, he will never be without spiritual consolation. "It is an eternal truth," writes Comenius, "that first impressions adhere most firmly to our mind." The Mother School, or as it has also been called, the School of Infancy, sets these first impressions, and without them, the future can never be quite as adequate or useful.

The whole spirit of education is weakened when children regard their schooling as a necessary evil. Nor should they be permitted to assume that they are simply learning a trade or profession so that they may attain economic success or security. All men should practice their trades skillfully, but the real purpose of education is to unfold the total human being, to strengthen his courage, enrich his insight, and prepare him to face his own years hopefully and serenely. If schooling fails to do this, it is because the foundations have not been deeply set in eternal values. It is therefore impossible for any educational system to separate the inner life of the child from his external activities.

Life must be lived from within, by a constant calling upon resources of character and disposition. Not to educate these resources, is to frustrate the real end of learning. Perhaps all things desirable may not be immediately accomplished, but without effort, matters drift from bad to worse. Men of one age may ridicule those few among them who have a vision of better times. Yet in a future age, that which has been ridiculed is accepted as normal, and so progress continues. The perfect school may still be a dream, but dedicated persons, recognizing the pressing need, can strive valiantly to build a foundation under that dream for the benefit of those who come after them.

PHILOSOPHICAL SONNET

(Attributed to the famous Saint-Germain)

Curious scrutator of all nature,

I have known of the great whole the principle and the end,

I have seen gold thick in the depths of the double mercury.

I have seized its substance and surprised its changing.

I explain by that art the soul with the womb of a mother,

Make its home, take it away, and as a kernel

Placed against a grain of wheat, under the humid pollen;

The one plant and the other vine-stock, are the bread and wine.

Nothing was, God willing, nothing became something,

I doubted it, I sought that on which the universe rests,

Nothing preserves the equilibrium and serves to sustain.

Then, with the weight of praise and of blame,

I weighed the eternal, it called my soul,

I died, I adored, I knew nothing more.

TRANSLATED FROM THE RARE ORIGINAL EDITION IN THE

BRITISH MUSEUM.

COMTE DE ST.-GERMAIN

Mystery shrouds the life and secret purposes of the Comte de St.-Germain. There is comparatively little authentic material available that does more than pick up the confused threads of a single life. Although his name occurs frequently in the memoirs of celebrated persons of the 18th century, most of the accounts are little better than fragments of opinion, often contradictory. A compilation of these fragments presents such a confused picture of the man and his work that much obviously is inaccurate.

In the *Royal Masonic Cyclopaedia*, Kenneth Mackenzie comments upon some of the stories in common circulation relating to the Comte's identity and origin. According to one writer, St.-Germain was born at Letmertz in Bohemia. By the Marquis de Crequis he was pronounced to be an Alsatian Jew named Simon Wolff, born at Strasbourg about the beginning of the 18th century. He was also identified as a Spanish Jesuit named Aymar. It was held with similar enthusiasm that he was the Marquis de Betmar, born in Portugal. An ingenious account makes him the natural son of an

213

Italian princess, born at San Germano in Savoy about 1710. Some contemporaries thought they detected a trace of Italian accent, but others were equally sure that he was Polish, Spanish, or Russian.

Out of the general uncertainty has arisen the belief now most generally held, and sustained by his own words, that he was a member of the Hungarian family of Rakoczy, and his Italian accent was derived from his education in that country under the patronage of the Medici.

All other explanations failing, he was identified with the Legend of the Wandering Jew.

THE CONFUSION OF NAMES

The name St.-Germain is a comparatively common one. The Chacornac Brothers, booksellers in Paris, have spent many years compiling data on the various men of the 18th century who bore the name of St.-Germain. They already have identified more than a dozen, and are convinced that these men have frequently been confused with the mysterious magician and alchemist.

One of the most illustrious of the St.-Germains was Claude Louis Comte de St.-Germain, 1707 to 1778, a French General and Minister of War under Louis XVI. Mr. Arthur Edward Waite in, *The Secret Tradition in Freemasonry*, published the portrait of the French general, believing it to be a likeness of the masonic mystic. This is a concrete example of the confusion. Error is unquestionably the key to many contradictions.

Further proof of this can be obtained by considering various examples of the Comte's supposed handwriting. A letter in the British Museum dated November 22, 1735, is en-

—From the painting by Thomas

COMTE DE ST.-GERMAIN

tirely different in its calligraphy from another letter written in Leipzig on the 8th of May, 1777. This letter is signed Count de Weldon, a name St.-Germain frequently employed.

At Maggs Brothers, in London, I examined the *Registre du T. R. Loge du Contrat Social, Mere Loge écossaise*, containing entries from 1775-1789. The name *St.-Germain* appears in bold letters among the signatures at the foot of one of the pages. The signature is irreconcilable with other available examples. Either the elusive Comte changed his handwriting at will, or else, as is far more probable, the signatures are by different men who have been confused by popular legend into one man.

BIOGRAPHICAL SOURCE MATERIAL

In recent years a number of books have appeared dealing with St.-Germain and his teachings. Some of these volumes are merely a collection of earlier opinions, and others are advanced with a considerable air of mystery as esoteric revelations on the subject. The conclusions of dubious clairvoyants hardly can be accepted as reliable sources of information. In the public imagination of our day St.-Germain has become everything from a mountebank to a *mahatma*, with the result that the general obscurity deepens. Biographies that emerge from the unknown to wax mighty en route overwhelm the gullible, but merely irritate the informed.

Incidentally, St.-Germain's complete name has not descended to us. In his letter of 1735 he signs himself *P. M. de St.-Germain*. None of the memoir writers has ever mentioned his first name, a circumstance curious in itself.

My own research on the subject has convinced me that while the Comte has been beatified by his admirers, the known facts of his life are generally disregarded to the point of

complete ignorance. The same may be said of the few fragments of his teachings which have survived.

According to Magre, in *Magicians, Seers, and Mystics,*
St.-Germain expounded his philosophy at Ermenonville and
Paris. His teaching was a Platonic Christianity which combined Swedenborg's vision with Martinez de Pasqually's
theory of reintegration. There was also to be found in it
Plotinus' emanationism and the hierarchy of successive
planes. St.-Germain taught that man has in him infinite possibilities and that from the practical point of view, he must
strive unceasingly to free himself from matter in order to
enter into communication with the world of higher intelli-
gences.

Deschamps in his work on secret societies states that St.-
Germain was a Knight Templar and that the ritual used at
Ermenonville was the ritual of the Knights Templars. In
Franc-Maconnerie by Baron du Potet there is a statement
that St.-Germain established a Theosophical Lodge in the
Castle of Ermenonville. This castle was 30 miles from Paris
and belonged to the Marquis de Girardin who was the chief
of the Lodge. This same de Girardin was a friend and pro-
tector of J. J. Rousseau.

Abbé Barreul in his great work on Jacobinism published in
1791, describes the rituals practiced at Ermenonville as those
of the theosophical Illuminists. He says that St.-Germain
was the lord of this group. Abbé Barreul was a personal
friend of St.-Germain.

The principal authentic works available which treat extensively of St.-Germain are: *Memoires* by Baron de Gleich-
en, Paris, 1868: *Memoires de mon temps* by Carl, Prince of
Hesse-Cassel, Copenhaguen, 1861; *Graf St.-Germain* by E.

M. Oettinger, Leipzig, 1846; *The Comte de St.-Germain* by
I. Cooper-Oakley, Milan, 1912.

With the exception of the last work, these books are exceedingly scarce and are quoted infrequently by modern
writers. Yet it is only after a thorough examination of these
writings that it is possible to arrive at any satisfactory conclusion.

Baron de Gleichen's book refers principally to a series of
personal experiences in which St.-Germain occupies a prominent position. There is special reference to the Comte's jewel
collection, his paintings, and his personal culture.

Carl of Hesse is most informative on that period of the
estates of Hesse-Cassel. There are references to alchemy, to
the Comte's manuscripts, and to his secret society which met
on the estates of Prince Carl.

Oettinger attempts an exposition of St.-Germain's personal life and is by far the most detailed of his biographers.
The book is in the form of historical fiction which presents
some difficulty, but on the whole appears reliable.

Mrs. Cooper-Oakley spent many years on intensive research, and has produced a highly colorful monograph,
trustworthy and dignified. Her research, though extensive,
is limited principally to the Comte's residence in Paris. There
are also many pages of letters by contemporary politicians
concerning the Comte.

Graf St.-Germain by E. M. Oettinger

It is our present intention to examine in some detail the
book by Herr Doktor Oettinger. According to all available
information, this German historian was the outstanding historical novelist of his day. His writings are always well
documented, and he takes few dramatic liberties with his

characters. There is circumstantial evidence to indicate that Oettinger met St.-Germain in Paris during the 1830's.

Everything dealing with the life of St.-Germain presents strange and irreconcilable contradictions. Oettinger's book is no exception. Most of the book is very sympathetic toward the Comte's activities. In the final chapter, however, Oettinger proceeds systematically to tear down the character that he has built up. This comes as a decided shock to the reader who has come to feel a definite attachment for the eccentric Comte, and to participate sympathetically in his misfortunes.

Oettinger's motives for his closing chapter are not entirely obvious. Furthermore, his conclusions pass into the sphere of personal opinion and definitely are inconsistent with his more serious research. It is possible that Herr Oettinger feared ridicule for himself if he seemed to sympathize unreservedly with the Comte's strange career. Such a precautionary method still is in vogue among the literati who dwell constantly in the fear that their fiction will reflect upon their own good names.

In his gentler mood the German historian is most informative, and as far as we have been able to discover, his research has never been translated out of the German, nor has it been adequately quoted in recent writing. Therefore, we shall take this opportunity to summarize briefly his most outstanding statements.

Oettinger quotes St.-Germain's own words that he was alive at the time of Christ; that he studied magic under the *doctor illuminatus* Raymond Lully (1235-1315), and painting with Cimabue (1240?-1302?). He knew Rabelais (1490?-1553); and on one occasion observed: "I had the fortune to meet Paracelsus (1493-1541) who was professor at Basel, in Switzerland." On another occasion he added of Paracelsus: "I studied his laudanum and he investigated my elixir. Each

of us was stubborn and held his own as the most potent."
Again he described his philosophical stone or elixir as being
composed of 777 ingredients.

He was with Francois I (1494-1547) when he was crowned
in 1515. He claimed to have assisted Nostradamus (1503-
1566) in the compilation of his celebrated prophecies. The
formula used by Nostradamus in his predictions has never
been recovered. St.-Germain mastered music under the guidance of Palestrina (died 1594?), thus explaining his extraordinary ability in musical technique and performance.

St.-Germain was a friend of Dr. John Dee of Mortlake
(1527-1608), the famous astrologer, mathematician, and
necromancer of Queen Elizabeth. He assisted Dr. Dee and
his *alter ego* Edward Kelley in the preparation of a great book
on spirits, one of the most inexplicable publications of the
17th century. The book, filled with strange ciphers and obscure lore, was not published until after the death of Dr.
Dee, when it was printed under the title of *A True and Faithful Revelation of what passed between Dr. John Dee and some
Spirits*. We might note in passing that John Dee was the
organizer of the English navy.

The Comte mentioned that he had learned from the magician Ruggieri (circa 1600) the secret of making wax
statues to be used in magic and the healing of disease.
Ruggieri was the outstanding sorcerer of his time. He was
with Montaigne (1533-1592), probably in Rome, in 1580.

Other authors add further names to Oettinger's list, but
those given are sufficient to reflect the measure of the problem. St.-Germain repeatedly referred to his friendship with
persons long dead, and spoke with an infinite knowledge that
confounded the ablest historians of his time.

Among other intimate details Oettinger notes that St.-
Germain always carried two books in his baggage, *Ars*

Reminiscendi by Guilio Camillo published in Venice in 1522, and *Pastor Fido* by Guarini published in Venice in 1604. He had received his copy of the *Pastor Fido* bound in red morocco from the author in 1612 as a personal souvenir. The Comte read a few passages from *Pastor Fido* every morning upon rising, and each evening before retiring he studied *Ars Reminiscendi* to train his mind.

St.-Germain also stated that he sharpened his marvelous memory by studying the *Dictionnaire Historique et Critique*, the four volume edition of Amsterdam, 1740. He had a considerable library, including books and manuscripts on the properties of the mandrake, a root resembling the human body which the ancients believed to have magical powers.

When St.-Germain was with William Pitt (1708-1778) in London, he told the Prime Minister, whose library he was examining, that he was the true author of the very rare anonymous work *De Tribus Impostoribus* of which only three examples were known in the world. The Comte said: "It is my work; I wrote it in 1512 while in Salamanca."

Herr Oettinger also casts some light, if we may call it that, upon the hitherto darkened subject of St.-Germain's private life. According to this historian St.-Germain met, in Venice, Angioletta Bartolomeo, a girl of humble station, the daughter of a gondolier. After some vicissitudes they were married, and St.-Germain took her with him to France. Here the Comte introduced Angioletta to Louis XV, not as his wife but as his sister.

While in Venice during 1756 St.-Germain, under the title of Comte Bellamarre or Aymar, was temporarily imprisoned, accused of traveling in the Republic of Venice under an assumed name. He was shortly liberated when he was able to prove that the estates of Bellamare belonged to his family. St.-Germain's release from prison was effected with the aid of Abbé de Bernis who was the French ambassador to Venice. St.-Germain was introduced to the Doge and amazed this dignitary by giving him intimate details of the lives of the various people whose portraits were displayed in the palace.

While in prison the Comte met Casanova (1725-1798). A few years later Angioletta committed suicide as the result of a compromising affair with Casanova.

At this time a new personality appeared in the foreground. Benjamin, St.-Germain's personal secretary and familiar, challenged Casanova to a duel without the knowledge of the Comte. Benjamin was killed in the duel, Casanova being one of Europe's greatest duelists. When the body of Benjamin was brought into the Comte's presence he lifted the covering from the face, and after looking at it intently for several seconds sighed deeply, and turning away remarked softly: "He was my son." The inevitable inference is that St.-Germain had been married prior to his marriage with Angioletta. Unfortunately, little information on this subject is available, except that Benjamin's mother was named Melle Couveur.

Years later Casanova, dying of an incurable malady, was offered the elixir of life by St.-Germain. Casanova was afraid to take the medicine for fear that the Comte intended to poison him for the murder of his son. A more dramatic situation would be difficult to imagine. Casanova's *Memoires* is the authority for this last incident.

THE ST.-GERMAIN MANUSCRIPTS

Let us now leave Herr Oettinger and investigate several other important records. Upon the authority of Prince Carl of Hesse, the Comte de St.-Germain was the author of several curious manuscripts. There is a phantom manuscript *Les Arcanes ou Secrets de la Philosophie Hermetique* which I have not been able to see. The existing copy is probably in the writing of the French esotericist Lenain. This may prove to be one of the books seen by Prince Carl.

Madame Blavatsky, in the *Secret Doctrine* quotes two long extracts from an essay by St.-Germain on the subject of numbers. Unfortunately she does not give us the name of the work or the place in which the original may be found. There is a rumor among the French transcendentalists that a small volume by the Comte, dealing with numbers, is in the files of the Bibliotheque Nationale. The Library was unable to produce the volume, however, when I requested to see it. They suggested that it may have been issued under an assumed name and therefore not so listed with his material.

Only two manuscripts, possibly by his own hand or prepared under his personal supervision, have been identified with reasonable certainty. The first is *La Tres Sainte Trinosophie* now reposing in the Bibliotheque de Troyes by right of purchase. It is a small quarto on paper, magnificently bound in crimson leather and illuminated with many strange and beautiful miniatures.

This manuscript was for some time in the possession of Cagliostro and was among the papers confiscated from him in Rome by the agents of the Inquisition. I published an English translation of this work in 1933, and a year later a second edition with a complete photostat.

The original of the other known manuscript is in my collection. This curious book was for many years in the Library of Lionel Hauser, *Ancien Membre du Conseil de Direction de la Societe Theosophique de France*. It was sold with the rest of his collection at Sotheby's celebrated Auction House in London. Later in Paris it was my good fortune to meet Monsier Hauser. He could give me no additional information about the manuscript which had come to him through the usual book-collecting channels. He showed me at the time a Masonic Lodge coin which had belonged to a member of St.-Germain's group.

While there is a rumor supported by some sketchy cross-cataloging that a printed form of St.-Germain's Hermetic Manuscript may have been privately circulated in France, it is unknown to the Comte's historians. The book is triangular in shape, on vellum, and written in cipher with the exception of the title page. The cipher itself is quite simple, belonging to the class found in Masonic documents, and decodes into French. This rare manuscript is entitled *LA MAGIE SAINTE revelee a MOSE, retrouvee dans un Monument Egyptien, et precieusement conservee en Asie sous la Devise d'un Dragon Aile.* (The Sacred Magic revealed to Moses, recovered in an Egyptian monument and carefully preserved in Asia under the Device of a Winged Dragon).

It is written on twenty-six leaves measuring 237mm x 237mm x 235mm. Though not dated, expert examination leads to the conclusion that it was written about 1750. The first leaf of this triangular manuscript is reproduced herewith, and from it we learn that St.-Germain prepared the work for an unknown person, presumably one of his disciples. The writing itself belongs to a class known as *Grimoire* or *Manuals of Ceremonial Magic.* A free translation of the opening pages of the text reads as follows:

"The orbit (magic circle) which thou seest on the preceding page will serve thee as a model to make others which shall be nine cubits in diameter. Thou shalt use these to perform marvels, a privilege which thy predecessors Beros and Sanchoniaton did not have. I give thee at the same time the intelligence of the characters in which is written my revelation so that thou mayest make use of them for three purposes: to find things lost in the seas since the upsetting of the globe (the Deluge); to discover mines of diamonds,

The first page of the cipher manuscript, *La Magie
Sainte*. Above a wyvern proper are the words: "By
the gift of the most wise Comte St.-Germain who
passed through the circle of the earth."

gold and silver in the heart of the earth; to preserve the
health and prolong the life to a century and over with the
freshness of fifty years and the strength of that age."

The balance of the manuscript is devoted to the consecration of magical implements and prayers to spirits. The writing ends with the following prayer addressed to attendant
spirits:

"In the name of the Eternal, of the True God, Master of
my body, my soul and my spirit, go; go in peace; retire ye.

Let it be that one of you accompany me always and that the others may be ready to come when I shall call."

Most of the formulas are magical rather than alchemical, and so involved in obscure symbolism and Cabalistic names as to be impractical to the modern reader.

La Magie Sainte is obviously based on a mysterious document of unknown antiquity called the *Clavicula Salomonis* or the Key of Solomon. This curious production was circulated widely during the Middle Ages and was supposed to have been derived from instructions in magic bestowed by King Solomon upon his son.

St.-Germain's manuscript is illustrated with drawings of magic circles executed in several colors, including gold. In the text are invocations to spirits, with the names of numerous spirits and demons. It is quite possible that the simple process of decoding does not reveal the true text. The document may have an under-meaning relating to matters of philosophy and esoteric Masonry.

La Magie Sainte was copied on several occasions for the use of the members of the French Masonic Order. The copies are inferior in workmanship and are usually written on paper. I have one such copy for comparison with the original. This copy which is magnificently bound, and decorated with masonic symbols, has an additional page at the beginning describing its original owner. The inscription reads:

"From the masonic collection of the F.·. illustrious F.·. Antoine Louis Moret founder, and venerable.·. honorary of the R.·. ☐ .·. Sincerity No. 122 Ex president of the Souv .·. Chap. .·. the triple union No. 5946, member of several G .·. — Now .·. master, Elu, chevalier commander, patriarch, Prince and Governor.:. Prince of all the masonic orders .·. and of all the Rites: French, Scotch, English, Irish, Prussian, etc., etc. Gov.·. G.·. insp.·. Gen.·. of the 33rd de-

gree S.: P.∴ D.∴ S.∴ E.· Now.·. of.·. New York, U.S.A,
5810. (5810 is the masonic date equivalent to 1810).

This manuscript passed from the collection of Moret to
the famous library of occult books and manuscripts formed
by the late Mme. Barbe of Paris. In the interval it had belonged to Stanislaus de Guaita, French transcendentalist, who
purchased it at the sale of books belonging to Jules Favre,
the French statesman and bibliophile.

Moret was one of the heads of Masonry in Europe and
America. He came to America and settled here for some
time. The manuscript, therefore, is of greatest importance in
the literature of early American Masonry.

During the middle years of the 19th century, a school
of transcendentalists came into being in France under the
able leadership of the Abbe Louis Constant, better known
under his pseudonym Eliphas Levi. He was a member of
the Fratres Lucis, and was devoted to the mysteries of the
Holy Cabala. Eliphas Levi gathered about himself a brilliant
group of European intellectuals who devoted much time to
searching out available information on St.-Germain. Most
of the rarer books and manuscripts relating to the Comte
passed through their hands, and in some cases copies were
made. These are almost as scarce as the originals.

We have summarized the various accounts given by Oettinger of St.-Germain's activities over a period of several
hundred years. These findings unfortunately are hopelessly
irreconcilable with the account left by Prince Carl of Hesse-
Cassel, who states specifically that he had St.-Germain's own
word that the Comte was born as the son of Rakoczy Ferenz
(Franz Rakoczy II of Transylvania, 1676-1735). Rakoczy
was crowned Regent of Transylvania by his nobles in their
struggle for independence from Austria. After the cause of

the Hungarians was hopelessly lost, Rakoczy Ferenz left Hungary and finally died in Turkey. He is the national hero of Hungary, and many weird legends surround the entire family. He had a mysterious secretary who was supposed to have been 150 years old, who assumes the attributes of a Merlin.

The Hungarians have a legend that one of the sons of Rakoczy Ferenz was sent away to be educated. At the age of 12 this child was so precocious that he seemed to know all the languages, and his teachers despaired of instructing him.

There is another legend among the Hungarian people that St.-Germain was in Hungary in 1848 during the Magyar Rebellion, under the name of Petofi Sandor (Alexander Petofi) the great Hungarian poet. He disappeared on the field of battle and was never heard of again.

Alexander Petofi seems to have been of Croatian origin, but in his enthusiasm for the Hungarian cause, changed his family name Petrovics to the Magyar form Petofi. He is said to have begun his poetic career at the age of twelve, turned to the theater as a means of livelihood, and played small parts in Shakespearean drama. His poems, which are fired with great enthusiasm for the Hungarian cause, brought him fame and a permanent place in the world of literary arts before his twenty-fifth year.

He joined the Hungarian army, and during the Transylvanian campaigns rose to the rank of Major, distinguishing himself in several heroic actions. It is supposed that Petofi was slain at the battle of Segesvar, July 31, 1894. Prosaic historians assume that his body was buried in the common grave of unidentified patriots. Hungarians who have carried on research in the subject are inclined to regard his disappearance as mysterious. To them it is unreasonable that a man of his fame and popularity should have perished without the fact being noted by any of his comrades.

Pictures of Petofi show a gentle and scholarly young man with an abundance of curly hair and a neatly trimmed moustache and Vandyke beard. His picture is startlingly reminiscent of portraits of the Master Rakoczy which have been privately circulated for a number of years among Theosophical groups. Petofi vanished at the age of twenty-six, an ardent champion of the rights of man.

St.-Germain Initiates Cagliostro

An important record concerning the philosophical activities of St.-Germain is contained in the *Memoires Authentique pour servir a l'Histoire du Comte de Cagliostro*, the first edition of which appeared in 1785. The work was published anonymously, but generally is attributed to the Marquis de Luchet. Arthur Edward Waite in *The Brotherhood of the Rosy Cross* dismisses the entire account as a "comedy." It is generally supposed that de Luchet was a dilettante who dabbled in sensational biography. A more careful investigation, however, reveals that de Luchet was a member of St.-Germain's secret society and therefore was party to the innermost workings of the order. This fact confirmed, the Marquis takes on a much more important character. His account deals with the initiation of the Comte and Comtesse de Cagliostro into the mysteries of the Illuminists at St.-Germain's castle in Holstein in 1785.

De Luchet describes the meeting of the two magicians in substance as follows:

Cagliostro had requested the favor of a secret audience to prostrate himself before the God of the Faithful. St.-Germain set the time at 2 a.m. The drawbridge of the castle was lowered for their reception and they were led into a dimly lighted room. Suddenly two great doors opened and a temple resplendent with the light of thousands of candles dazzled their vision. On an altar in the midst of the room sat the mysterious St.-Germain. At his feet knelt two acolytes holding golden bowls of perfume. The God of the Faithful wore upon his chest a pectoral of diamonds of such radiance that the eye scarcely could bear their brilliancy.

A voice which appeared to come from everywhere interrogated the visitors: "Who are you? Where did you come from? What do you want?"

Cagliostro prostrated himself before the altar and his wife did likewise. After a long pause he uttered this short address in a low voice:

"I come to invoke the God of the Faithful, the Son of Nature, the Father of Truth. I come to ask one of the fourteen thousand and seven secrets that he bears in his bosom. I come to give myself up as his slave, his apostle, his martyr."

Later in the same ritual a mysterious book was opened and Cagliostro listened while his own future was read to him with a detailed description of his persecution, trials, dishonor, and imprisonment.

In this account St.-Germain assumes a new form. He is deified by his followers, regarded as worthy of veneration and referred to by them as a god. Here again, the elements of the Illuminist ritual reveal the true estate of the mysterious adept. The account of the ordeals that follow are evidently allegorical, but the reference to St.-Germain scarcely can be regarded as such.

St.-Germain as a man of Letters

It is usual to regard mysterious persons or such as affirm the reality of magical arts as impostors and charlatans. This general condemnation has been turned upon St.-Germain without, however, the usual results. It has been impossible to prove that the elusive Comte ever actually dealt in misrepresentation. Wherever his extraordinary pretensions were susceptible of verification, they were proved to be true.

That the Comte was a man of culture was beyond question. He was a personification of refinement, and all his habits and ways testified to a natural gentility of mind and breeding. His abilities were diversified and intense. His judgment was trained and skillful. His tastes were above criticism. He carried his mysterious estate with charm, with ease and dignity. All this is most discouraging to those looking for evidence of imposture.

He lived modestly in an aura of grandeur, always abundantly supplied with appropriate means. He emerged socially with the resources of a Count of Monte Cristo. He used no bankers and carried no letters of credit. He entertained lavishly, and yet in his own habits practiced complete moderation. He seldom ate in public, but when attending banquets as guest or host, devoted his time exclusively to the comfort and pleasure of the guests. On one occasion, a guest arriving unexpectedly found the Comte in the capacity of a waiter, serving his own retainers.

He was a member of the smoking club of Frederick the Great, an exclusive circle which could only be entered by one owning a pipe. In all gatherings his presence insured a delightful and informative occasion.

The Count was small and slight of person, always immaculately groomed in black velvet and satin. His studs were clusters of diamonds, and his shoe buckles gleamed with the ransom of a king. His hair was powdered according to the prevailing fashion and tied at the back with a black ribbon. His lace and linen were of the finest quality, probably

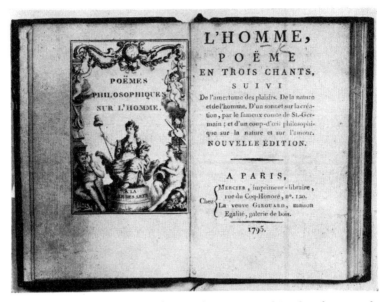

St.-Germain's Philosophical Sonnet first appeared in the above work.

oriental. His one slight ostentation was his rings. Although he is known to have possessed many military and diplomatic decorations he never wore them. His sword was magnificently jeweled and his capes and hats appropriate to the ensemble. Many efforts were made to trace him by his clothes but none of these carried any labels or markings. One inquisitive French Marquis tried to quiz one of St.-Germain's secretaries by asking him if it was true that the Comte had been a personal friend of the Queen of Sheba. "Alas, Monsieur le Marquis," replied the decorous secretary, "I cannot say. I have only been with his excellency for five hundred years."

St.-Germain was an acknowledged connoisseur of fine arts, and could identify the paintings of ancient and obscure artists at a single glance. He was an authority on precious gems and could detect the slightest flaw by merely touching the stone. He painted with an admirable technique, mixing powdered mother-of-pearl with his pigments to increase luminosity. He had a small but refined collection of art selected not for the fame of the artists but on the basis of merit alone. He was an expert in the mixing of perfumes and had a liberal acquaintance with rare oriental drugs. So attractive was his manner and so abundant his accomplishment that even the greatest skeptics could not doubt his aristocracy.

For court intrigues he had an ever ready ear but never committed himself. He was the confidant of many great nobles and illustrious ladies. Their confidences died with him. He is never known to have betrayed a trust. All these things are disconcerting to a public opinion which has searched vainly for traces of infamy and double dealing.

When St.-Germain moved his headquarters from one country to another certain arrangements were made in advance. A suitable residence awaited him. His servants in snuff colored livery, appeared at precisely the correct moment. The arrangements created an appropriate atmosphere of anticipation, and when St.-Germain appeared he was immediately master of the situation. There were no unnecessary pretensions, but nothing in any way essential was overlooked or slighted. Each move was utterly correct.

In a letter to the British Museum, St.-Germain reveals a thorough knowledge of the art of printing and its origin. He offers the museum his copy of the second edition of the Bible published in 1462. The volume is in a perfect state of preservation, bound in wood covered with pigskin, ornamented with *fleur-de-lis* crowned with rosettes, enclosed in a frame of dragons. This Bible is now in the British Museum collection.

ST.-GERMAIN THE MUSICIAN

As writer, poet, musician and literary critic, he humbled many of the most brilliant men of his time. It was a privilege to have his opinion on almost any subject. He performed exquisitely on the violin and the viola da gamba, composed with a keen sense of values and was a master of melodic line and counterpoint. On at least one occasion he conducted without a score the private orchestra of Frederick the Great.

St.-Germain composed an opera and a number of sonatas. The London music publisher Walsh who handled only the works of the best composers, published favorite selections from the opera, and a collection of Six Sonatas for Two Violins etc.

The Comte's Opera *La Inconstanzia Deluza* was written before the year 1740, and is now among the rarities of music. The only copy (known to be in America) of Walsh's extracts from this opera is in my collection. Three selections from this work were played for the first time in America, arranged from my copy, and presented in 1940 by the Junior Chamber of Commerce Music Foundation.

THE DEATH OF ST.-GERMAIN

The death of St.-Germain, like his life, is shrouded in deepest mystery. He is supposed to have died on the estates of Prince Carl of Hesse. According to Waite "the last authentic record is that of the Church Register of Eckernforde, which has this entry: 'Deceased on February 27, buried on March 2, 1784, the so-called Comte de St.-Germain and Weldon — further information not known — privately deposited in this church.' "

The usual uncertainties attended this great man's demise. Some who saw him but a few weeks before his death, found him in splendid health; others report years of lingering illness. One group comments upon the exalted calmness which radiated from his person, and still others are certain that he was devoured by a corrupting melancholy. Perhaps each interpreted the Comte's moods according to his own nature. To some calmness might convey the impression of despair. According to Oettinger, St.-Germain passed away peacefully in his sleep. M. de Genlis is the authority for the melancholy. And Prince Carl of Hesse himself acknowledged that the Comte was in robust health at the time of his decease.

It is curious that so illustrious a person should not lie in state or be accorded an appropriate funeral. Apparently no one of importance, with the exception of Prince Carl, saw the Comte's body. Without will or any document testamentary, the settling of St.-Germain's various estates and titles should have presented quite a problem. If such a dilemma did exist, the executors, whoever they may have been, suffered their burden in silence. It is also unusual that such an illustrious man should have no heirs, real or fictitious. No one ever came forward to claim kinship. A rich man with no relations is a circumstance phenomenal in itself.

No one would have doubted his death had he not been seen on several occasions, years after his supposed demise.

The secrecy attending his final illness, his funeral, and the distribution of his effects, all incline the mind to suspect a mock funeral. This possibility is strengthened definitely by later records of his activities.

In support of the belief that reports of St.-Germain's decease were exaggerated we can mention a few of his subsequent appearances. He was present at a Masonic conference of the French Higher Bodies in 1785, and put in an appearance at the Lodge of the Philalethes in 1786. His faithful historian Mme. D'Adhemar saw him in 1788, and

according to Franz Graffer, he was in Vienna with the Rosicrucian lodges in 1788-90. His friend M. Grosley saw him
in France just before the execution of the Princess de Lam-
balle in 1792. For a number of years thereafter he appeared
briefly in several places.

The celebrated French writer and critic Jules Janin kept
open house for intellectuals at Rue Tournon 8. In 1835
St.-Germain appeared among the guests at one of M. Janin's
soirees. Several of those present had known him before his
supposed death in Schleswig. One of these was Dr. Oettinger,
previously mentioned. M. Janin is said to have known that
St.-Germain was alive and addressed him by name.

Between the years 1842 and 1845 a literary group of
importance met with some regularity at the Cafe de Dwan
in Paris. The group included such men as Vandam, Alexander
Dumas pere, Honore de Balzac, and Eugene Sue. It is believed that Lord Bulwer-Lytton occasionally met with them.
Among the habitues of the Cafe de Dwan was an interesting
and curious man who went by the name of Major Fraser,
from his Britannic Majesty's Indian Army. There is a persistent rumor that Major Fraser was in fact our elusive Comte.

The description of Major Fraser appears in the memoirs
of Albert Vandam entitled *An Englishman in Paris*. Major
Fraser possessed an extraordinary knowledge of arts, sciences,
literature, and history, and implied that he had lived for
hundreds of years. The Major resembled St.-Germain in appearance and build and was the author of a book describing his journeys in the Himalayas. When his friends expressed
interest in his personal life and history, he disappeared, re-
moving his possessions overnight and was not seen afterward.

There is a record in India of a European answering the
description of St.-Germain who lived in Darjeeling for a

number of years. He was buried under the name of Count Cosmo or Cosmos about 1840 in a small cemetery connected with the town.

THE MAGIC AND MYSTERY OF THE NAME OF ST.-GERMAIN

It sometimes appears as though some mysterious force in nature conspired to preserve the secrecy which surrounds the memory of the mysterious Comte. In his *Magicians, Seers, and Mystics,* Maurice Magre records an incident of this almost providential intervention:

"Napoleon III, puzzled and interested by what he had heard about the mysterious life of the Comte de St.-Germain, instructed one of his librarians to search for and collect all that could be found about him in the archives and documents of the latter part of the 18th Century. This was done and a great number of papers, forming an enormous dossier, were deposited in the library of the Prefecture of Police. The Franco-Prussian War and the Commune supervened, and the part of the building in which the dossier was kept was burned. Thus once again an 'accident' upheld the ancient law which decrees that the life of the adept must always be surrounded with mystery."

It is not difficult to understand why St.-Germain should be a name to conjure with. He is mystery in the modern world, almost within the memory of the living. Yet no sorcerer of the Middle Ages, no witch of Thessaly, had a more dramatic or mysterious life. The unknown remains forever the proper foundation for conjecture. We are challenged by the mysterious, and the inventive faculty of man soon fills in where history fails. Today the Comte is more talked about than in his own time. Years have added to his fame. A world longing for eternal life sees in him the justification for this hope. Such personalities as St.-Germain are necessary to the escape mechanism of the mind. This is no fiction like the *Markropoulos Secret*. This is fact stranger than fiction.

Therefore we can understand easily why modern theosophical and mystical movements include this man among their patron saints. St.-Germain was rich, he gave away emeralds on invitation cards, he owned some of the finest jewels in Europe. Most men desire to be rich; the appeal is obvious. St.-Germain was the friend of kings, the associate of princes; all men naturally like to associate with that which is superior. St.-Germain was mysterious. His birth and death are unrecorded. His ways were strange and inexplicable.

Men, tired of being prosaic, take him to their hearts as he was—or is. But above all, he possessed the secret of life. He did not live forever by growing old and full of the ills of age. He remained in his prime, surviving from century to century, if we are to believe his own words, always accomplishing, always adventuring. Is there any wonder why he becomes the personification of the very philosophical elixir which preserved the youth of Madame de Pompadour for twenty years? It is all very natural, reasonable, and therefore, an admirable foundation for exploitation.

There is an adage that if you wish to get somewhere in this world and do not know how, find a man who is going somewhere and follow him. Also, if you have an organization that is not doing well, a fraudulent cult that is hopelessly obvious, the only way to give it pre-eminence is to hang it onto some illustrious name and follow in the wake of that name to prosperity.

So, in this modern world of thoughtless people who want things they do not earn and desire frantically to evade those things that they have earned, an adept is more than a luxury, he is a necessity. St.-Germain has been accredited with some extraordinary opinions and beliefs. Most of these are entirely inconsistent with what he is *known* to have believed and taught, and the only possible conclusion left is that either he is not responsible for that which is ascribed to him, or he has suffered a complete mental breakdown since the end of the 18th century.

The teachings of St.-Germain partook of the doctrines ascribed to the Illuminati, a group of social reformers established in 1776 by Adam Weishaupt, professor of canonical law at Ingolstadt. The society flourished for a few years, but after the decease of its principal members, sank into comparative oblivion, to be revived in part by the French Transcendentalists of the 19th century.

There is no evidence to be found among historical documents to establish that St.-Germain was a Rosicrucian, although he is suspected of membership in the society. In fact, it has even been advanced that he was the *magus* of the society. This is purely conjectural, all claims notwithstanding. There is considerable evidence to support the belief that St.-Germain was a profound Orientalist; in fact, practiced Hindu breathing exercises and other meditative and contemplative disciplines. There is no evidence that the modern organizations which include him in their hagiology have preserved any balanced program in the various subjects which claimed his interest during the historical period of his life. These interests were most varied, including language, art, invention, science, military tactics, statesmanship, alchemy, astrology, Orientalism, wool-dying and manufacturing, hatmaking, herbalism, ceremonial magic, cryptography, comparative religion, medicine, psychology, music, cabalism, and in his spare time, he was an excellent judge of horses.

It is incredible that a man of such accomplishment, had he rulership over any modern order, would govern it less wisely now and with less skill and prudence than he displayed in 1770. Nor is there any evidence that St.-Germain ever delivered his manifestoes through automatic writing, slates, or table tilting. He came in person, and there was no power in Europe that could stop him when he chose to leave. Nor was he nationalistic, desiring the supremacy of any nation over any other nation. In a few short years he served Persia, Great Britian, France, Germany, Italy, Austria, and Russia, being fully accepted in each of these countries as a gentleman of rank and authority. In several countries, he possessed lands, titles, and military rank. He came as he pleased, had very few friends and only one intimate recorded in history. And in the words of one of his biographers, "Those who knew him best knew him least."

Those of the rationalist persuasion have attempted repeatedly to destroy the character of St.-Germain by asserting that he was an impostor and a charlatan, but they have never been able to make either of these accusations stick. He could not be an impostor without imposing upon someone, which he has never been known to have done. Nor could he be a charlatan without misrepresenting, and he has never been known to make an erroneous statement. About the best his traducers have been able to accomplish is to affirm vigorously that "it cannot be so."

The average student of the old philosophies may legitimately ask the question: "What does this whole controversy mean to me?"

Its merit lies in its protective aspect. A person properly informed is not easily deceived. But a person whose opinions must rest entirely on hearsay and pretensions is not properly equipped to preserve his own integrity.

There have been so many claims and so many statements made about St.-Germain that it seems important to clarify and organize the available and reliable data. Thus a measuring rod is established in the mind by which intelligent comparisons can be made. Faith in human nature and a belief in the fundamental integrity of people is regarded as a virtue. But in these times when every ideal of the human being is exploited for the profit of others, a blind faith will lead only to misfortune and disillusionment. Most people who are deceived in spiritual matters have only themselves to blame.

Philosophy demands no blind acceptance from anyone. It deals not in promises but in principles and law. Philosophy does not insult the common sense; it does not cause people to believe under the influence of some glamorous, fantastic, and irrational doctrines. From what we know of St.-Germain, we know that he was a trained thinker and a trained scientist and as such, any work attributed to him must reveal in its very fabric the evidence of a superior mind. The two manuscripts now existing attributed to St.-Germain, the *Holy Trinosophia* and the *Sacred Magic* are consistent in every way with what he is known to have taught. There are other manuscripts by him in European libraries; of this there can be no reasonable doubt. These libraries belong to organizations and individuals, who have preserved these secret works from century to century, revealing their contents only to those qualified to receive such important information.

In closing, therefore, let us simply restate what we have previously indicated. Only adequate knowledge, adequate preparation, and adequate mental capacity developed through years of self-improvement, entitle the seeker after wisdom to expect that he will be made party to any body of knowledge worthy of his consideration.

MYSTICISM OF WILLIAM BLAKE

To attempt an interpretation of the mysticism and artistry of William Blake may appear little short of audacity. No other personality in the field of esoteric speculation presents as numerous or as diversified difficulties. Unsympathetic critics have suggested that Blake lived in such a state of internal confusion that neither he nor anyone else could make heads or tails of his philosophy. A superficial reading certainly invites such criticism, but the more we investigate the curious productions of this extraordinary genius, the more convinced we become that a broad pattern underlay and motivated his vision of the universal scheme. As in the case of Dante, splendid particulars have obscured the framework of his project.

To the modern world, Blake is known principally for his drawings and engravings. For nearly a century, these turned up in English auction galleries where they brought no great price. The compositions were too intellectual and were in violent contrast to the altogether charming and intensely meaningless products of Gainsborough, Lawrence, and Romney. The public taste was so addicted to Mrs. Siddons and Lady Emma Hamilton in various poses and impersonations that it had slight sympathy for what it considered the wretched distortions of Mr. Pars' most individualistic pupil. We now recognize Blake as the first important English artist to break the nostalgia surrounding "Pinky" and the "Blue Boy."

It has long been a moot question as to whether a great work of art should appeal to the mind or merely interpret the obvious to no purpose. The schools that bestow upon the waiting world an endless stream of buxom nudes insist that we should be satisfied with color, line, and mass—especially mass. Blake broke the prevailing concept and, for that matter, the entire modern concept by selecting his subject matter from a sphere of cosmic symbolism entirely beyond the human experience. He gained a reputation for madness, outraged most of his contemporaries, and suffered the full weight of that penalty which is reserved for courage and originality.

It was only after the turn of the present century that the artistic world began to take Blake seriously. Of course he had a few earlier champions, but these were regarded as touched by the same malady from which Blake himself had suffered—a sickly mysticism. Then the art world caught up to William Blake. Modernism had overthrown the academic tradition, and art was emerging as a vehicle of impression and interpretation. The prints and water colors of the master commanded high, even fabulous prices, and today the private collector seldom has an opportunity to purchase an original.

The great galleries of the world are now proud to own even sketches and unfinished drawings.

The mature style of William Blake cannot be mistaken for the work of any other artist, although there are certain doubts about some of his earlier productions. The keynote of his technique may be termed Gothic, with the dynamic elongations and exaggerations common to that school. He was also considerably influenced by the work of Michelangelo, and is known to have made an extensive study of the figure composition of "The Last Judgment," in the Sistine Chapel in Rome. There is also a fascinating quality of naivete in all of Blake's delineations of the human face and figure. Even his "Fallen Angels" appear virginal, and his numerous representations of Mother Eve would indicate that she was entirely uncontaminated by the unfortunate episode in the Garden of Eden.

In order to estimate the mind of William Blake, we must first examine his background and early life. He was born in London, Nov. 28, 1757, the son of James Blake, a dealer in hosiery. The mother's maiden name is not recorded. William was the second son, in a family of four sons and one daughter. With the exception of the youngest son, who died in his twenties after showing some artistic talent, there was little promise of genius among the Blakes; nor is there anything to indicate a tendency toward scholarship.

London of the period is preserved for us in the later caricatures of Hogarth, and was a rough-and-ready metropolis, to say the least. There may have been important conditioning circumstances, but, unfortunately, no one had the wit or wisdom to preserve the records, and even Gilchrist, Blake's principal biographer, rescued little of importance from the prevailing obscurity. We learn that young William showed early promise of artistic talent, and his father,

PORTRAIT OF WILLIAM BLAKE

From the painting by T. Phillips, R.A. This portrait appears in
The Grave, a poem by Robert Blair. (London, 1808.)

strangely enough, encouraged the boy. This in itself must have been quite a decision for a man with a solid business in knitted goods.

James Blake, Senior, arranged that William should attend a school of drawing in the Strand, presided over by one, Mr. Pars. It appears that Pars followed the profession of enchasing until that type of ornamentation went out of fashion. He then opened an "art academy" for infant prodigies. There is an amusing line referring to the precocious youngsters who graced the memoirs of that day. It was said that they "commence their career at three, become expert linguists at four, profound philosophers at five, read the Fathers at six, and die of old age at seven."

Mr. Pars naturally did not provide any facilities for drawing from the living figure, but he supplied a fair assortment of plaster casts "after the antique." Blake's father was moderately successful and of an indulgent turn of mind, and he supplied his son with such pin money as was necessary to purchase additional casts and to attend auctions, where useful copies of celebrated masterpieces could often be secured for a shilling or two. William early indicated a preference for Raphael, Michelangelo, Duerer, and Hemskerk.

In describing the childhood of Blake, Gilchrist indulges in that type of literary daydreaming which distinguishes Sidney Lee's woolgathering about the early life of Shakespeare. These pleasant nothings, choicely expressed, contain only two or three matters of serious interest. When young Blake was eight or ten years old he seems to have experienced his first vision: "Sauntering along, the boy sees a tree filled with angels, bright angelic wings bespangling every bough like stars. Returned home he related the incident, and only through his mother's intercession escapes a thrashing from his honest father, for telling a lie." Other visions followed, and about his twelfth year Blake began to write blank verse, selections from which were published many years later.

The most famous engraver of the time was Ryland; and in order to give his son every opportunity, Blake senior negotiated to have William apprenticed to this great man. The boy himself frustrated the plan by announcing that he did not like Ryland's face, adding: "It looks as if he will live to be hanged." The prophecy was fulfilled twelve years later—Ryland was hanged for forgery.

When William Blake was fourteen years old, he entered the workshop of Basire; and the second of these famous engravers, James Basire, was especially associated with the young man's studies. During this apprenticeship of seven years, Blake met Goldsmith and, according to speculation, may have contacted Emanuel Swedenborg. Young William received a thorough training in illustration and portraiture, and made a number of contacts which were valuable to him in later years. In order to escape the wrangling caused by other apprentices, Blake spent much time in Westminster Abbey and other old churches about London, preparing illustrations for books and chimney places.

Blake completed his apprenticeship in 1788, and four years later he married Catherine Sophia Boucher of Battersea, the daughter of a market-gardener. At the time of the wedding, it appears that Catherine had not been greatly burdened with schooling, for she signed the parish-register with an X. Evidently, however, she had a ready mind, and her husband taught her to read and write. Later, he gave her lessons in art, and she learned to draw and paint so creditably that she contributed considerably to his work. Catherine has been described as an almost perfect wife. She outlived her husband by four years, and the marriage was without issue.

So much for the physical career of William Blake during the first twenty-five years of his life—those formative years which established his character, his taste, and his philosophy. There is nothing to indicate the scope of his educational opportunities beyond Pars' academy and Basire's workshop. The old apprenticeship system involved a continuous drudgery each day from dawn to dark. The masters grumbled if their boys so much as burned an inch of candle after hours.

Even presuming that Blake's abilities brought him considerable preferment, we cannot but wonder how he enriched his mental life under such conditions. Of course, he lived in the great city of the world with libraries and galleries and numerous groups of outstanding intellectuals. It remains, however, a little difficult to marry a profound scholarship to a man whose father was a stocking merchant and whose wife could not write her own name. This state of affairs has influenced the minds of biographers and led them to assume that Blake was but a dabbler in the abstract doctrines which dominate his artistry. But let us examine the facts, as these can be assembled from the actual productions of Blake's genius.

First, we must bear in mind that only an interpreter versed in the lore with which Blake was completely familiar can hope to estimate the depth of the artist's learning. Blake was a mystic and an occultist, and such addictions are sufficient in themselves to frustrate the average biographer. In a day when free thinking was considered a dishonorable type of mental activity, Blake was not only an iconoclast but a profound scholar. Early, by means unknown, he had mastered Locke, Bacon, and Descartes. He knew the works of Boehme, Paracelsus, and dared to criticize Newton. His understanding of Greek mythology and the Hellenic mysteries was prodigious. He was a master of the subtle transcendentalism of Plotinus and the Alexandrian Neoplatonists, but in some matters he chose to follow the Syrian and Egyptian Gnostics. As a cabalist and alchemistical philosopher, he can be described as the last of the illumined Hermetists. He had imbibed deeply of the wisdom of the Troubadours, and showed familiarity with the tenets of the Rosicrucians, early Illuminists, and Freemasons.

To him the Bible was the book of books, but he interpreted it with a grandeur of concept that would have bewildered the Archbishop of Canterbury and the Dean of St. Paul's. It is hard to decide whether he was a great pagan Christian or a Christian pagan. One may suspect that he had some contact with the celebrated Platonist, Thomas Taylor, for these two men had much in common.

Blake refused to be limited by the boundaries of any theological despotism. Literally, he created a universe of his own, administered it by laws originating within his own conviction, and populated it with creatures fashioned by his own high fantasy. Yet, he was in no sense of the word merely a repository of ancient doctrines. His vision was his own, a strange compound of inspiration and prophecy flowing from deep hidden places within himself.

As we examine the illuminated manuscripts of the mystics, alchemists, and thaumaturgists of old, we see the pages filled with curious symbols and designs. Many of the emblems are daring and original, belonging to a world entirely beyond the common ken. Vast were the dreams, but unskilled the hands that committed the symbols to paper or parchment. Blake was the first to bring a superb and dynamic artistry to the esoteric tradition. Through him, abstract concepts took fantastic forms of such intrinsic merit that they are now included among the greatest productions of human skill.

Although Blake illustrated many works and even drew astrological faces for his friend, Varley, the astrologer-water-colorist, and at times descended to artistic potboiling in order to survive, most of his productions are parts of one vast pattern. The names which he gave to his prints and books often had little to do with the subject matter. Whoever paid the bill was secondary; Blake always worked for himself. He might label his mystic vision of Christ as the personification of art with such a title as "Lord Nelson." No one understood just what he meant, but the work itself was admirable.

Having overlooked the basic fact that all of Blake's so-called prophetic works are chapters of one book, and that the text which accompanies them is reminiscent of the subtlety of the Sufi mystics, the interpreters are at loose ends. It seems easier to deny so vast a plan than to acknowledge such genius in the artist. As the merit of his drawings and prints has already been the subject of many learned comments and remarks, it would serve no useful purpose to devote space here to this phase of the artistry. We are concerned primarily with Blake the Illuminist and his generally unknown contributions to the descent of the secret doctrines of antiquity.

Although Blake, the artist, had a considerable market for his illustrations and engravings, Blake, the mystic, was without any practical medium for the distribution of his ideas. By the end of 1788, Blake had completed the first section of his wonderful series of esoteric prose-poetry and poetic prose. He anticipated by more than twenty years the school of free verse, and pioneering is a thankless task. He was entirely capable of preparing the illustrations for his mystical writings, but no publisher was available who would risk money

Engraving by William Blake to illustrate *Night Thoughts*, by
Edward Young. (London, 1797.)

and reputation to compose the text. At this critical moment, Blake had on hand less than twenty shillings in the coinage of the realm, and was in no position to finance reluctant printers.

In his emergency, Blake believed that he received guidance from his younger and favorite brother, Robert, who had already passed beyond the grave. Robert appeared to him in a vision at night and supplied the solution to the pressing difficulty. The answer was amazingly simple, and the necessary materials were purchased at the cost of approximately two shillings by Mrs. Blake. There were other complications, but his friends in the spirit world assisted, and the result contributed a large part of the distinction peculiar to Blake's prophetic books. If an artist could prepare the plates for his illustrations, he could also draw the plates for the text by hand. Thus, he could combine text and design in one artistic structure. The writing was done on the metal with a kind of varnish which was impervious to acids, and the rest of the metal was afterwards eaten away with aqua fortis.

Mrs. Blake was entrusted with the delicate task of making the prints for the new plates, which she did in various colored inks which her husband prepared. Later, the printed outlines were hand-colored by Blake or his wife. To reduce expenses, the plates were small, a limitation greatly to be regretted. Somewhere along the line, good Catherine also became a successful amateur book binder, and the volumes were produced complete and ready for the market by these two patient persons. It has been said that they made everything except the blank paper.

Of course, the curious works thus produced had a limited sale and distribution, but the costs were so low that they became the principal source of income, and continued a limited popularity throughout the life of the artist. Occasionally, the books were issued uncolored, which shows the basic technique to the best advantage. In this way, between the years 1789 and 1795, Blake issued *The Book of Thel, The Marriage of Heaven and Hell, The Songs of Innocence, The Songs of Experience, America, Visions of the Daughters of Albion, Europe, Urizen, The Book of Los, The Book of Ahania,* and *The Song of Los.* Although the originals of these are now great rarities, accurate hand-colored facsimiles are available through the industry and patience of William Muir. Most are now procurable by modern lithographic processes.

These are the prophetic books, and to them Blake entrusted the principal parts of his philosophy. As the mood grew within him, however, a number of supplementary engravings invented for other purposes extended the symbolism by using the same characters, and occasionally incorporating fragments of text. As the prophetic books expanded their doctrines, Blake became more and more completely immersed in his mystical pre-occupations. The mood of the evangelist grew upon him, and the artist became the teacher, the seer, the sage, and the prophet.

During this period also, Blake seems to have felt an increasing guidance and overshadowing from the invisible worlds. Like Swedenborg, he became the enraptured spectator of a mystery in the spirit. It never seemed to concern him greatly whether his message was immediately perceived or understood; in fact, he became almost unintelligible even to his nearest friends. He depended almost entirely upon the dramatic impact of his productions for the survival of his ideas.

Blake's metaphysical philosophy was enclosed within one dominant concept, which an interpreter of his work has called "the circle of destiny." As the power of his own vision increased, the pressure brought with it the kind of urgency so often present among Adventists. Blake was convinced that the possibility of a great spiritual regeneration was immediate, and that it was his duty to herald the dawn of a new age.

It is interesting to observe the consistency with which those motivated by internal illumination are dominated by this sense of immediateness. All the rounds, cycles, and circles of the Blakean anthropology and psychology converged toward the time, the place, and the person that was Blake himself. Unless humanity released its consciousness from the prevailing delusions, it must plunge back into darkness and despair for another vast circle of time. Blake believed himself to have been entrusted with the secret of human liberation. Only by recognizing the universal truth which he revealed at the critical moment, when one cycle ended and another was about to begin, could the world preserve itself from the disaster of reason without faith. We may or may not agree that Blake was the prophet of a new order, but we cannot deny that in the century following his death humanity became the victim of a despotic materialism.

It never occurred to Blake that it was necessary for him to justify or prove even the most abstract of his concepts. To him, his doctrine was self-evident. He proved his principles from his particulars, and his particulars from his principles. To question the inner reality of that which was outwardly consistent was to reject the testimony of the senses themselves. To accept part of the grand scheme was to accept all, and to reject part was to reject all.

Blake's mood was not so different from Kant's, to whom pure reason must lead to the complete acceptance of the

Kantean concept. To differ was to stand condemned of ignorance or intolerance. Blake did not have the belligerence of
personality that distinguished the little professor of Koenigs-
berg. Blake did not dislike those who failed to appreciate
the profundity of his visions; in fact, he did not require the
approbation of anyone. He lived in a state of almost complete absorption in the magnitude of the cosmic and moral

BEHEMOTH AND LEVIATHAN

Fragment from the *Book of Job* engravings by
William Blake.

scheme that his mind had conjured out of the abyss of false
doctrines.

It has been said that Blake became almost obsessed by
his own ideas. The creatures he had fashioned gained such
reality for him that he suffered by them, with them, and for
them. The imagination of great artistry opened the sensitive

consciousness to the impact of his own symbolism. Then, as
he drew the physical likenesses of his mental progeny, they
became even more tangible and substantial. Psychologically
speaking, Blake possessed a strangely involved personality,
which gradually introverted until it had but slight existence
apart from the concepts with which it was merged.

The Blakean metaphysics will be most comprehensible to
those who have some familiarity with the doctrines and tenets
of Gnosticism. The grand scheme of the Gnosis—its doctrine
of emanations and their female counterparts, the fall of man
from a paradisiacal state, the intercession of the Soter, or
Messiah, the final redemption of the human family—re-
occurs in the mystical revelations of William Blake. In metaphysics, *Gnosis* means *positive knowledge, especially of spiritual truths*. To the Gnostic, therefore, his eons and emanations,
though imperceptible to his external faculties, were an absolute reality to his contemplative faculties. His invisible
world, with its powers and planes and creatures, was held
empirically as demonstrable to those who accepted rather
than to those who questioned the substance of the doctrine.

The principal figure in Blakean metaphysics is Albion,
who corresponds closely with the anthropos of the Gnostics.
Albion is the universal man, the Being "whose body Nature
is, and God the soul." Albion is the ideal or archetypal man
of Plato. He is both the pattern and the fulfillment of the
pattern. He is Adam Kadmon, the man fashioned of the red
earth, who occurs in the doctrine and literature of the Cabala.
He is the Grand Man of the *Zohar*, whose parts and members
form the world. Albion is humanity itself as one person, and
he is the universe likened unto a man. While Albion remains
aware of his own eternal unity, he dwells in the light and
in a spiritual state, which Blake calls Eden. When sleep
comes upon Albion and he experiences division within him-

self, the fall is the inevitable consequence. Division, therefore, is itself the illusion and the disaster.

The division that is set up in Albion by the loss of the consciousness of unity brings into existence an infinite diversity
of parts within Albion. These parts then enter into an intricate combination of moods, motions, and modes, and it becomes the final duty or responsibility of the parts to redeem
their own sense or awareness of wholeness. Thus, in a strange
way, the sleeping Albion is awakened and "saved" by the
re-integration of his own divided nature. Here Blake shares
the vision of Jakob Boehme, who saw in Adam, Satan, and
Christ one force moving under three compulsions. The
heavenly man, Albion, is redeemed by his own fulfillment
in the mundane sphere—the man of heaven, Christ.

Albion personifies universal consciousness, which abides
naturally in the consciousness of universals. He possesses
without effort that all-sufficiency which the fragments of
himself must attain through ceaseless striving. He is, therefore, the true and selfless Self in all men who partake of
unity through him, even as they partake of diversity through
a false Ego, or illusion of separate sufficiency. Only Albion
lives, dies, and is reborn in glory. These vast occurrences
underlie all the motions and impulses which manifest in
human affairs. Thus, Albion is the universal hero, whose
adventures in space make up the legend that is more than
legend.

The primary division of Albion is reminiscent of the doctrines held by the Brahman mystics of India. All universals,
including *the Universal*, contain the potential of polarity.
Albion, as Universal Knowing, emanates a feminine counterpart whom Blake calls Jerusalem, the universal to be known.
This is the same Jerusalem adorned as a bride referred to
in the *Apocalypse*. This "Bride of the Lamb" is popularly

supposed to represent the Church, which will ultimately be
married to Christ. Blake uses it, however, in a larger sense.
It is the assembly, the Ecclesia, as those brought into union.
The Redeemer, the redemption, and the redeemed are one
mystery, and Blake is careful to point out that this is the
supreme mystery in which factually there is no secret at all.

In Brahman theology, four castes or orders or life (later
classes of humanity) emerged from the body or meditation-
unity of Brahma. These emerged from the head, the heart,
the loins, and the feet of the Supreme Deity. In Blake's system, Albion, as he sinks into the condition of non-identity,
releases from himself the four Zoas. The term is derived
from the Greek *zoion*, meaning an animal; and there is
definite analogy with the four beasts of Ezekiel's vision and
the four creatures of *The Revelation of St. John*.

According to Blake's concept, the four Zoas are released
into a state of separate existence by the differentiation of
the powers of the head, the heart, the loins, and the body
of Albion. Once these centers of separate awareness or power
emerge, they take over the administration of a divided world-
consciousness and enter into a state of competition for dominion, in this way bringing about the tragedy of disunity.
We might point out that the Blakean perspective is psy-
chocosmical, for like Buddhism, it emphasizes the creative
processes as moods of life primarily metaphysical. These
moods react upon the world-form and the world-body, thus
producing the complex physical phenomena.

The first of the Zoas, which emanates from the head of
Albion, is Urizen, usually represented as an aged man. In
Blake's drawings, this patriarchal figure, performing various
stately functions, resembles the popular artistic concept of
God. This majestic being measures Infinity with compasses,
hovers in clouds and whirlwinds, and seems to create, by

decree alone, the creatures of this world. But as we proceed to a more careful study, we see that this ancient man appears also humbled, bound, blinded, and melancholy. Like Odin, the splendid All-father of the Nordics, Urizen is subject to moods of fear, despair, revenge, and fretfulness. This Jehovistic being personifies the power of reason which inherits the world when truth goes to sleep.

When the Zoas abide together with Albion in Eden, they are internally lighted and may properly be termed *the Eternals*. As reason descends into the corruption of Ulro, the material sphere of spiritual death, the internal light gradually extinguishes and the majestic demiurgus is reduced to a fretful, uncertain old man, bound and blinded, like Samson, who was chained to the millstone of the Philistines. Of course, the millstone itself is a symbol of cycles, the very power of reason, which in its spiritual state redeems; in its material state destroys. The god becomes the tyrant; for the mind, naturally the servant of spirit, once it loses its inward light, attempts to make itself master over matter and the creatures of the material world. Reason degenerates into intellectual despotism, and Urizen is transformed into an ungainly giant, a Titanic monster that plunges the human nature into a deeper abyss of doubt, fear, and false knowledge.

The female aspect of Urizen, Blake calls Ahania, or the repose of reason. She is the mind's desire, ever pressing Urizen by the mystery of the unconquered unknown. In a way, Ahania is the mistress of every materialistic intellectual. She eternally invites the reason to speculate upon those universal workings which are in substance beyond the capacity of the reasoning power. She is responsible for the illusion that man is placed in a material world to conquer it for the fulfillment of small personal projects and conceits. Reason would lie dormant unless it contemplated the repose of space.

URIZEN BROODING OVER THE WORLD

—From William Blake's prophetic work, *America.*

Fired by the determination to explore and exploit all things for its own survival, reason changes from the kindly god who walked in Eden to the Lord of Battles, of vengeance and of sin.

In the prophetic works, Blake uses the character of Urizen to personify restraint or repression manifesting through vested authority. In his *America,* which Blake issued in 1793, Urizen attempts the restraint of the rights of man through his angel, Albion. In this instance, Albion certainly refers to England, and Albion's angel is King George III. The second of the Zoas, under the name Orc, quickening the souls of men like Washington, Franklin, and Payne, leads them to rebellion against the tyranny represented by the plagues and blights of restraint. To Blake, the American Revolution was the beginning of a world motion toward the eternal liberty which constitutes the perfect existence as decreed by the eternal order of life.

Thus we see that Blake, having established the symbolic instruments of his concept, applies them variously to human institutions, finding the ageless warfare between repression and expression at the root of mortal confusion. We must not, however, assume that Blake was an advocate of spiritual, moral, or political anarchy. He points out that entrenched despotism always regards the rebel as evil. To repress rebellion is to maintain the status quo, a condition which binds the mortal creature in a state of intellectual or physical slavery. But it is impossible to chain man merely by enslaving his body; the mind also must be held, and to accomplish this, fear is the accepted weapon. The common man must be kept afraid. He must fear life, fear death, fear God, fear the Devil, and fear those mortal masters and overlords who have proclaimed themselves the keepers of his destiny.

Although Blake is not entirely correct in his timing, he anticipated in his prophetic mood those revolutions of States and Empires by which tyranny should finally be shaken to its foundation. To him, the American Revolution was the shadow of things to come, an indication of the internal resolution of the oppressed to cast off the shackles of their oppression. The physical political changes, however, were not merely accidental and incidental phenomena. They bore witness to immutable laws abiding in space, which decreed that in the fullness of time man should be free.

Incidentally, one of Blake's most interesting examples of extrasensory perception occurred in connection with Thomas Payne. In September, 1792, in the modest home of Johnston, the bookseller, Blake was present when Payne summarized an inflammatory speech in favor of liberty, which he had given at a public gathering the previous evening. As he was leaving, Blake stepped up to him, saying: "You must not go home, or you are a dead man!" Blake hustled Payne to the Dover docks and put him on board a ship for France. By that time, the police were in his house, and a detaining order reached the docks twenty minutes after Payne had been passed through customs. He never returned to England.

By way of interlude, it should be pointed out that any explanation of Blake's philosophy must be considered, to a degree at least, an interpretation. The poetic style of the mystic, the brevity of his text, and the fantasy which permeates his literary form make it impossible to dogmatize upon his meanings. Often Blake, the metaphysician, applies his symbolism to several particulars almost simultaneously. He must be explained in the terms of the convictions of his commentator. Therefore, there is considerable confusion about the more obscure phases of his metaphysical images.

We have already mentioned the character Orc, the second of the four Zoas. Orc is a mode or qualification of a being called Luvah, the personification of the emotional (spirit-soul) life of Albion, enthroned in the heart of the universal man. Luvah, as the true emotion of the soul, appears in several forms on the various planes of emotional energy, but he is always directly or indirectly the liberator of that which is oppressed or repressed.

In *America*, the prophetic book, Luvah as Orc is the fire of liberty, the flame that blazes in the heart of the patriot. Luvah also appears as Satan, personifying negative rebellion. Satan is not essentially evil, but is liberation without love. Goethe sensed this mystery when he caused Mephistopheles to describe himself as "part of the power that still works for good, though ever scheming ill." Blake also used Luvah as the divine imagination-in-art, identifying ultimate liberation or redemption and the power which produces it with the true figure of Christ. Aspiration toward the universal beauty of freedom under the law of love has its passive phase, or female counterpart, in Valla, whose demon form becomes Lilith.

From the loins of Albion comes the third of the Zoas, Urthona, the generative and regenerative power which manifests as Los, and whose feminine counterpart is Enitharmon, or pity. From the body of Albion comes the fourth of the Zoas, Tharmas, which is the bodily union of things, and his feminine counterpart, Enion, the great earth-mother. In the descent through the worlds brought about by the mystery of the fall, these Zoas come into dominion over the creatures which emanate from the composition of the universal man, within whom these creatures live and move and have their being.

The descent itself is through four spheres, planes, or states, which are really the psychic organisms of the Zoas themselves, and therefore are divisions of the body of the universal Albion. Here we have the cabalistic doctrine of emanations, with the four Adams existing in the four worlds which emanate from the Ancient of the Ancients. The first world is Eden, the home of eternals, and the natural abode of all the Zoas in their inward state, with their faces turned toward the Eternal Light. The second world is Beulah, the etheric paradise where facts are no longer evident or dominant, but whose creatures have certain abiding beliefs about facts and, therefore, have not descended completely into error. It is here that Urizen fashioned the Mundane Shell to encircle the higher spheres and to prevent the fall of the creation into the abyss. The third world is Ulro, the sphere of spiritual death and physical generation. Here beliefs have degenerated into opinions, and men are led in darkness. The fourth sphere seems without clear definition, and may not be included among the worlds except as a fourth-dimensional quality. It is something added by the power of the soul. It is a world or sphere of regeneration or redemption, a state achieved by high imagination-in-art.

Blake also introduces a ghostly and demoniac character called the Spectre. This Spectre, often represented crowned and bearing a flaming lance, is the personification of the consequence of reason without faith, and Blake implies that his strange symbol signifies doubt, which haunts all things with a mortal fear. Some interpreters believe that the Spectre is man himself, the personification of unreasonable uncertainties. The preachment is clear: The mind developed without the heart can never attain tranquillity. We live in a sphere of unknowns, extending the feeble powers of our minds toward infinities, only to discover that we lack the very faculties necessary to answer our eternal questions. The conviction of inability, the realization that we abide in an unknown and probably unknowable universal, has given to mankind an over-shadowing inferiority complex and bound mortals with the shackles and chains of endless opinions.

Although Blake was a devoutly religious man in his own way, he had little respect for those revealed doctrines which men must accept without question or endanger their immortal souls. To him, all these institutions of infallibility, grounded in ignorance and perpetuated by playing upon the fears and doubts of mortals, were the work of Urizen, striving desperately to maintain the tyranny of mind over the natural aspiration of truth-seekers. All the "thou shalts" and the "thou shalt nots" are part of a dictatorship of reason without faith. In a way, doctrines set up tension in the mind and emotions, and tension itself is the destroyer of reality. Man cannot find truth by doubt, by fear, or by concepts forced upon him by human institutions. Truth belongs to

From *Illustrations of the Book of Job,* in twenty-one plates, invented and engraved by William Blake. (London, 1826)

the free and to those who seek it without pressure or restraint. It can never be ours until as free men we incline to a natural and beautiful faith, embraced through love and gladness.

The Blakean vision of the universal redemption is reminiscent of the alchemistic doctrine of "art perfecting Nature." By art the alchemist implied a spiritual chemistry, a science of human regeneration. Man himself becomes master of a method or discipline by which he can ascend to a state of conscious unity, in this way discovering and experiencing internally the substance of Albion. Although Blake did not agree with Francis Bacon's political policies, there is evidence that the artist appreciated the ideas underlying the concept of the philosopher.

Bacon referred frequently to the power of art and to the possibility of moral and ethical improvement by personal effort according to law. Art is a kind of divine ingenuity possible to man. The human creature is possessed of capacities by which he can cause two blades of grass to grow where one has grown before. Skill enlarges, improves, and enriches; and man is the only animal endowed with this quality of skill. As Luther Burbank could improve plants and flowers, so all men have the innate ability, if they exercise their birthright, to improve both their world and themselves.

This power to be more than we are by an effort that we alone can make is the secret of redemption. On the material plane, we use this skill only to increase our goods or to advance our fortunes. This does not mean, however, that material industry exhausts the potentials of our strength. Physical advancement is only the shadow or symbol of essential growth. If we can organize our world, we can organize our own natures. If we can free a garden of weeds so that the plants that are useful can flourish, it is also possible for us to free our minds and souls of their infirmities, thus permitting the spiritual life within us to bear its perfect fruit.

Salvation cannot be bestowed; it must be discovered by the experience of art. If the scientist thinks of art as method, the mystic defines art as a sensitive appreciation for all that is noble, beautiful, and true. Appreciation in turn results in a kind of awareness. The human being must be taught to see with the dimensions of his own mental and moral nature. As long as we see only the outer forms of things and are satisfied to live in a world of forms, explaining one in the terms of another, we abide in separateness and discord. From the eternal roots of our own being, however, we derive the inalienable right to love the beautiful and to serve the good.

The technique of art, then, is regeneration through clarification. We set ourselves the task of revealing through an obstinate personality the unity-in-glory, which is eternal life. The kingdom of Urizen is overcome, not by a warfare of the reason, but by each man in himself forgiving the world sin. In a strange way man himself becomes Christ, and achieves through the Christ in himself the salvation of the God which fashioned him. The creature attains the state of forgiveness *by forgiving and not by being forgiven.*

Thus Blake emerges as a champion of positive rather than of negative attitudes. He had no place for a concept of life under which men are forever begging their bread and depending for survival upon crumbs from the banquet table of a universal tyrant. He shared with Thomas Payne a general aversion to despots, whether celestial or terrestrial. He had no patience for doctrines which regarded the universe as a vaster England, or Deity as a highly glorified George III.

Nor could he bend the knee to those dogmas of the Church which taught salvation to result from the sacrifice and suffering of one good man. Blake did not believe in salvation by the grace of God. He preferred to think of men themselves growing in grace, and in the fullness of time rescuing God from the clutches of higher ecclesiasticism. Most gods are but men seen from below, and all men are gods when seen from within.

Blake's understanding of the Christian mystery was completely mystical in the best sense of that term. He used the word *forgiveness* in an unusual way. It implied an enlargement of understanding by which things become truly known. True knowing in turn leads to true loving. The human soul, cleansed of unreasonable and unnatural fears, relaxes from error to a state of grace. As the child, confident of the strength and wisdom of its parents, lives without fear, so the enlightened man, sure of the integrities which preserve him, can cease the unnatural struggle against phantoms and abide in a peace that surpasses understanding.

There is much of the Oriental in this positive recognition. Man is resigned to the good and not to the evil. Virtue is thus a simple gesture of acceptance, and not a tyranny upon the wayward. As an artist, Blake lived on a plane of intense emotional activity. He interpreted life in terms of tone, symmetry, and design. He experienced the complete satisfaction which comes through the use rather than the abuse of artistic principles. He sensed right use as the natural remedy for misuse. More than this, he knew that the power within him by which he was impelled, gently but inevitably, to the appreciation of the beautiful, was a spirit of redemption and regeneration.

Like so many mystics, he required no intermediary between himself and the universe. True religion is not institutional but intimate and internal. Theologies, conjured into existence by Urizen, were concerned primarily not with the salvation of man but the preservation of themselves. They had substituted the passing glory of this world for the eternal glory of the divine world. Even as they taught redemption, they were binding men to the machinery of sect and creed and dogma. Human destiny could not be fulfilled by setting up democracies in the physical world and at the same time worshipping a concept of spiritual autocracy. Yet Blake was in no way an atheist or agnostic. He was devoutly religious, as we have said, but he stood on the threshold of an era of emancipation. He acknowledged the rights of man, but required that men themselves be right.

The Christ of Blake was perfect spiritual freedom, guided by the gentle power of enlightened love. It was the practice of the brotherhood of man, developed and perfected by inner conviction. Men united in action become aware through their own union of the universal One. They restore the broken body of Albion, not by innumerable ineffective remedies or learned debates about the physiology of First Cause, but by discovering that they, and not God, are divided. It is man who has decreed the division. He has seen his own enraged and distorted visage reflected from the mirrored surface of space, and named this reflection a god of vengeance.

In this part of his philosophy, Blake approaches basic tenets of Buddhism, the great Eastern school which teaches that the universe exists primarily in consciousness rather than in matter. The Eastern way of union is through disciplines of realization. What the Easterners call realization, Blake covers by his interpretation of the act of forgiving. Forgiveness is a loving acceptance which has seen through appearances and discovered the reality. It is difficult to confine the dreams of the mystic to the narrow and inadequate

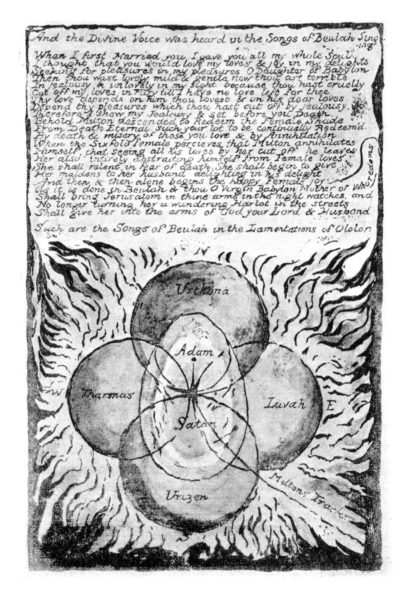

And the Divine Voice was heard in the Songs of Beulah Sing

When I first Married you, I gave you all my whole Soul
I thought that you would love my loves & joy in my delights
Seeking for pleasures in my pleasures O Daughter of Babylon
Then thou wast lovely mild & gentle now thou art terrible
In jealousy & unlovely in my sight because thou hast cruelly
Cut off my loves in fury till I have no love left for thee
Thy love depends on him thou lovest & on his dear loves
Depend thy pleasures which thou hast cut off by jealousy
Therefore I shew my Jealousy & set before you Death.
Behold Milton descended to Redeem the Female Shade
From Death Eternal such your lot to be continually Redeem'd
By death & misery of those you love & by Annihilation
When the Sixfold Female perceives that Milton annihilates
Himself that seeing all his loves by her cut off he leaves
Her also intirely abstracting himself from Female loves
She shall relent in fear of death. She shall begin to give
Her maidens to her husband delighting in his delight
And then & then alone begins the happy Female joy
As it is done in Beulah & thou O Virgin Babylon Mother of Whoredoms
Shall bring Jerusalem in thine arms in the night watches, and
No longer turning her a wandering Harlot in the streets
Shall give her into the arms of God your Lord & Husband

Such are the Songs of Beulah in the Lamentations of Ololon

A cosmological figure illustrating the principles of William Blake.
From his poem, *Milton*, in two books engraved in 1804.

structure of words. We must even ask words to forgive us for the sins we have committed with them.

The Utopia of Blake is a social order of civilized human beings. It is the kingdom of heaven set up in the hearts of men. When human beings have attained to a state of spiritual democracy, then and then only can physical States and nations abide together in a true comradeship of enlightened understanding. Mortals can never protect themselves against the consequences of their own actions except by outgrowing their own insufficiencies. Man masters the world by overcoming the specter of worldliness, conjured into being by fear, ambition, and selfishness. The negative forces of life cannot control us unless we acknowledge their sovereignty. We must accept the illusion or we cannot be the victims of the illusion. This does not mean that the physical world does not exist, but rather that material things are themselves parts of an eternal beauty until man disfigures them with his own ulterior motives.

The redeemer is not a separate creature either human or divine, but the eternal rightness of things, ever present and ever awaiting acceptance. Truth knocks at every man's door, but for most is an unwelcome guest. Even at best, reality is the stranger, and we all fear and doubt that which is strange. The Last Judgment is not a weighing of souls, but is the judgment of man himself judging righteous judgment. This final judgment results in the selection of that which is unchangeably good. To weigh all things and to cling to that which is beautiful and true is the high decision and the Last Judgment.

If, then, we may not fully share in Blake's vision, nor completely comprehend the strange wild beauty of this great artist, let us at least be patient and sympathetic in the presence of his vision. He was one of those who "saw God in flames and heard him in the winds." The wild grandeur of space was not to Blake the savagery of tortured elements, but the free beauty of eternal spirit. This freedom, perfected by imagination-in-art, makes possible the emergence of a free man. To Blake, freedom was the right to be beautiful, noble, kind, and wise. Only the free man can serve truth and redeem the world which he has betrayed.

THOMAS TAYLOR,
THE ENGLISH PLATONIST

In England, a protestant who disputes the authority of the Church of England is called a Dissenter, or a non-conformist. In the 18th century, these Dissenters were subject to numerous indignities, and special abuse was reserved for Dissenting ministers. The father of Thomas Taylor was such a minister and, as a result, was impoverished by his convictions. He was described as a worthy and God-fearing man, but it also appears that he was set in his ways and strongly opinionated. He was one of those good souls who made life difficult for himself and others. Into this meager and frustrated atmosphere, Thomas Taylor was born in London, on the fifteenth day of May, 1758. Early admirers referred to this event with philosophical elegance, declaring that on his natal day the soul of the philosopher "descended into this mundane sphere." While Thomas was still in his trim, his reverent father decided that his son should follow in his

footsteps and become a Dissenting minister. It seems, however, that the muses and those tutelary spirits which attend
such matters decreed otherwise.

When Thomas reached his ninth year, he was sent to St.
Paul's school, a proper atmosphere in which to absorb theology and non-conformism. Even at this early age, the boy
gave indications of a contemplative turn of mind. He also
revealed a strong spirit and a profound aversion to pedantry
and pedagogy. He disliked to listen to the opinions of those
whose wordiness indicated no depth of personal understanding. A certain Mr. Ryder, who was one of the masters of
St. Paul's school, became interested in the serious and pene-
trating mind of young Taylor. When the lesson involved
some especially grave or meaningful passage by a classic
author, Mr. Ryder would turn to Thomas, saying "Come,
here is something worthy the attention of a philosopher."
After remaining three years in this school, young Taylor
became so thoroughly disgusted with the superficial manner
in which classical languages and sciences were taught that
he finally persuaded his father to take him home. There
were then further family councils and Thomas succeeded in
convincing his father that he was not designed by natural
endowments for the ministry. This was a great blow, for it
seemed to the good man that the career of a Dissenting
minister was the highest, noblest, and most enviable employment which the world could offer.

Young Thomas was an impetuous fellow, and shortly after
his twelfth year he fell deeply in love with a Miss Morton,
the oldest daughter of a respectable coal merchant in Doctor's Commons. She must have been an extraordinary person, for it is recorded that she was younger than Thomas
and he had recently passed his twelfth year. Miss Morton,
the coal merchant's daughter, was already highly and technic-

ally educated with a profound interest in the most advanced subjects of philosophy. Young Thomas sang her praises constantly, and declared himself to be as much in love as any of the famous heroes of romance and chivalry. His greatest joy was to converse with his beloved or to describe her charms and attainments to any who would listen. It was considered almost incredible by his biographers that this boy, scarcely in his teens, should have been so deeply and lastingly smitten, but future events seemed to indicate that destiny had decreed this association.

Taylor's father found difficulty in deciding a new direction for his son's future. He was not overly enthusiastic when young Thomas indicated a strong preference for higher mathematics. As a Dissenting minister, the senior Taylor was deeply skilled in modern theology, but was hopelessly deficient in the classical sciences and philosophies. It seemed to him that the boy had chosen a difficult and unpromising field of endeavor. Thomas found it necessary to study at night and to conceal his books, and the long and constant sacrifice of sleep may have contributed to the delicacy of the young man's constitution.

In 1773, when Thomas was about 15 years old, he was placed under his uncle, who was one of the officers of the dock-yard at Sheerness. This worthy uncle believed in keeping young people as busy as possible. Leisure hours were few, but these were used to advance the speculative parts of mathematics, for Thomas was early of the opinion that those sciences were degraded when applied to practical affairs. Thomas was also reading Bolingbroke and Hume at this period. Young Taylor remained with his tyrannical and uninspiring uncle for about three years and, unable to endure longer what he considered a state of abject slavery, sought liberation by returning to the Church. He left Sheerness and studied for two years with the Reverend Mr. Worthington, a celebrated Dissenting preacher. Here he recovered his basic knowledge of Latin and Greek. He did not advance very rapidly, however, because the text with which he worked did not challenge his mind. While he was a pupil of the Reverend Mr. Worthington, Taylor renewed with increased ardor his acquaintance with Miss Morton. It would seem that he maintained a rigorous program. He studied Greek and Latin all day, courted his fair lady in the evening, and read the Latin Quarto of Simson's *Conic Sections* at night.

In some way, Taylor found it possible during these congested years to approach the study of modern philosophy and, armed with the subtler parts of mathematics, he attacked Newton's *Principia*. He never finished the book, however, because he regarded a number of Newton's Propositions to be plainly absurd. He particularly disapproved of Propositions VI, VII, and VIII in the Third Book. The biographers have noted that up to this point, Mr. Taylor's life had flowed "limpid and unruffled." They meant that in comparison to his future adventures, his childhood was scarcely noteworthy.

Conspiracy now entered the picture. It was time for Thomas to enter the university, so he bade Miss Morton an impassioned farewell. Her father, the respectable coal-merchant, intended during Taylor's absence to marry his daughter to a wealthy man who was also courting her most ardently. The young lady, who returned our hero's devotion with full measure, seeking to protect herself from the tyrannical weight of parental authority, consented to marry young Taylor secretly, under the condition that the marriage would be only a formal one until he had finished his studies at Aberdeen. And so it came about that these remarkable young people were bound in holy matrimony.

The secret was soon discovered, however, and a series of distressing parental outbursts followed. Fortunately, the times were such that even the most desperate and embittered parent would scarcely think of divorce. In time, the rages subsided, and the young couple attempted to establish themselves in a home of their own. It was then that young Thomas discovered that his selection of interests scarcely fitted him for successful employment. For nearly a year, the two young people lived on seven shillings a week. Mrs. Taylor was cheated out of her inheritance by a relative who was left the executor of her father's estate. The young couple was abandoned by both friends and relatives and, in an emergency, could not borrow ten shillings and sixpence. Finally, Mr. Taylor secured a position as usher in a school at Paddington. He did not earn enough money so that his wife could be with him, and he was permitted to see her only on Saturday afternoons. He later found the situation of a clerk in Mssrs. Lubbock's bank in London. This paid him 50 pounds a year, and he received his money quarterly. He was unable to take care of his wife and keep enough funds for his own living. On a number of occasions when he reached his room in the evening, he fell senseless on the floor from malnutrition. At last, he managed to rent a house at Walworth through the assistance of a schoolmate, and here, for the first time, the Taylors were able to experience a frugal family existence. Already, however, Thomas was showing serious impairment to his physical health and, in the years that followed, there was no remedy for this impairment.

Settled in his new home, Taylor directed his attention to the study of chemistry, but his selection of texts indicated an inclination toward alchemy. He remained true, however, to mathematics, and having given much attention to the quadrature of the circle, which he believed could be verified

geometrically, he published, in 1780, a pamphlet entitled
"A New Method of Reasoning in Geometry." A very small
edition of this little work was printed and it attracted slight
attention. Later, the substance was incorporated into the first
volume of Taylor's translation of *Proclus on Euclid*.

Up to this time, Taylor's studies were merely preparing
him for the specialization which was to establish his reputation in the literary world. He became acquainted with the
treatise of Sir Kenelm Digby *On Bodies and Man's Soul*.
Digby was a celebrated physician and philosopher of 17th-
century England, and is remembered especially for his famous theory of "the weapon salve," a method of treating
wounds by placing the medication on the weapon that caused
them rather than upon the injury itself. The remedy was
startlingly successful, but one factor in the cure had been
generally overlooked—Digby insisted that the wound be kept
scrupulously clean. Taylor considered Sir Digby to be a
great logician, metaphysician, and universal scholar, whose
name should never be mentioned but with reverence for his
unparalleled worth. Through Digby, Taylor's attention was
directed to the philosophy of Aristotle, and he had no more
than read Aristotle's *Physics* when he determined to make
the study of parapatetic philosophy the principal work of
his life. He was so enthusiastic that he soon fitted himself
to read Aristotle in the original, and later remarked that he
had learned Greek through Greek philosophy, rather than
Greek philosophy through Greek.

All this time, Taylor labored in the banking house from
early morning to seven o'clock in the evening, and when
business was pressing was expected to remain until 9 or 10.
He was therefore obliged to do most of his studying at night,
and for several years seldom retired before two or three
o'clock in the morning. He trained his mind to free himself

PORTRAIT OF THOMAS TAYLOR, THE GREATEST OF
THE MODERN PLATONISTS

from all interruption during those precious hours which he devoted to the classics. Neither poverty nor daily responsibility interrupted his dedicated pursuit of knowledge.

It was said that, like Penelope of old, Taylor's ability to pursue his studies under the most trying circumstances was due to the mental discipline which he imposed upon himself. He organized his daily employment so efficiently that he was able to satisfy the exacting requirements of banking and at the same time carry on philosophical reflections during working hours. As he made out bills, balanced accounts, and interviewed depositors, his mind was busily engaged in expanding lines of thought without making mistakes in either.

Through Aristotle, Taylor passed naturally to the contemplation of the works of Plato. As these researches unfolded, Taylor came to the conclusion that the philosophies of Aristotle and Plato might be likened to the Lesser and Greater Mysteries of the Greeks. It was only a step from Plato to Plotinus, whose mystical apperception brought a new and deeper light to Taylor's soul. He also studied Proclus' *On the Theology of Plato*, a work so abstruse that he observed that he did not thoroughly understand its full meaning until he had read it three times. While Taylor was reflecting upon the writings of Proclus, the celebrated Mary Wollstonecraft lived in his home for nearly three months. Taylor considered her a very modest, sensible and agreeable young woman, and she referred to the little room where Taylor studied as "the abode of peace." When Taylor published his little book *A Vindication of the Rights of Brutes*, he declared that he had been induced to this particular labor because Mr. Thomas Payne had convinced thousands of the rights of man, and Mary Wollstonecraft had indisputably proved that women are in every respect equal to men.

After Taylor had served nearly six years in Lubbock's Bank, he found it necessary to make an important decision. His health had been so undermined by long hours of uncongenial employment combined with his intensive program of reading and research, that he could no longer continue this double life. He therefore resolved to find a means of creating a career in his chosen field. His first effort was most curious. He attempted to construct a perpetual lamp such as is reported to have been found in ancient tombs. He used phosphorus, and exhibited his creation at the Freemasons Tavern. Due to circumstances beyond his control, the experiment was not a success, but it did attract several devoted and influential friends through whose assistance he was able to sever his connection with the banking world.

Next, at the suggestion of Mr. John Flaxman, the distinguished sculptor and artist, Taylor composed twelve lectures on Platonic philosophy, which he delivered at Mr. Flaxman's house to a respectable and distinguished audience. His lectures were enthusiastically received and a Mr. Bennett Langton was so impressed that he mentioned Thomas Taylor to the King of England. His majesty, though reminded several times of Taylor's work, went no further than to express his admiration, although it was hoped for a time that he might become a patron of the scholar. During his lectures, Taylor also met and formed a lasting friendship with Mr. William Meredith, a man of large fortune and liberal mind. Meredith became a staunch supporter of Taylor, and assisted him financially in the publication of several of his books.

In 1787, Taylor became acquainted with Dr. Floyer Sydenham, a learned Platonist, who died in prison because he was unable to pay a debt which he owed to the keeper of a restaurant. Dr. Sydenham had come to the study of Plato

late in life, but might have advanced to a greater knowledge
had he not been so limited by infirmity, poverty, and a tragic
death. On April 1, 1787, Taylor composed an eloquent
panegyric dedicated to Dr. Sydenham, which appeared in
seven journals and was reprinted, with some changes, in
Taylor's *Miscellanies*.

According to the outline in *The Platonist*, Taylor's life
after his attaining the support of a few sincere and enthusiastic friends was largely devoted to his literary work.
In 1787, he published his translation of *The Mystical Hymns
of Orpheus*, and this was followed in regular order by most
of his other translations and original writings. To conserve
space, a check list of these important books will be found
at the end of this biographical outline.

In 1788, the Marquis de Valadi, a French nobleman with
philosophic inclinations, visited England in search of Pythag-
orean lore. He presented himself to Thomas Taylor and,
with true French enthusiasm, is said to have thrown himself
at the master's feet. He presented Taylor with a small sum
of money, which constituted his entire fortune at the moment, and begged with great humility to become a disciple.
Taylor received him most graciously, and for a time instructed the Marquis in the essentials of philosophy. In due
course, however, Valadi decided that the contemplative life
was not for him, and he returned to France to take part in
the political commotion then agitating the country. He bade
adieu in full military attire, remarking, "I am going back
to Alexander."

About 1791, while working in the British Museum, Taylor
discovered a remarkable Hymn of Proclus to Athena. Taylor was fortunate in having the facilities of the Museum at
his disposal, for while it was not the institution it is today,
it was rich in ancient works, most of which were unknown

to 18th-century scholars. It was Mr. Samuel Patterson who recorded the incident which led to the translation of *Pausanias, The Description of Greece,* which appeared in 1794. Patterson was present, and remarked that the assignment was "enough to break a man's heart." The bookseller replied easily, "Oh, nothing will break the heart of Mr. Taylor." The work was completed in ten months, including all the notes and addenda, and for his labor Taylor received sixty pounds. The strain of this assignment was so great that when the manuscript was finished Taylor lost the use of the forefinger of his right hand, which he never regained.

As may be expected, the critics attacked the translation of *Pausanias,* intimating that Mr. Taylor was no scholar. He answered his principal critic, Mr. Porson, as follows: "I only add that their invidious insinuation that I do not understand Greek is too contemptible to merit a reply, unless they mean that my knowledge of Greek is by no means to be compared with that of Mr. Porson, because I am not, like him, unable to do anything without accents; for I confess, that in this respect I am so far inferior to him, that I can read a philosophic Greek manuscript without accents with nearly as much facility as a book written in my native tongue."

During the six years between 1795 and 1801, Taylor translated the remaining dialogues of Plato which had not been completed by Dr. Floyer Sydenham, and continued his work upon the writings of Aristotle. During this period also, he contributed to several periodicals, where some of his most important writings first appeared. About 1799, Taylor became assistant secretary to the Society for the Encouragement of Arts, Manufactures, and Commerce. Through the efforts of his friends, he secured a large majority of votes for this office, but he was forced to relinquish it because his health would not permit the additional exertion. Soon after this, he engaged in a philosophical controversy with Dr. Gilles, whom he vanquished to the satisfaction of every-one except Dr. Gilles. About this time also, Taylor paid a special tribute to William George Meredith to whom he expressed deepest friendship and the most profound grati-tude for his continuous assistance and inspiration. He also answered Dr. Gilles in a pamphlet published in 1804. The *Miscellanies in Prose and Verse*, which appeared in 1805, is especially interesting because it contains Taylor's original summary of Platonic philosophy under the title *The Creed of the Platonic Philosopher*.

At this time, Taylor was also at work on his original trans-lation of the complete Aristotle in ten volumes, which is the most rare of his productions. He said that only fifty copies would be printed of each volume, and that they would be distributed according to his own discretion. Unfortunately, this monument to erudition has never been reprinted, and complete sets are almost unobtainable. Mr. Bridgman, the critic who reviewed this work, was as unpleasant as possible; but he is forgottten, and Taylor's memory remains green. In 1809, the audacious Mr. Taylor published anonymously his *Arguments of the Emperor Julian Against the Christians*. This book had the distinction of being rigidly suppressed and most of the copies destroyed. We are fortunate in hav-ing an original copy of this book, which belonged to an intimate friend of Taylor's, in our library.

In 1818, Taylor was heartened by a very pleasant letter which he received from Dr. Copleston, provost of Oriel College. This letter paid high tribute to the depth and dignity of Taylor's translation of Aristotle's *Nicomachean Ethics*, which enjoyed a second edition. Such encouragement was cherished by the scholar because it was rare, especially com-

The inside front cover of a rare first edition copy of Taylor's translation of *The Arguments of the Emperor Julian Against the Christians.* Pasted on to this cover are the book-plate of Dr. Ingals (one of Taylor's personal friends), a rare portrait of Thomas Taylor, and two figures representing Julian and Christ.

THE PLATONIC PHILOSOPHER'S CREED

ing from an advanced authority in the field. After 1818, Taylor gave special consideration to the Neo-Platonic philosophy, and in 1822 he produced his well-known translation of the philosophical works of Apuleius, from the original Latin. This is probably the most often reprinted of Taylor's translations. The last of his works appeared in 1834, and consisted of several treatises of Plotinus. It is noteworthy that there was no indication that his faculties or powers were diminishing.

Thomas Taylor passed from this life early on Sunday morning, the first day of November, 1835. The Reverend Alexander Dyce, the distinguished editor of Shakespeare, was with Taylor the day before his death. He recorded this visit as follows: "That he [Taylor] endeavored to carry into practice the precepts of the ancient philosophers is sufficiently notorious; that he did so to the last hour of his existence I myself had a proof: the day before he died I went to see him, and to my inquiry, 'how he was?' he answered, 'I have passed a dreadful night of pain,—but you remember what Posidonios said to Pompey,' (that pain was no evil)."

Thomas Taylor wrote his own epitaph, and it would be difficult to imagine lines more appropriate.

"Health, strength, and ease, and manhood's active age,
    Freely I gave to Plato's sacred cave.

With Truth's pure joys, with Fame my days were crown'd,
    Tho' Fortune adverse on my labors frown'd."

The following description of Mr. Taylor will help to complete the picture. He was described as of medium size, well-proportioned, with an open, regular, and benevolent countenance. There was a quiet dignity about him, but no intellectual affectations of any kind. His manner was such that he won the friendship and affection of all who knew him well. His dress was simple, and his conduct irreproachable. Even among friends, he would never compromise his principles, but he was free and easy, and never attempted to dominate situations. As he grew older, his appearance became memorable, but his manner was always gracious, without pride, haughtiness, or vanity. He had an extraordinary memory, which was always available, and he was an acute observer with a profound understanding of human nature. A wonderful conversationalist, he possessed an inexhaustible fund of anecdotes, and was able to entertain his associates without ever becoming personal or referring to his own joys or sorrows. Though a profound mathematician, he had none of the attributes of a traditional scholar. His abilities were diversified, but his purpose always the service of truth. Taylor has been called the *Great English Pagan,* and it seems that he even attempted, in a quiet way, to re-establish some of the rituals of the Greek religion. Early in their marriage, he taught his wife the Greek language, and it was used extensively in their home. There is a report that in order that he might more readily comprehend the times and circumstances of the great philosophic era, he lived in a Grecian fashion, even in matters of food and clothing, but of this we can find no documentary proof.

The interest in the work of Thomas Taylor has increased through the years, and his books, which have remained scarce from lack of reprinting, are highly regarded by all students who wish to understand the soul of classical thinking. A tribute to his memory is both proper and timely.

TO THE ARTIFICER OF THE UNIVERSE

BY THOMAS TAYLOR

To thee great Demiurgus of the world,
With various intellectual sections bright,
My soul the tribute of her praise shall pay,
Unfeign'd and ardent, mystic and devout.

Thee shall she sing, when Morning's rosy beams
Lead on the broad effulgence of the day,
And when the hand of softly-treading Eve
Invests the world with solitary shade.

Artificer, and father of the whole!
With perfect good, and deity replete,
Through which the world perpetually receives
Exhaustless stores of intellectual good.

To thee belongs that all-sustaining power,
Which mind, and soul, and mundane life supports.
To thee, their fabrication bodies owe,
And things the due perfection of their kinds.

Through thee, each part of this amazing whole
Is link'd by Sympathy's connecting hand,
And in the strongest, best proportions join'd;
And the world's various powers and pondrous weights
Are bound by thee in beautiful accord.

By thee, the world is form'd a perfect whole,
From age exempt, unconscious of disease,
And with a shape adorn'd by far the first,
Most simple, most capacious, and the best.

By thee, this *all*, was self-sufficient fram'd,
And with a self-revolving power endu'd;
And motion intellectual owes to thee
Its never-ceasing energy, and life.

The Platonic Philosopher's Creed

By Thomas Taylor

(Note: In his preface to the volume from which the following extract is taken, Thomas Taylor writes: "The Creed of the Platonic Philosopher is added for the purpose of presenting the *intelligent* reader with a synoptical view of that sublime theology which was first obscurely promulgated by Orpheus, Pythagoras and Plato, and was afterwards perspicuously unfolded by their legitimate disciples; a theology which, however it may be involved in oblivion in *barbarous,* and derided in *impious* ages, will again flourish for very extended periods, through all the infinite revolutions of time. The reader who wishes to have a more ample view of it, may peruse the author's Introduction to his translation of Plato, from which the whole of this Creed is nearly extracted.")

1. I believe in one first cause of all things, whose nature is so immensely transcendent, that it is even super-essential; and that in consequence of this it cannot properly either be named, or spoken of, or conceived by opinion, or be known, or perceived by any being.

2. I believe, however, that if it be lawful to give a name to that which is truly ineffable, the appellations of *the one* and *the good* are of all others the most adapted to it; the former of these names indicating that it is the principle of all things, and the latter that it is the ultimate object of desire to all things.

3. I believe that this immense principle produced such things as are first and proximate to itself, most similar to itself; just as the heat *immediately* proceeding from fire is most similar to the heat in the fire; and the light *immediately* emanating from the sun, to that which the sun essentially contains. Hence, this principle produces many principles proximately from itself.

4. I likewise believe that since all things differ from each other, and are multiplied with their proper differences, each

289

of these multitudes is suspended from its one proper principle. That, in consequence of this, all beautiful things, whether in souls or in bodies, are suspended from one fountain of beauty. That whatever possesses symmetry, and whatever is true, and all principles are in a certain respect connate with the first principle, so far as they are principles, with an appropriate subjection and analogy. That all other principles are comprehended in this first principle, not with interval and multitude, but as parts in the whole, and number in the monad. That it is not a certain principle like each of the rest; for of these, one is the principle of beauty, another of truth, and another of something else, but it is *simply principle.* Nor is it simply the *principle of beings,* but it is *the principle of principles;* it being necessary that the characteristic property of principle, after the same manner as other things, should not begin from multitude, but should be collected into one monad as a summit, and which is the principle of principles.

5. I believe, therefore, that such things as are produced by the first good in consequence of being connascent with it, do not recede from essential goodness, since they are immoveable and unchanged, and are eternally established in the same blessedness. All other natures, however, being produced by the one good, and many goodnesses, since they fall off from essential goodness, and are not immoveably established in the nature of divine goodness, possess on this account the good according to participation.

6. I believe that as all things considered as subsisting *causally* in this immense principle, are transcendently more excellent than they are when considered as effects proceeding from him; this principle is very properly said to be all things, *prior* to all; *priority* denoting exempt transcendency.

Just as number may be considered as subsisting occultly in the monad, and the circle in the centre; this *occult* being the same in each with *causal* subsistence.

7. I believe that the most proper mode of venerating this great principle of principles is to extend in silence the ineffable parturitions of the soul to its ineffable co-sensation; and that if it be at all lawful to celebrate it, it is to be celebrated as a thrice unknown darkness, as the god of all gods, and the unity of all unities, as more ineffable than all silence, and more occult than all essence, as holy among the holies, and concealed in its first progeny, the intelligible gods.

8. I believe that self-subsistent natures are the immediate offspring of this principle, if it be lawful thus to denominate things which ought rather to be called ineffable unfoldings into light from the ineffable.

9. I believe that incorporeal forms or ideas resident in a divine intellect, are the paradigms or models of every thing which has a perpetual subsistence according to nature. That these ideas subsist primarily in the highest intellects, secondarily in souls, and ultimately in sensible natures; and that they subsist in each, characterized by the essential properties of the beings in which they are contained. That they possess a *paternal, producing, guardian, connecting, perfective*, and *uniting* power. That in *divine beings* they possess a power fabricative and gnostic! in *nature* a power fabricative but not gnostic; and in *human souls* in their present condition through a degradation of intellect, a power gnostic, but not fabricative.

10. I believe that this world, depending on its divine artificer, who is himhelf an intelligible world, replete with the archetypal ideas of all things, is perpetually flowing, and perpetually advancing to being, and, compared with its paradigm, has no stability, or reality of being. That considered,

however, as animated by a divine soul, and as being the receptacle of divinities from whom bodies are suspended, it is justly called by Plato, a blessed god.

11. I believe that the great body of this world, which subsists in a perpetual dispersion of temporal extension, may be properly called a *whole, with a total subsistence*, or a *whole of wholes*, on account of the perpetuity of its duration, though this is nothing more than a flowing eternity. That the other wholes which it contains are the celestial spheres, the sphere of aether, the whole of air considered as one great orb; the whole earth, and the whole sea. That these spheres are *parts with a total subsistence*, and through this subsistence are perpetual.

12. I believe that all the parts of the universe are unable to participate of the providence of divinity in a similar manner, but some of its parts enjoy this eternally, and others temporally; some in a primary and others in a secondary degree; for the universe being a perfect whole, must have a first, a middle, and a last part. But its first parts, as having the most excellent subsistence, must always exist according to nature; and its last parts must sometimes exist according to, and sometimes contrary to, nature. Hence, the celestial bodies, which are the first parts of the universe, perpetually subsist according to nature, both the whole spheres, and the multitude co-ordinate to these wholes; and the only alteration which they experience is a mutation of figure, and variation of light at different periods; but in the sublunary region, while the spheres of the elements remain on account of their subsistence, as wholes, always according to nature; the parts of the wholes have sometimes a natural, and sometimes an unnatural subsistence: for thus alone can the circle of generation unfold all the variety which it contains. I be-

lieve, therefore, that the different periods in which these mutations happen, are with great propriety called by Plato, periods of *fertility* and *sterility*: for in these periods a fertility or sterility of men, animals, and plants takes place; so that in fertile periods mankind will be both more numerous, and upon the whole superior in mental and bodily endowments to the men of a barren period. And that a similar reasoning must be extended to irrational animals and plants. I also believe that the most dreadful consequence attending a barren period with respect to mankind is this, that in such a period they have no scientific theology, and deny the existence of the immediate progeny of the ineffable cause of all things.

13. I believe that as the world considered as one great comprehending whole is a divine animal, so likewise every whole which it contains is a world, possessing in the first place a self-perfect unity proceeding from the ineffable by which it becomes a god; in the second place, a divine intellect; in the third place, a divine soul; and in the last place a deified body. That each of these wholes is the producing cause of all the multitude which it contains, and on this account is said to be a whole prior to parts; because considered as possessing an eternal form which holds all its parts together, and gives to the whole perpetuity of subsistence, it is not indigent of such parts to the perfection of its being. And that it follows by a geometrical necessity, that these wholes which rank thus high in the universe must be animated.

14. Hence I believe that after the immense principle of principles in which all things causally subsist absorbed in super-essential light, and involved in unfathomable depths, a beautiful series of principles proceeds, all largely partaking of the ineffable, all stamped with the occult characters

of deity, all possessing an overflowing fulness of good. That
from these dazzling summits, these ineffable blossoms, these
divine propagations, being, life, intellect, soul, nature, and
body depend; *monads* suspended from *unities*, deified natures proceeding from deities. That each of these monads is
the leader of a series which extends to the last of things, and
which, while it proceeds from, at the same time abides in,
and returns to its leader. Thus all beings proceed from and
are comprehended in the first being; all intellects emanate
from one first intellect; all souls from one first soul; all
natures blossom from one first nature; and all bodies proceed from the vital and luminous body of the world. That
all these great monads are comprehended in the first one,
from which both they and all their depending series are unfolded into light. And that hence this first one is truly the
unity of unities, the monad of monads, the principle of
principles, the god of gods, one and all things, and yet one
prior to all.

15. I also believe that man is a microcosm, comprehending in himself *partially* every thing which the world contains
divinely and *totally*. That hence he is endued with an intellect subsisting in energy, and a rational soul proceeding
from the same causes as those from which the intellect and
soul of the universe proceed. And that he has likewise an
ethereal vehicle analogous to the heavens, and a terrestrial
body composed from the four elements, and with which also
it is co-ordinate.

16. I believe that the rational part of man, in which his
essence consists, is of a self-motive nature, and that it subsists between intellect, which is immoveable both in essence
and energy, and nature, which both moves and is moved.

17. I believe that the human as well as every mundane
soul, uses periods and restitutions of its proper life. For in

consequence of being measured by time, it energizes transitively, and possesses a proper motion. But every thing which is moved perpetually, and participates of time, revolves periodically, and proceeds from the same to the same.

18. I also believe that as the human soul ranks among the number of those souls that *sometimes* follow the mundane divinities, in consequence of subsisting immediately after daemons and heroes the *perpetual* attendants of the gods, it possesses a power of descending infinitely into the sublunary region, and of ascending from thence to real being. That in consequence of this, the soul while an inhabitant of earth is in a fallen condition, an apostate from deity, an exile from the orb of light. That she can only be restored while on earth to the divine likeness, and be able after death to reascend to the intelligible world, by the exercise of the *cathartic* and *theoretic* virtues; the former purifying her from the defilements of a mortal nature, and the latter elevating her to the vision of true being. And that such a soul returns after death to her kindred star from which she fell, and enjoys a blessed life.

19. I believe that the human soul essentially contains all knowledge, and that whatever knowledge she acquires in the present life, is nothing more than a recovery of what she once possessed; and which discipline evocates from its dormant retreats.

20. I also believe that the soul is punished in a future for the crimes she has committed in the present life; but that this punishment is proportioned to the crimes, and is not perpetual; divinity punishing, not from anger or revenge, but in order to purify the guilty soul, and restore her to the proper perfection of her nature.

21. I also believe that the human soul on its departure from the present life, will, if not properly purified, pass into other

terrene bodies; and that if it passes into a human body, it becomes the soul of that body; but if into the body of a brute, it does not become the soul of the brute, but is externally connected with the brutal soul in the same manner as presiding daemons are connected in their beneficent operations with mankind; for the rational part never becomes the soul of the irrational nature.

22. Lastly, I believe that souls that live according to virtue, shall in other respects be happy; and when separated from the irrational nature, and purified from all body, shall be conjoined with the gods, and govern the whole world, together with the deities by whom it was produced.

BIBLIOGRAPHY OF THE PUBLISHED WORKS OF
THOMAS TAYLOR

* In the Library of the Society

An Answer to Dr. Gilles' Supplement (London, 1804)

*Arguments of the Emperor Julian Against the Christians (London, 1809)

*Aristotle's Great Ethics (1811)

*Aristotle's Metaphysics (1801)

The Commentaries of Proclus on the Timaeus of Plato (2 vols., 1820)

*Cratylus, Phaedo, Parmenides, and Timaeus of Plato (London, 1793)

*The Description of Greece, by Pausanias (London, 1794)

*The Dissertations of Maximus Tyrius (London, 1804)

*A Dissertation on the Eleusinian Bacchic Mysteries (Amsterdam,—)

*A Dissertation on the Philosophy of Aristotle (1812)

*The Elements of a New Arithmetical Notation, and of a New Arithmetic of Infinites (London, 1823)

*Eleusinian and Bacchic Mysteries (New York, 1891)

*Extracts from the Scholia of Olympiodorus on the Phaedo of Plato (1793)

*The Fable of Cupid and Psyche, To which are added A Poetical Paraphrase on the Speech of Diotima, in the Banquet of Plato; Four Hymns, &c. &c. (London, 1795)

*Five Books of Plotinus (London, 1794)

Fragments of Porphyry, Julian Celsus, and Others Against the Christians (1830)

*Fragments of The Lost Writings of Proclus (London, 1825)

Fragments of a Work Written by the Emporer Julian Against the Christians, preserved by Cyril Bishop of Alexandria—A part of the third book of Proclus on Plato's Theology (1789)

*The Hymns of Orpheus, With a Preliminary Dissertation on The Life and Theology of Orpheus. Contains also The Initiations of Orpheus and An Essay on The Beautiful, from the Greek of Plotinus (London, 1792)

Iamblichus on The Mysteries (London, 1895)

*Iamblichus on The Mysteries of The Egyptians, Chaldeans, and Assyrians (1821)

*Life of Pythagoras by Iamblichus (London, 1818)

*The Metamorphosis, or Golden Ass, and Philosophical Works of Apuleius (London, 1822)

*Miscellanies. in Prose and Verse: Containing The Triumph of The
    Wise Man Over Fortune, The Creed Of The Platonic Philoso-
    pher; A Panegyric On Sydenham, &c. &c (London, 1805)
  Miscellaneous Extracts in one Vol. (n.d.)
  Mystical Hymns of Orpheus (London, 1896)
*Ocellus Lucanus on The Nature of The Universe. Taurus, The
    Platonic Philosopher, On the Eternity of The World. Julius
    Firmicus Maternus of The Thema Mundi; in which the Po-
    sitions of The Stars at the Commencement of the Seven Mun-
    dane Periods is Given. Select Theorems on the Perpetuity of
    Time, by Proclus. (London, 1831)
*Phaedrus of Plato (London, 1792)
  Philosophical and Mathematical Commentaries of Proclus (Lon-
    don, 1788)
*The Platonist. Periodical, ed. by Thomas M. Johnson. (St Louis,
    Mo.. 1881—)
*Political Fragments of Archytas, Charondas, Zaleucus, and other
    Ancient Pythagoreans, Preserved by Stobaeus; and also Ethi-
    cal Fragments of Hierocles (Chiswick, 1822)
*Pythagoric Sentences of Demophilus (London, 1804)
*Rhetoric. Poetic. and Nicomachean Ethics of Aristotle (3 vols.
    London, 1818)
*Sallust on The Gods And The World; And The Pythagoric Sen-
    tences of Demophilus, Translated from the Greek; and Five
    Hymns by Proclus (London, 1795)
*Select Works of Plotinus (1817)
*Select Works of Porphyry; Containing His Four Books on Ab-
    stinence From Animal Foods; His Treatise on The Homeric
    Cave of The Nymphs; and His Auxiliaries to the Perception
    of Intelligible Natures. With an Appendix explaining the
    Allegory of the Wanderings of Ulysses. (London, 1823)
  A Selection of Arguments Against Modern Astronomy, and also
    Theological Questions with Their Solutions (n.d.)
*The Six Books of Proclus on The Theology of Plato (2 vols. 1816)
*Theoretic Arithmetic (1816)
*Treatises of Plotinus: Viz. On Suicide, to which is added an Ex-
    tract from the Harleian MS. of the Scholia of Olympiodorus on
    the Phaedo of Plato Respecting Suicide, Accompanied by the
    Greek Text; Two Books on Truly Existing Being; and Ex-
    tracts from His Treatise on the Manner in which the Multitude
    of Ideas Subsists, and Concerning The Good (London, 1834)
*Two Orations of the Emperor Julian (London, 1793)
  Two Treatises of Proclus, translated from the French (1833)
*A Vindication of the Rights of Brutes (London, 1792)
*The Works of Aristotle (8 vols. London, 1812)
*The Works of Plato (6 vols. London, 1804.)

GANDHI
A Tribute

The reaction of the public to the assassination of Mohandas Gandhi reveals clearly the general state of confusion dominating this generation of uncertainties. The Press of the world, though divided as to the feasibility of the Mahatma's political program, was united in a spontaneous expression of genuine sorrow over the tragic end of the kindly little man himself. Seldom has the "fourth estate" been so deeply moved, and the memorials and tributes were for the most part dignified, thoughtful, and respectful.

Public reaction was intense. Persons of all races and faiths and practically every political allegiance joined in accepting the death of Gandhi as a personal loss. To all of them, he represented a rare quality of integrity, which appealed to the highest sentiments in human character. No other man in

299

modern times has been accepted so completely as a personification of the principles of enlightened leadership.

Even while the ashes of Mohandas Gandhi were being
scattered upon the sacred rivers of India, the shocked and
outraged public mind, rallying from the first impact of the
tragedy, began to think in terms of causes and consequences.
It was inevitable that history and tradition should supply
the materials for certain obvious comparisons. The story of
civilization includes numerous records of heroic idealists
who paid with their lives for the contributions which they
made to the essential progress of the human race.

Pythagoras, the first philosopher of the Grecians, was
burned to death with his disciples by an angry mob of il-
literates, led by a disgruntled man who had been rejected
by the master as unfit for higher learning. Zoroaster, the
fire prophet of Persia, had a spear thrust into his back while
kneeling in prayer before the altar of his temple. Socrates
was sentenced to death by the court of Athens on a trumped-
up charge supported by perjuring witnesses. Jesus was executed as a common criminal for teaching the brotherhood
of man. The death of Mohammed was hastened by poison.

We can all understand how ancient nations might have
been so deficient in spiritual understanding that they could
have persecuted the prophets without realizing the magnitude
of these crimes. But we like to think that modern man has
outgrown these destructive, primitive instincts. The assassination of Gandhi brought with it the sickening realization that
even in the 20th century a gentle, tired old man, who gave
his life wisely and lovingly to the service of humanity, could
be brutally murdered on his way to prayer.

Time magazine compared Gandhi and Lincoln, and found
them both martyrs to ideals beyond the comprehension of

the mass-mind. It also pointed out that both men were astute
politicians, a fact generally overlooked. Each skillfully used
the forces at his command to accomplish those ends which
he regarded as necessary. Both were essentially practical,
and their programs revealed rare judgment in making use
of every available opportunity. They were men of vision,
but not visionary men.

As might be expected, George Bernard Shaw came to the
profound conclusion that trying to help folks is an exceedingly dangerous occupation, and could assemble an immense
amount of evidence in support of his conclusion.

A number of editorial writers developed quite an instinct
for semantics, and tried to draw a clear line of distinction
between a *good* man and a *great* man. In my opinion, the
distinction which they tried to make is completely worthless,
for the simple reason that only a good man can be truly great.
Anyone who attains fame without virtue is merely notorious—
a term applicable to most outstanding rascals in history.

When we attempt to estimate the qualities of Gandhi's
personality, we must arrive at conclusions contrary to most
of our prevailing concepts of greatness. The appearance of
the little Mahatma was scarcely heroic, with none of the
attributes of the matinee idol. Certainly his success was not
measured in terms of wealth or the supremacy of money
over morals. He built no palaces, and neither practiced nor
encouraged cupidity. He inspired no fear, and demanded
no allegiance. In an age of dictators, industrial tycoons, and
wizards of high finance, he remained untouched by those
extravagant personal ambitions which contaminated most of
his contemporaries.

It is somewhat embarrassing for a success-mad world to
realize that this humble little man, with his loin cloth, safety
pin, and dollar watch, received as his natural right that uni-

versal admiration which material success is unable to demand. The incongruity of the situation is best summarized
in the distress of the important motion picture executive
when Gandhi declined an offer of one million dollars to appear in a super-colossal Hollywood production.

The canonization of Gandhi by the popular mind is inevitable. Even during his life, there was a timelessness about
him, and he belonged to the ages while yet he still lived.
His tragic death fulfilled one of the oldest patterns in the
spiritual experience of the human race. Already the myth
of the world hero is forming about him. He appealed to the
common man, the poor and the down-trodden, the weak and
the oppressed, and it is among these classes that the legend
of immortality always originates.

A number of serious thinkers regret the immediate sanctification of this venerated leader. This is not because they
wish to withhold honors so obviously merited, but because
this deification is likely to obscure the vital human purpose
for which the Mahatma gave his life. It is much easier to
deck a man's shrine with flowers than to unite for the attainment of his objectives. Worship so easily becomes static,
and at this critical time the world is in desperate need of a
dynamic vision. The loss of a practical champion of the cause
of human rights is a serious disaster. The mere veneration
of Gandhi's memory is not sufficient to fill the empty place
which he left behind him in Asia.

What were the forces responsible for the brutal murder
of Mohandas Gandhi? Enough evidence is already at hand
to prove that he was not the victim of an unbalanced fanatic,
but that his death was part of a deeply laid plot to remove
the one man who was capable of maintaining a degree of
religious and political unity in India. He was an obstacle
in the path of those who were resolved to force the two

newly created nations—Hindustan and Pakistan—into a state of religious and political strife. The man of peace was murdered by men who wanted to make war. He stood in the way of traditional hatreds and intolerances, and was sacrificed to the greeds and ambitions of those who make profit from human misery.

We cannot agree entirely with some of the emotional editorial writers who insist that the assassination of Gandhi is a general indictment of human morals and ethics. Outside of a few essentially dishonest opportunists, Mohandas Gandhi could have traveled unguarded in almost any part of the world with complete safety. Scarcely a door would have been closed to him. The rich and the poor alike would have been honored to accept him into their hearts and homes. The English people gave Gandhi a tremendous ovation when he was in London, even though his program of non-co-operation was working a serious hardship in England. Even religious groups, with many prejudices against the Hindu faith, acknowledged and admired the personal virtues of the humble little man.

No doubt there were many who realized that Gandhi's program was too far from the common experience of mortals to be likely to succeed. We believe in ideals, but we fear them and we fear for them. In our hearts we know that we are living under a highly competitive concept. We will go so far as to admit that the concept itself is basically unsound, but we lack the power and the wisdom to change the patterns which afflict all of us in varying degrees. The world did not wish this lovable man to die; but even from the beginning of his career, tragedy was ever nigh unto him.

In many ways Mahatma Gandhi was the most universal person of his time. His philosophy was derived from many sources. He found inspiration from the writings of Thoreau and other New England Transcendentalists. He read carefully the social writings of Count Leo Tolstoy and other European liberals. He was most sympathetic to the teachings of Jesus, and naturally was well informed in the doctrines of Mohammed, which dominated such a large group of the Indian people. Himself a devout member of the Hindu faith, he was in every sense of the word the outstanding modern example of the highest ideals of that religion. But at no time was it reported that his conduct was influenced by any religious prejudices. In his personal living, many faiths met and mingled; and by living the spirit of one faith, he lived the spirit of them all. To him, true religion was the practice of the brotherhood of man.

So many accounts are now available dealing with the historical incidents in the life of Mohandas Gandhi that there is no need to repeat such anecdotes. He was the father of Indian independence, but the very day it was attained, he was rewarded by extremists throwing rocks through the windows of his apartment. It is reported that the unhappy incidents following India's freedom caused Gandhi to feel that his mission had failed. He found no worldly peace in the closing months of his life, and at least one unsuccessful attempt was made to assassinate him with a bomb. We can remember the last words of the great Chinese sage, Confucius, "I have failed." There is comfort in the thought that the philosophy of Confucius became the most powerful and constructive force in China.

The assassination of Gandhi provides the substance for a general re-estimation of the spiritual achievement of the human race. We have so long assumed that we are a mature creation on the very threshold of perfection that we have

developed a highly aggravated form of the superiority complex. It is time to face the facts. While we glimpse a distant Utopia, our conduct is inconsistent with our concept of
the shape of things to come. Between us and the golden time
we look for is an abyss which can be bridged only by a vast
human effort over a long period of time.

Actually, we have solved very few of the problems which
we have inherited from the past. Peace is still a dream, and
war a fact. Co-operation is a beautiful ideal, but competition is the moving force of our life-pattern. Man is still
a blundering adolescent, dominated by those uncontrollable
impulses and emotions natural to these difficult years. Like
small children, we like to dress up in our parents' clothes,
but the masquerade deceives no one but ourselves.

We are not really wicked, but we are really stupid; and
the final proof of our stupidity is that we do not know or
realize our own limitations. There is little virtue in precocity.
Children are not any better by appearing to be in advance
of their ages. The infant prodigy is seldom a success in life.
Humanity would be no better off if a maturity beyond its
years were forced upon it by artificial means. The wiser
course is to understand things as they are, and build forward slowly and intelligently. We can never put the world
in order until we recover from the delusion of the infallibility of our current conceits.

The average man, in any country of the world and in
any class of society, has the internal rational and emotional
equipment approximating the standard of values of a twelve-
to fourteen-year-old child. This is his true age in the universe, even though he may be an octogenarian in physical
years. His notions and opinions may have the appearance of
maturity, but his actions are impelled by his internal capacity to estimate the consequences of his own conduct. It

is in his conduct that he reveals clearly his psychological immaturity.

It was Confucius who pointed out that the superior man was one so firmly established on his own ethical foundation that he was incapable by nature, and not by self-discipline, of performing an inferior action. In other words, we are never really good until we have attained this state without trying to be good.

When gracious instincts are graciously expressed, we have accomplished the true integration of the personality. As long as there are conflicts in ourselves between the things we believe and the things we do, this conflict will manifest itself in all of our larger social and political patterns. This conflict cannot be overcome merely by instruction; it must be outgrown by the evolving consciousness of the human being. Until he reaches this state, man is merely a child in a mature body.

The common mistake of idealists is to overestimate the human being, even as it is the common mistake of the realist to underestimate the spiritual potencies in man. Regardless of all estimates, the creature remains itself, and its reactions are consistent with its inner understanding or lack of understanding. This is one of those inevitables about which we cannot afford to grieve. Man is growing up in an infinite universe, or, as some physicists believe, a finite universe, infinitely beyond our comprehension. In either case, there is abundant space and opportunity for growth and development. Man, a million years from now, will be a far better creature than he is today; but only a million years, with their vast sequences of experience, can accomplish this improvement.

The power of Gandhi is that of noble example. He revealed through his life a spiritual dimension beyond the comprehension of his followers and well-wishers. As one writer puts it, Gandhi was not a person; he was a phenomenon. Just as the good examples of parents are the most powerful environmental force operating in the life of a child, so the example of a mature human being is the most powerful force operating in the lives of those less mature in terms of spiritual growth. No great ethical leader, regardless of his internal strength, can bestow security upon his race. His standard of life is too remote to be understood, even if its proportions are partially appreciated. Admiration may cause us to wish to be like that which we admire, but wishing is too weak a sentiment to bear fruit unless it is supported by strong, continuous resolution.

Instead of feeling that Gandhi was betrayed by those he sought to serve, we should realize that he possessed a strength of character that others lacked. They wished to be true, but they could not follow in his path. It is useless to say that the followers should have been bigger and stronger and wiser. They did their best, and many will continue to do so. Some will grow and become powers for good, and others will fall by the wayside, unable to bear the strain.

Political convictions are extremely difficult to rationalize. Many who differed from Gandhi were equally sincere. One of the forces working against the Mahatma was the pressure of tradition. We are all creatures of habit, and in India especially, where all traditions are sanctified, Gandhi violated many of the most ancient and sacred habitual practices.

More than three thousand years ago, the Egyptian Pharaoh Akhenaten attempted to defy the long-established religion of Amen-Ra. He succeeded for a short time, but the cult he created was overwhelmed by the pressure of ancient rites and practices. He, too, was a man born out of time, and died of a broken heart before he reached his thirtieth year.

In India, the caste system is deep and strong. Buddha attempted to break it down with the most powerful system of ethics ever to oppose an entrenched tradition. But slowly the old ways came back, and Buddhism vanished from the life of the Indian people. If the religion of the Hindus is ancient and powerful, the faith of Islam, though younger, is dynamic and intense. It is one of the most rapidly growing religions in the world today. The Moslem and the Hindu have mingled for centuries, but in the main they have found little common ground. Each group owes allegiance first to its faith, and until these faiths are reconciled, the followers cannot meet on terms of spiritual equity.

It is not enough to point out that Hinduism and Islamism have much in common. Even if this were proved beyond any doubt, the proof would not be acceptable. We still think in terms of Moslem virtue, Hindu virtue, Christian virtue, and Confucian virtue. To all appearances the Golden Rule is the same in each faith, but in fact, to the devout believer, there are theological differences which transcend reason and understanding. While such differences are accepted as the reality, unity is impossible.

Gandhi as a man transcended these differences, and to a considerable degree reconciled them among his followers. By the strength of his own personality, he set up a state of amity. In many cases, the love for the man himself was the binding force, but beneath the surface, the old antagonisms remained. The various groups loved him, but they had not learned to sincerely love one another. In all parties there were reactionaries who regarded the Mahatma as a menace to the traditional institutions. To them, these institutions were divine, above fault, and beyond reform. Even though these reactionaries might admire the man, they could not forgive the attack which he made upon their competitive concepts of doctrinal infallibility. To the man who already regards himself as superior, the doctrine of equality is seldom acceptable.

One thing is certain: The majority of mankind agreed that Mohandas Gandhi was a good man and a great man. Even those extremists who accomplished his destruction probably would concur with this estimation of his character. To them, however, it appeared expedient to remove this good man who was interfering with the natural inclinations of discordant factions. Friend and enemy alike will honor Gandhi's memory, relieved of his further interference with their immediate plans.

Already the inevitable critics are attempting a negative estimate of the qualities and attributes of Mohandas Gandhi. They point out the peculiarities of his disposition, and seek out the flaws in his diplomacy. Those who understood nothing of either the man or his work will pass judgment upon both. They will attempt to tear down the hero and reduce him to their own level. They will discover impulses in him which exist only in themselves and will assume that his appearance of virtue concealed an array of ulterior motives. This is called rationalization.

Simple virtue is the most difficult to explain of all moral convictions. We must complicate natural human impulses to justify our preconceived definitions of behavior patterns. But the critics labor in vain, for the heart of humanity has taken this little brown man to itself. The world does not love him primarily because he was wise or great or powerful or, for that matter, just because he was good. It loves him because he was the most lovable man in the last thousand years of history. Naturally, we admire his virtues, but we instinctively return, in like measure, the sincere devotion he gave to us.

Gandhi proved the possibility of solving the disputes of nations by peaceful means. We are attempting to do the same thing by means of the machinery of the United Nations Organization. It is doubtful if we will be as successful with our ponderous project as the Mahatma was with his simple program. Western nations have not accepted the most essential element in Gandhi's concept; namely, the supremacy of soul power over brute force.

The Mahatma was a devoutly religious man. His spiritual convictions gave him an inner security, unavailable to those functioning only on a material plane of thinking. The materialist may have noble ideals and aspirations, but he is insufficient within himself. He lacks the kind of courage which comes only to those whose inner life is lighted and warmed by the flame of a holy dedication.

Gandhi was not a religious fanatic, but he was strengthened and sustained by a deep and abiding love of God. Like Washington and Lincoln, he turned to prayer for guidance in critical times. Although physically frail and infirm, his indomitable spirit never failed. Through him moved a force so tremendous that it transcended all the natural limitations of his personality. It was this God-power that carried him from comparative obscurity to a position of universal esteem and regard. Western leadership cannot succeed until the Occidental world produces heroic spirits moved to action by enlightened principles rather than by ulterior motives, political or economic.

While public opinion is widely divided over the proposed architectural structure that is to house the United Nations Organization, the pressing world concerns of the moment

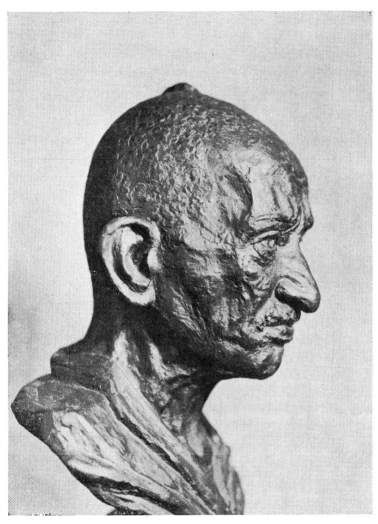

—Modeled by Manly P. Hall

PORTRAIT HEAD OF MAHATMA GANDHI

receive scant consideration. In true Western fashion, we spend millions of dollars to house our hope of future peace, forgetting that an honorable friendship under a buttonwood tree will advance the human cause much further than intrigue in a palace. The American tragedy of high finance originated under a buttonwood tree, and this might be an appropriate place to discover the remedy.

Gandhi was the outstanding exponent in modern times of the doctrine of the ultimate victory of right over might. He realized that it was impossible to organize the resources of the masses so that they could oppose the entrenched institutions of vested interests on their own level. It was useless for an unarmed, underfed, untrained and disorganized population to oppose the military might of powerful nations or combines of nations.

It is not possible to attain peace by making war. It is equally useless to call together conferences of politicians and diplomats concerned only with maintaining the status quo at all costs. The only possible solution is to stand firmly on right principles, willing to sacrifice life, liberty, and worldly goods rather than to compromise these principles in any particular. The impact of principles works a serious hardship on the unprincipled. We can destroy men, but we cannot destroy truth. That which is established upon truth must ultimately win.

If a nation like America would take its stand firmly on the principles set down by its founding fathers and rise up as a champion of eternal values, it could accomplish much more than one dedicated man. Gandhi started with nothing. We have everything to work with except the abiding conviction of a divine destiny. Nations do not fall because of the strength of their enemies, but because of the weaknesses of themselves. All nations and all individuals are weak unless they have faith in the right, and, like Lincoln, have the courage to perform the right, as it is given them to know the right.

Even today we are overshadowed by innumerable fears: further wars, waves of crime, depressions, and those other misfortunes which result from man's inhumanity to man. We have no solution beyond competitive armament, and we are in constant apprehension of the infiltration of subversive elements resolved to overthrow the American way of life. Mahatma Gandhi faced all the problems that we face, or are likely to face, in the next hundred years of our national history. He had no vast appropriations at his disposal, and no organization to ferret out the purveyors of alien political and social doctrines. He had nothing but his own courage, his own faith, and his own integrity with which to defend himself and the four hundred million whose futures depended largely upon him.

Gandhi accomplished what the statesmen of the world solemnly declared to be impossible. It is true that he was not entirely successful, but he proved beyond any reasonable doubt that his method was practical, and not merely the abstract theory of a mystic. There is no way in which the average human being can estimate correctly the potential power of the human soul over the pressures of its environment. Man can emerge victorious in his struggle for individual and collective security.

The assassination of this inspired Indian leader only revealed more clearly the desperate need for a higher ethical concept in world affairs. Although he was struck down at the most critical time in the destiny of his people, he lived to attain the freedom of India. The use and abuse of that freedom is now in the keeping of those he emancipated. That which was attained with the ever present help of God must be preserved by the ever constant vigilance of man. It must be preserved with the same spirit by which it was attained, or it cannot survive. That which men build with high convictions must afterwards be defended with high convictions. Continuous dedication to principle is the price of security.

With the death of Gandhi, a great dream must fail, unless those who found comfort and inspiration in that dream carry on the work. Each of us has received a fragment of his conviction as a priceless heritage. All the world is better because he proved the power of an inspired life. If we can feel enough of this inspiration within ourselves to live nearer to the truth, we can carry his concept forward as a vital force in world affairs.

Years ago it was the common belief in India that the day would come when the Hindu people would reckon history before and after Gandhi, as Christians measure their annals before and after Christ. The tragic death of the Mahatma adds to the probability that such an honor will be conferred upon his memory. His picture, draped with garlands of flowers, already is venerated and carried in solemn procession. In a strange way, this sanctified ascetic has become the symbol of modern India. He personifies something deep and strong in the life stream of this distant people. He was different in many ways from most Hindus, and yet he was the fulfillment of their pattern. He was part of the classical lore, the cultural heritage of the first Aryans.

India has drifted far from its own concept of life. It has been invaded and conquered and converted so often and so long that the proportions of its natural philosophy are dim and uncertain. Most of all, the significance of its mystical convictions has been distorted and obscured. The world had long thought of the Hindu holy man as a fanatic, a curiosity, someone given to fantastic practices, a survivor of old superstitious rites and systems. We pictured in our own minds the Hindu ascetic seated on a bed of spikes, or wandering about the countryside with long unkempt hair and beard and his body plastered with gray mud.

The example of Mahatma Gandhi has corrected many of these erroneous conclusions. He proved that a powerful and practical inspiration flows through the *Vedas*. With his shaven head, gold-rimmed spectacles, and quaint manner, he was like thousands of recluses who meditate their lives away in the sheltered gardens of old ashrams. But suddenly the holy man emerged as prophet, inspired leader, astute diplomat, skillful lawyer, and enlightened friend. He was the living proof of the vitality of India's mysticism and esoteric philosophy.

The title *Mahatma*, which the Indian people have conferred upon their inspired teacher and friend, means simply "great soul." It was in this sense that they used the term when referring to Gandhi. It was not that he was some conjurer or fabled arhat, but in his own way, he was the greatest magician in modern Asiatic history. He wrought a miracle by the power of his love, and he has revealed to a tired and disillusioned humankind the magic powers of unselfishness, sincerity, kindliness, and self-sacrifice. Already, orthodox Hindus are praying that soon he will come back to his people in a new body. As one Hindu expressed it simply: "How can we live in this world without him?"

With the eyes of our hearts, we can see the tired little man, leaning heavily on his crooked stick, trudging along a

road that leads away from this earth, with its pains and
burdens, to a distant place beyond the glittering stars. But
we share in the feeling that he will not be long away. He
was not the kind of man who sought rest and peace and
liberation for himself. He will be back, laboring not only
through years, but through lives, to bring that peace and
rest and liberation to those millions and hundreds of millions
whom he loved. This is India's belief, and there are many
outside of India who feel the same way. The beloved little
man has left us, but he has not gone far, nor will he be gone
long.